ORGANIZING WOMEN

Gender Equality Policies in French and British Trade Unions

Cécile Guillaume

Translated by
Katharine Throssell

BRISTOL
UNIVERSITY
PRESS

First published in Great Britain in 2022 by

Bristol University Press
University of Bristol
1–9 Old Park Hill
Bristol
BS2 8BB
UK
t: +44 (0)117 954 5940
e: bup-info@bristol.ac.uk

Details of international sales and distribution partners are available at bristoluniversitypress.co.uk

English-language translation © Katharine Throssell 2022
Originally published as *Syndiquées. Défendre les intérêts des femmes au travail* © Presses de la Foundation Nationale des Sciences Politiques 2017

British Library Cataloguing in Publication Data
A catalogue record for this book is available from the British Library

ISBN 978-1-5292-1369-0 hardcover
ISBN 978-1-5292-1371-3 ePub
ISBN 978-1-5292-1372-0 ePdf

Cover design by Nicky Borowiec
Front cover image: iStock-1069739918

Contents

List of Figure, Tables and Boxes

Figure

Tables

Boxes

List of British Unions

ACT   Association of Cine-Technicians, created in 1933, becoming the Association of Cinematograph Technicians in 1956 and the Broadcasting, Entertainment, Cinematograph and Theatre Union (BECTU) in 1991. Merged with Prospect in 2017.

AMICUS   created in 2001 following the amalgamation of the Manufacturing Science and Finance (MSF), Amalgamate Engineering and Electrical Union (AEEU), UNIFI and the GPMU.

APEX   Association of Professional, Executive, Clerical and Computer Staff, created as the Clerks Union in 1890, amalgamated with GMB in 1989.

ASTMS   Association of Scientific, Technical and Managerial Staffs, created in 1969, amalgamated with the Technical, Administrative and Supervisory Section (TASS) in 1988 to form the MSF.

BIFU   Banking, Insurance and Finance Union, created in 1979, succeeded to National Union of Bank Employees created in 1946, then merged in 1999 with Natwest Staff Association and Barclays Group Staff Union to constitute the UNIFI (which then amalgamated with AMICUS in 2004 and is today part of UNITE).

COHSE   Confederation of Health Service Employees, created in 1946, merged in 1993 with NALGO and NUPE to form UNISON.

CWU   Communication Workers Union, created in 1995, following the merger between the Union of Communication Workers and the National Communications Union.

GMB   National Union of General and Municipal Workers, created in 1924 following the amalgamation between the National Amalgamated Union of Labour (NAUL), the National Union of General Workers (NUGW) and the Municipal Employees Association. Since then, other unions have merged with the GMB: Association of Professional, Executive, Clerical and Computer Staff (APEX), Furniture, Timber and Allied Trades

Union (FTAT) and the National Union of Tailors and Garment Workers (NUTGW).

MSF — Manufacturing, Science and Finance, created in 1988 following the merger of the Association of Scientific, Technical and Managerial Staffs (ASTMS) and the Technical, Administrative and Supervisory Section (TASS). Amalgamated in 2001 with the Amalgamated Engineering and Electrical Union to form AMICUS.

NALGO — National and Local Government Officers' Association, created in 1905, merged in 1993 with COHSE and NUPE to form UNISON.

NAPO — National Association of Probation Officers, created in 1912.

NASUWT — National Association of Schoolmasters Union of Women Teachers, created in 1976, following the amalgamation between the National Association of Schoolmasters and the Union of Women Teachers.

NATSOPA — National Society of Operative Printers and Assistants, created in 1889, merged with the National Union of Printing, Bookbinding and Paper Workers in 1966 to form the Society of Graphical and Allied Trades (SOGAT).

NUPE — National Union of Public Employees, created in 1908, amalgamated with NALGO and COHSE in 1993 to form UNISON.

NUTGW — National Union of Tailors and Garment Workers, created in 1920, merged with GMB in 1991.

POA — The Professional Trades Union for Prison, Correctional and Secure Psychiatric Workers, founded in 1939, has remained autonomous ever since.

SOGAT — Society of Graphical and Allied Trades, created in 1966 following the merger between National Union of Printing, Bookbinding and Paper Workers and the National Society of Operative Printers and Assistants (NATSOPA). In 1991, SOGAT merged with the National Graphical Association to form the Graphical, Paper and Media Union, which subsequently merged with AMICUS to become that union's Graphical, Paper and Media industrial sector.

TASS — Technical, Administrative and Supervisory Section, founded in 1913.

TGWU — Transport and General Workers' Union, founded in 1922, merged with AMICUS in 2007 to form UNITE.

TUC — Trades Union Congress, founded in 1868.

UNISON — created in 1993 following the merger between COHSE, NALGO, and NUPE.

UNITE
Unite the Union, created in 2007 following the merger of TGWU and AMICUS.

USDAW
Union of Shop, Distributive and Allied Workers, created in 1947 following the merger of the National Union of Distributive and Allied Workers and the National Union of Shop Assistants, Warehousemen and Clerks.

List of French Unions

CFDT French Democratic Confederation of Labour (*Confédération française démocratique du travail*), established in 1964 when members of the CFTC decided they wanted a secular union.

CFE-CGC French Confederation of Management – General Confederation of Executives (*Confédération française de l'encadrement–Confédération générale des cadres*), founded in 1944 under the name *Confédération générale des cadres*, from the amalgamation of a number of federations of engineers and managers (FNSI, CGCE, GSCD, FIATIM) who argued that the existing labour organizations could not adequately represent their interests. It adopted its current name in 1981, covering all management professions.

CFTC French Confederation of Christian Workers (*Confédération française des travailleurs chrétiens*), founded in 1919. In 1964 an internal schism led to the creation of the secular CFDT, while a minority defended the union's spiritual role and retained the name CFTC.

CGT General Labour Confederation (*Confédération générale du travail*), formed in 1895. The initial professions represented were the publishing industry and the railway workers. Today it has around 30 affiliated federations in vastly different sectors and also covers temporary workers.

CGT-FO General Labour Confederation – Workers' Force (*Confédération Générale du Travail–Force Ouvrière*), created in 1948 as a result of internal division within the CGT leading to a schism in which members critical of the influence of the French Communist Party formed their own union.

CNT National Confederation of Labour (*Confédération nationale du travail*), created in 1946 by exiled anarcho-syndicalist members of the Spanish CNT.

FSU United Trade Union Federation (*Fédération syndicale unitaire*), the largest union in the education sector. It was formed in

	1992 following a breakaway from its predecessor, the National Education Federation (*Fédération de l'Education nationale*).
SUD	Solidarity or Solidarity Unity Democracy (*Solidaires* or *Solidaires Unitaires Démocratiques*), created in 1981 as the 'Group of Ten', a group of ten independent unions who refused to belong to a confederation. The first SUD unions were created in 1988 following the departure of CFDT's postal and telecommunications federations. There are now numerous SUD-affiliated unions in a range of sectors such as health, education, or transport, among others.
UNSA	National Union of Autonomous Trade Unions (*Union nationale des syndicats autonomes*), created in 1993 by five autonomous trade unions. Among them was the National Education Federation, following the 1992 schism which led to the creation of the FSU.

Series Editors' Preface

We are very pleased to launch this new book series, Understanding Work and Employment Relations, with Cécile Guillaume's monograph *Organizing Women: Gender Equality Policies in French and British Trade Unions*. This is the first book to be published within this series and we are delighted to have such a strong contribution as our starting point.

The purpose of this book series is to create a space for monographs and edited volumes highlighting the latest research and commentary in the academic field of employment relations. The series is associated with the British Universities Industrial Relations Association (BUIRA), which marked 70 years of existence in 2020, and seeks to draw on the expertise of the membership of BUIRA and their contributions to its annual conference, as well as employment relations academics from around the world. Employment relations is a mature field of study and continues to be of relevance to academic and practitioner audiences alike. BUIRA has always been deliberately broad in scope as the field of employment relations has evolved and changed over time. BUIRA regards employment relations to be the study of the relation, control and governance of work and the employment relationship. It is the study of rules regarding job regulation and the 'reward–effort bargain'. These issues remain relevant today, in an era where the standard employment relationship has become increasingly fragmented due to employers' pursuit of labour flexibility and we see the continued expansion of the gig economy. Employment relations (and adjacent research areas including human resource management [HRM] and the sociology of work) is taught widely in universities around the world, most commonly in business and management schools and departments. The field of study is multidisciplinary, encompassing law, politics, history, geography, sociology and economics. HRM has a tendency to focus uncritically on management objectives, without exploring issues of work and employment in their wider socioeconomic context, and has its disciplinary roots in psychology, whereas employment relations retains a strong critical social science tradition. However, as scholars in this area we feel that there is a need for regular, up-to-date, research-focused books that reflect current work in the field and go further than more introductory texts. This book series aims to take an interdisciplinary approach, and we welcome proposals from academics across this range of disciplines as well as from a broad range of international and comparative perspectives in order to reflect the increasingly diverse and internationalized nature of the field both in the UK and globally.

Originally published in French in 2018 as *Syndiquées: Défendre les intérêts des femmes au travail*, this revised and translated edition of Cecile Guillaume's monograph is a fascinating comparative study of unions in Britain and France and their relative, albeit slow, progress in representing the interests of women and increasing levels of female representation within their structures. Guillaume draws on the careers of 100 activists across four major unions (the CFDT and Solidaires in France, and GMB and Unison in Great Britain) and a longitudinal study of union campaigning for equal pay in the UK. Analysis of this rich data is centred on the social, organizational and political conditions that contribute to the reproduction of gender inequalities or, conversely, support the promotion of equality. The underrepresentation of the interests of women within unions, including those with predominantly female memberships, is a long-standing issue of concern within the field of employment relations and more generally, and this book constitutes an important and timely contribution to these ongoing debates.

We hope you enjoy reading this first book in the series. If you would like to discuss a proposal of your own, then e-mail the series editors. We look forward to hearing from you.

Andy Hodder and Stephen Mustchin

1

Introduction

In recent years there has been significant improvement in the feminization of unions in both Great Britain and in France. Today, union membership generally reflects the presence of women in the labour market in these countries. However, this descriptive representation of women is not the result of a mechanical adjustment to the transformations of the labour market or the development of an 'egalitarian conscience' among unions. Large numbers of women moved into paid work between 1970 and 1990, but their union representation improved only in the 2000s (Boston, 2015; Kirton, 2015), thanks to the implementation of targeted recruitment strategies in highly feminized sectors and voluntarist equality policies within unions. In the UK, around 43% of women were in paid employment in 1987, but they represented only 29% of union members. Union representation increased over time, reaching 39% in 2000 and 48% in 2012. Today, the unionization of women has outpaced that of men (26.2% compared to 20.7% in 2018), like in other countries (Cooper, 2012; Milkman, 2016; Gavin et al, 2020). However, this feminization is variable between unions, depending on their size and sector (Kirton, 2015). In France, the rate of unionization is lower among women than men (10% compared to 12%) but, according to the most recent data, some unions, like the CFDT, have levels of women members that on average reflect the proportion of women employees. Other organizations in more traditionally male-dominated industrial sectors, like the CGT, or in occupations that are still male dominated (CFE-CGC), have lower levels of women members (see Table 1.2).

The progress of gender equality in unions remains selective. There is a resistance to granting women access to leadership roles, such as General or Regional Secretaries, or including them in decision-making bodies. In Great Britain, Frances O'Grady was elected as the head of the Trade Union Congress (TUC) in 2013, and three of the ten largest British unions are today led by a woman (all leading education unions). Many smaller professional unions also have a woman as General Secretary, such as the Society of

1

Table 1.1: Women's aggregate representation in the ten largest UK unions in 1989 and 2012

	Membership		National Executive Committee (elected)		National paid officers		General Secretaries	
	1989 % women	2012 % women	1989 % women	2012 % women	1989 % women	2012 % women	1989 % women	2012 % women
Male-dominated unions	24	22	13	28	10	29	10	0
Gender-balanced/female-dominated unions	67	64	32	43	19	43	0	40

Source: Data collected by Gill Kirton (Kirton, 2017).

Chiropodists and Podiatrists (SCP) or the Association of Educational Psychologists (AEP). But women still struggle to access leadership positions in the major unions. In 2021, Christina McAnea was elected as the new general secretary of UNISON – the first woman to head the UK's largest union. Only 14 (29%) of TUC-affiliated unions currently have a woman leader. Moreover, women remain vastly underrepresented on union staff, whether in elected or employed positions (Table 1.1).

In France, the situation is comparable, with a small proportion of women at the head of union organizations, even in feminized sectors like education (Haller, 2017), and lower levels of participation in union conferences and decision-making bodies (see Table 1.2). This glass ceiling is associated with a form of horizontal gender segregation according to the types of union role. In both countries, women are particularly underrepresented in negotiation roles (Contrepois, 2006). But they are present in roles to do with the everyday representation of workers or the promotion of equality/diversity in the union or in the workplace.

Even when they are unionized, women continue to be subject to a range of forms of workplace discrimination. Many of them remain stuck in low-paid, insecure jobs. Even when they are in highly skilled positions, they have less chance of being promoted than men, and the gender pay gap remains around 17 to 20% in both countries, depending on calculations (Silvera, 2014). How can we understand this underrepresentation of women's interests in the workplace? What connections might be made between the increasing but selective presence of women in unions and their abilities to defend

Table 1.2: Data on the position of women in French unions in 2013–15 (%)

	CGT	CFDT	CGT-FO	CFTC	CFE-CGC
Proportion of women union members	37.5	47	45	42	29.1
Proportion of women as union conference delegates	44.5	39	43	32	13.5
Proportion of women in national committees (or councils)	23.3	28.5	10	16	37
Proportion of women in executive committees	50	33	6	16	33
Proportion of women among General Secretaries of union federations	15	17	9	14	17.1
Proportion of women among General Secretaries of departmental unions	22	18.6	11	30	6

Source: Data collected by Rachel Silvera (Silvera, 2010; Silvera and Rigaud, 2016).

gender equality in the labour market? How can women have an impact from within unions to prioritize and advance 'women's issues', given they are still underrepresented in negotiating and decision-making bodies? Is it enough to simply have women (and which women?) in unions to improve the employment and working conditions of women workers? These are some of the research questions that have guided this comparative study on the relationships between the descriptive and substantive representation of women in different union contexts in France and the UK.

Structure of the book

The book is made up of three main chapters. The first is dedicated to an overview of the literature on gender and trade unions, and of how gender has progressively been considered in the field of employment relations. It also presents the methodology used in this comparative research. The second chapter explores the way in which four unions – the CFDT and Solidaires in France, and GMB and UNISON in Great Britain – have dealt with women's representation within the organization. These two countries were chosen for their differences in attitudes towards gender equality. In the British unions, equality policies are both older and more voluntarist than in their French counterparts, even in those that are the most proactive on the subject. This section of the book is therefore dedicated to the analysis of the 'inequality regimes' (Acker, 2006) specific to the four unions studied here, and the effects of equality policies put in place within unions. Through the comparison of 100 'trade unionist careers' (Guillaume and Pochic, 2021) the book analyses the social and organizational processes that contribute to the making of gender inequalities and limit the effects of the policies that are adopted.

The third chapter looks more specifically at how British unions have represented women's interests, based on a study of the struggle for equal pay since the 1970s. To shed light on this remarkable union mobilization, 40 interviews were conducted with women unionists, lawyers, and experts who were involved in equal pay litigation. These interviews were associated with an analysis of emblematic legal cases and statistics on the evolution of equal pay litigation since the implementation of the first legislation in 1975. This history provides a complex, evolving, and in-depth reading of the presumed links between descriptive and substantive representation of women. It reveals the involvement of critical actors; men and women inside institutions, including unions, some of whom were very hostile to the defence of equal pay. Whether internally in their unions, or externally through bodies like the Equal Opportunity Commission (EOC), women have mobilized to obtain their rights and ensure those rights were implemented. Less well known is the fact that local union men, mostly low paid and from male-dominated unions, seized on the existing legislation to obtain equal pay for their female colleagues. At the periphery of institutions, these actors were able to mobilize allies in the legal and political spheres both at the national and European level, to build networks and work towards the interpretation, implementation, and spread of legal norms within organizational practices.

The book concludes with an examination of possible directions for future (comparative) studies of women and trade unions, looking into methodological and theoretical challenges.

2

Unions' Representation
of Women and Their Interests
in the Workplace

In comparison with other academic fields, the underrepresentation of women and their interests in and by unions has attracted attention only relatively recently in France, with the exception of pioneering work on women's strikes in sociology (Maruani, 1979; Borzeix and Maruani, 1982; Kergoat, 1982) and history (Guilbert, 1966; Perrot, 1974; Zylberberg-Hocquard, 1978; Auzias and Houel, 1982). Research in employment relations has long been criticized for its 'classist obsession' (Kirton and Healy, 2008), its institutional bias (Wajcman, 2000), and its lack of consideration for the gendered dynamics that characterize union representation and the labour market. Yet, as early as the 1980s, Sylvia Walby (1986) argued that trade unions were one of the three patriarchal institutions that intervene in gender relations in paid employment, the others being the state and employers. In both France and Great Britain an overview of the literature shows the clearly marginal place of women in the 'classical' study of industrial relations; when they are not literally left out of the analysis, women feature only as a descriptive variable, or are studied in relation to specific issues like equal pay, workplace discrimination, and sometimes organizing.

In the UK in the 1980s, work by socialist-feminist researchers on working-class women's work led to a condemnation of the unions' hostile attitude to women in traditional industries and raised the question of the underrepresentation of women and their interests more generally (Pollert, 1981; Glucksmann, 1982; Cockburn, 1983). The convergence between feminism, the feminization of the workforce, and the increasing union membership of women contributed to the emergence of a 'subfield of research' (Ledwith, 2012) in the 1990s. Research was conducted with public sector unions like UNISON, which have a large female membership (Lawrence, 1994; Cunnison and Stageman, 1995; Colgan and Ledwith,

1996). Special issues in academic journals focusing on employment relations (Dickens, 1989) developed a gendered perspective and research groups were set up in specialized organizations like the British Universities Industrial Relations Association. In France it was not until the 2000s that research in this area developed, with work by Josette Trat and Marie-Hélène Zylberberg (2000), Yannick Le Quentrec and Annie Rieu (2003), Chantal Rogerat (2005), and Rachel Silvera (2006, 2010) on the CGT, my own research and that of Sophie Pochic (Guillaume 2007, Guillaume and Pochic, 2009c, 2011, 2013), and Pascale Le Brouster (2006, 2009, 2011) on the CFDT. Since then, this field of research has attracted young researchers, such as Maxime Lescurieux (2019) and Zoé Haller (2017) in France or Vanessa Monney (2020) in Switzerland, and has been enriched by the ongoing work of anglophone researchers such as Sue Ledwith, Gill Kirton, and Geraldine Healy in the UK, Linda Briskin in Canada, and Ruth Milkman in the US, whose references irrigate this entire book.

The roots of women's underrepresentation within unions

Like in the political field, research on gender and trade unions initially focused on the analysis of the processes that contribute to the underrepresentation of women in unions, both at the base and, especially, at the peak. It emphasized the role of both internal and external factors (Dunezat, 2005), such as the characteristics of the female workforce and the domestic constraints of women members, but also the dynamics specific to gender relations within the union movement.

Mechanisms of excluding women and undervaluing their work

These studies have helped to challenge 'false ideas' regarding the difficulties in unionizing women (Yates, 2006), by focusing the analysis on employers' management of the female workforce and union practices targeting women. Far from the myth of the unified working class, the labour market has always been stratified, with a clear hierarchy between skilled male workers, organized in powerful unions, and low-paid workers (women, young people, immigrants) who were often excluded from unions and therefore less unionized. Unions have often been reluctant to open their doors to women, fluctuating between discourses proclaiming women's right to work and those aiming to keep women in the home. In France, before 1914, the first union conference saw impassioned debates on the low wages of women workers and the threat that they posed to male employment (Silvera, 2014) at a time when women represented 36% of the working population, but only 9% of union members (Guilbert, 1966). These hostile reactions occasionally led to open confrontations between the male-dominated union federations and the (bourgeois women) representatives of the first-wave feminist movement. This played out in several highly mediatized disputes (Zylberberg-Hocquard, 1978; Chaignaud, 2009), such as the Berger-Levraut case in 1901[1] or the Couriau affair in 1913.[2] These exclusionary practices were particularly typical in industries like printing and publishing which were traditionally male dominated. The unions' attitudes were slightly more subtle in traditionally feminine employment sectors – the textile or clothing industries (see Box 2.1), for example – where women were less organized or only sporadically so. The exception here is the tobacco industry, which was highly feminized and very unionized (Guilbert, 1966).

Box 2.1: Women's unions: an unusual case

Excluded from men's unions, women organized themselves within women-only unions. In France, a few Christian women's unions were set up in non-unionized feminized sectors (clothing and textile – whether working from home or in factories – and office workers) as early as 1906, later affiliated with the CFTC, which had 37% female members when it was created in 1919 (Bard, 1993; Ratto and Gautier, 1996). The CFTC promoted the role of women as wives and mothers in accordance with the doctrine of the Church, suggesting that women participate in the Christian Youth movements (JOC-F or LOC-F, see Loiseau, 1996). However, social Catholicism also accepted women's work out of pragmatism (particularly for single women and widows) and sought ways to fight against the blatant discrimination female workers were subject to in the name of the protection of family life (low wages for long working hours). Quite apart from the feminist movement, and overseen by Catholic networks and lady patronesses, these reformist women's unions (Chabot, 2003) set out to help female employees and workers defend their interests by means other than strikes. They provided union training and assistance with appeals to employment tribunals, along with other services such as mutual assistance societies and professional schools for women. This segregation, justified by the ideology of the complementarity of the sexes, created a space for the expression of female union members, the defence of their interests, and their participation in leadership positions (37% of the national officers in 1927 were women). After 1936, some of these unions accepted mergers with male unions in return for commitments to internal equality (Ratto and Gautier, 1996). This formal equality, which involved the creation of a women's commission and representation in decision-making bodies, nevertheless marked the beginning of the decline of women's power in the CFTC in the period between the two world wars (Bard, 1993). In Great Britain, the women's trade unions created at the end of the 19th century with the support of the Women's Trade Union League (WTUL) in the textile and cotton industries also hoped to one day be accepted by male unions, and they encouraged the membership of men. These women's unions were dissolved as soon as it became possible to incorporate them within mixed-sex unions (Boston, 2015).

After 1918, women were tolerated within mixed-sex unions, in particular because of their involvement in the major strikes of 1917–18 and 1936, and because of their progressive entry into the labour market, particularly in the public sector. Limited inclusion or separate practices developed in different ways and according to different timelines in the two countries, but these also depended on the ideological framing of the different unions and their connections to the political parties and movements (Frader, 1996). From 1922, the French Communist Party began to see the recruitment of women as a way to build a mass movement and encouraged the establishment of women's commissions. Following this model, the CGT set up a 'women's sector' that oversaw women members and young members, with separate women's commissions within the federations and local unions (known as women's groups in 1963). They also offered educational work placements for women workers and produced a magazine for women called *Antoinette* (launched in 1955, producing up to 85,000 copies in 1976). These separate structures were considered essential to 'domesticating women' in the 1920s and then to 'helping women find their place in the union' in the 1960s (George, 2011). Alongside this, after the Second World War, the CGT supported women's right to work and launched campaigns for equal pay, reduced working hours and workplace equality (pay, training, and promotion). It was one of the only French unions to celebrate International Women's Day in workplaces, on 8 March. The CGT nevertheless promoted a 'conservative-egalitarian' framing which continued to emphasize women's primary role as mothers (defending pro-natalist policies after 1945). Class struggle remained the absolute priority, which often led to a paternalistic control of women's groups at the local level (Olmi, 2007).

In Great Britain, craft unions were strongly opposed to the inclusion of women (as illustrated by Frances Galt's excellent 2021 book on the film industry), using a gendered understanding of skill to exclude low-paid women from their membership. But they were even more opposed to the idea of equal pay – and in some cases remained so for a long time. When they did grant women equal pay, as the ACT did in the 1930s, only a minority of women were covered by these agreements because sex segregation confined women to grades in which few men were employed (Galt, 2021). In the name of the 'family wage' for men and domesticity for women (Rose, 1988), many unions defended – or even promoted – strict occupational segregation for women and young workers, even opposing women's recruitment in certain sectors or professions, and the maintenance of differentiated and gendered grades. The image of the male breadwinner and the mother at home was the bedrock of working-class respectability (Seccombe, 1986). This image of working-class masculinity was thrown into question, however, by employers who began to use underpaid female labour at the end of the 19th century as a way to control skilled male workers. The hostility of the trade unions to women's work can therefore be interpreted as the result of a combination of material factors related to employers' strategies, creating competition between different categories of workers, the emergence of new technologies (Cockburn, 1983), the economic context, and ideological factors. Employers rapidly associated specific characteristics with women workers, assuming these to be 'natural' qualities (skill, dexterity, attention to detail, patience), and they used women to push down labour costs and rationalize production. In the interwar period, women constituted a workforce that was particularly preferred in industries that were beginning mass production and assembly lines (Glucksmann, 1986).

In her historic study of a strike among low-paid women workers at the Rover factory in Coventry in 1930, Laura Lee Downs (2002) emphasized the interconnectedness between the recruitment of a female labour force, the undervaluing of labour, the development of managerial control, and a desire to increase productivity within a system of stratified labour force management, with separate pay and negotiation practices depending on the categories of workers. More recently, in her study of the printing sector, Cynthia Cockburn (1983) has shown how skilled male workers – and their unions – helped to keep women at the bottom of the wage hierarchy, refusing them access to apprenticeships and training until 1950. She also showed how employers used new technologies to replace skilled male workers and push men to do 'women's work', the ultimate attack on their gender identity. The hostility of craft trade unions can be seen in terms of not only the symbolic aspects linked to the definition of gendered roles and skills but also their strategies for maintaining a hierarchy of jobs and wages in industries that were undergoing rapid transformation (Savage, 1988). Research has shown that, during the Second World War, unions such as the ACT in the film industry negotiated agreements that specified that women performing men's work would be employed on a temporary basis, initially receiving women's rates before progressing to full male rates (Galt, 2021). They also consistently criticized women workers' (supposed) lack of commitment to their work, conveying the belief that women threatened the craft identity of male members, associated with dedication to their trade (Galt, 2021). By comparison, (semi-skilled) general or industrial unions did more to unionize women and young people.

Equality policy at the crossroads of democratic and instrumental concerns

Three main factors were involved in changing unions' attitudes towards women and workplace equality (Colgan and Ledwith, 2002): the activism of women's groups in the workplace and in union branches; the influence of second-wave feminists, very visible within the CFDT in France or the TUC and NALGO[3] in Great Britain; and the changes in union structures resulting from de-unionization and mergers between unions.

By the mid-1960s, women made up 70% of new union members in Great Britain. But this feminization of the membership did not mechanically result in women making real gains within trade unions and in the labour market. It was not until a series of strikes by women (see Box 2.2), and particularly by the women workers at the Ford factory in Dagenham in 1968, that there was a real coalescence between unionism and feminism (Boston, 2015). Increased educational opportunities for girls in the post-war period and the changing composition of the workforce contributed to women workers' growing discontent with their continued low status in sex-segregated jobs during the 1960s (Galt, 2021). As Ruth Elliot (1984) emphasized, women's strikes often drew their solidarity from outside existing union structures, or even in opposition to them. Connections also developed through campaigns such as the Working Women's Charter, launched in 1972 by feminists from the London Trades Council, which raised a number of questions relating to abortion, contraception, wages, and training and shook up standard negotiation practices by demanding the establishment of a minimum wage.

Box 2.2: Mid-1970s to mid-1980s: the decade when women workers got active (again)

During the period between 1973 and 1984 there were at least 12 strikes by low-paid women workers in Great Britain (Pugh, 2000). Some of the documents linked to these strikes (photos, leaflets, posters) can be seen on the TUC website *Equal Pay Archives*. In 1973 there was a strike in Coventry (GEC Spon Street Works) against a drop in piecework wages following technical changes. In 1974 there was one in Liverpool (Wingrove and Rogers Company) against a redundancy plan particularly targeted at women workers. In 1976 there was one in Brentford (Trico) for equal pay for women, and another in a North London factory (Grunwick Film Processing) with mostly female workers for better wages and working conditions. The latter led to a violent clash and the women eventually won the right to organize. In 1978–79 there was a movement against a pay freeze in the public service entitled 'End Low Pay' and in 1981 there was a period of collective action with strikes coordinated by NALGO to improve typists' wages in local government. 1982 saw a movement against low wages for textile workers (Smethwick Supreme Quilting), and 1984 a new strike for a pay regrade for women workers in Dagenham (Ford).

Despite this wave of mobilizations for equal pay, the Labour Party and the TUC did not discuss many of these disputes (for example, the one at Trico) at major conferences, prioritizing other issues such as concerns over unemployment (Stevenson, 2016). In the 1970s, the TUC simply published a booklet on the women's issues that had been raised. However, within the TUC and in other public sector unions, feminists challenged the 'democratic deficit' (Cockburn, 1995) and fought for voluntarist feminization in decision-making bodies, to promote an image of openness toward women and attract new female members. In 1979 the TUC finally adopted a Charter for Equality for Women within Trade Unions, which included ten recommendations focused on internal and organizational dimensions. They encouraged unions to establish procedures to facilitate the defence of women's interests at all levels of the union. The TUC then changed its own statutes to increase diversity and gender equality within its structures, playing a driving role for most of the unions affiliated with it. The move was pushed through internally by a few unions spearheading this issue (NALGO, MSF,[4] CWU[5]) and defended by leaders convinced of its importance. In these unions, the emergence of these policies was often linked to the conjuncture of internal factors, like the decentralization of union organization that made it possible to constitute local groups, as well as external impetus provided by the emergence of the New Urban Left in certain borough councils in Greater London in the late 1970s (Humphrey, 2000) and certain feminist organizations, some of which no longer existed by the end of the decade (Galt, 2021). The unions began to be subject by deep divisions around race, class, and sexuality.

Two kinds of policies were put in place. There were 'liberal' measures (Jewson and Mason, 1986) aiming to lift barriers to individual ambition but without changing union culture (family-friendly meeting times, training for women, childcare, and so on) and measures described as 'radical'. The latter were focused on equal-opportunity policies with the goal of achieving more systemic outcomes such as political awareness raising and the transformation of union organizations 'in order to ensure fair distribution of rewards according to merit and value' (Jewson and Mason, 1986). This approach justified equal-opportunity policies such as quotas or seats reserved for women, proportional representation for elections and delegations to Congress, women's committees and conferences, and, finally, self-organized groups. The two last kinds of structures, exclusively reserved for women and/or minority groups, were adopted in only a handful of unions and aimed to transform the organizations over the long term (Briskin, 2002). They sought to raise awareness of the status of the dominated group and provided the foundation for alliances to empower these oppressed groups while working with and within existing union structures.

Some policies fluctuate between the two models, depending on the way they are used, and the dichotomy between radical and liberal has been challenged by Cynthia Cockburn (1989), who prefers to talk about short- or long-term goals, between correction of discrimination bias and transformative goals. Thus, the 'women-only schools' within the TUC that were created in 1932 developed in the 1960s thanks to impetus from recently affiliated women's unions, and a few male unions that wished to address criticism from their (rare) female leaders, but without devoting substantial resources to this. At the beginning, these schools for women were created as protected spaces for acquiring the skills and empowerment that were needed for union roles (Kirton, 2006a). Under the influence of second-wave feminists these spaces took on a more political dimension and other objectives were added: debating questions specific to women and prioritizing women's issues; mobilizing internal pressure groups working for equality and encouraging women to take on leadership positions, including as trainers and educators. Above all, these 'safe spaces' were designed as places for the politicization of social identities, where feminist awareness and unionist awareness could come together, be shaped, and be activated (Kirton, 2006a). This impetus at the union level was consolidated by a legislative and political context prioritizing the fight against discrimination. In response to pressure from civil rights and feminist movements, three laws were passed in Great Britain: the Equal Pay Act (voted in 1970, implemented in 1975), the Sex Discrimination Act 1975, and the Race Relations Act 1976. From the late 1970s, the TUC committed to anti-racist campaigns and unionization of ethnic minorities (Virdee and Grint, 1994; Kirton, 2019) under pressure from militant anti-racist union members and strikes against racist practices among employers and some unions. However, although women made remarkable gains within unions in the 1980s, it is worth remembering that women workers 'progressed little between 1976 and 1986 and in important aspects slipped backwards' (Boston, 2015: 309–11). Women's employment declined. They were increasingly employed in a narrow range of jobs, and the gender pay gap widened. In the face of the political and economic challenges induced by Thatcherism, women's demands increasingly became seen as a 'campaigning luxury' by union members (Loach, 1987: 67), demonstrating that the specific needs of women are often 'eclipsed in times of economic crisis' (Loach, 1987: 67). Women union activists and the labour movement were forced to adopt a defensive strategy.

In France, the women members of the CFDT pushed for the incorporation of feminist (abortion, contraception, shared domestic labour) and egalitarian (reduced working hours for all, retirement at 60 for all) demands into the union's agenda (Gallot and Meuret-Campfort, 2015) in the 1970s, particularly through the local women's groups that were being set up in the service sector and in the region around Paris (Marauni, 1979). But these women's groups did not receive much support from the Confederation because it was difficult to control them politically (Le Brouster, 2011). Moreover, women-only structures progressively lost legitimacy, due to the egalitarian universalist framing that characterized the French legislation and the dominance of the class paradigm in the French union movement (Guillaume, 2018a), but the CFDT developed training sessions for female workers between 1962 and 1982 (Le Brouster, 2009). Initially restricted to women, these training programmes were progressively opened up to men and became less central in the development of a union strategy for women. From 1982 the CFDT adopted a quota-based policy for gender diversity in national-level structures, and prioritized collective bargaining following the adoption of the Roudy Law on workplace equality in 1983. This shift was the reflection of a de-politicization of the equality policy and renewed focus on labour issues, in a context of increasing distance from the feminist movement, accentuated by the departure of historic feminist figures. Yet women continued to join the CFDT because of its implantation in the service sector – in 2019 50.15% of members were women. Moreover, between 1992 and 2002 the leader of the organization was a woman, Nicole Notat, an ex-teacher; she was not, however, particularly sensitive to the feminist movement.

As for the CGT, which had promoted the idea of separate structures, these were abandoned in 1985 in favour of a diversity approach focusing on the age groups and social class of women workers. After a certain torpor in the 1980s, this organization seemed to actively take up the issue of workplace equality, organizing training programmes for both men and women on the subject, in partnerships with other unions – FSU and Solidaires. It also ran a network of 'Women and diversity' (*femmes mixité*) groups, even though its membership remained largely male. Although the idea of quotas was adopted only later, parity was directly imposed in the executive body of the union in 1999. As was the case in politics, unions were influenced by the evolution in gender equality occurring at the European level, promoting affirmative action in businesses and instances of power (along with the adoption of new national laws on parity and workplace equality). The European Trade Union Confederation tried to promote policies for increasing the representation of women from the mid-1990s (Cockburn, 1999) and adopted a Charter on Equality in 2007. The integrated and cross-cutting approach of this charter was a source of inspiration for certain French unions, including the CGT. However, this equal-opportunity and gender-mainstreaming perspective often resulted in a de-politicization of policies promoting women (Cristofalo, 2014), to the benefit of more instrumentalist approaches linked to the 'modernization' of union practices and union renewal.

These equality policies were indeed clearly influenced by instrumental considerations to do with survival strategies in a context of declining union membership, particularly among male workers, and steadily increasing employment rates for women in both countries. In a context of dwindling bargaining power, the focus on underrepresented categories that could provide new sources of union members was accentuated towards the end of the 1980s with the development of organizing campaigns in Great Britain (Simms et al, 2013; Galt, 2021). Apart from recruiting members, these campaigns aimed to breathe new life into unions that were servicing passive members and declining in number. Described as a new model for unionism and a radical break away from past practices, the 'organizing' approach theoretically aims at reviving a grassroots perspective, emphasizing activism and member participation along with the representation of minority groups. It intends to redefine the union as a structure for mobilization aiming to promote social justice, particularly through the pursuit of coalitions with other social movements. From a similar perspective, in France, the CFDT sought to develop a 'members–led unionism' initially considered participative (Guillaume and Pochic, 2009a), before being reframed as more representative and passive. In France, like in Great Britain, equality policies and unionization policies therefore moved forward in 'tandem' (Parker, 2003). Minority groups (particularly young people) were involved in organizing campaigns and union leaders acknowledged the need to respond to concerns from underrepresented groups in order to be able to unionize them (Heery et al, 2000). Radical reforms were therefore introduced by trade unions, including reserved seats, electoral reform, women's conferences, and women's committees to increase women's participation and improve union democracy (Kirton, 2006a).

In the early 2000s, progress on the question of equality within unions affiliated with the TUC nevertheless remained 'limited, fragmented, and progressive' (Colgan and Ledwith, 2002). The context of the 1990s was marked by numerous mergers between unions to cope with the financial difficulties related to declining membership and to consolidate union power. This further reduced the opportunities for women and other minority groups to increase their representation in leadership positions and gain access to positions as officers in the unions (Ledwith, 2009; Galt, 2021). This also applied to the French case. From the mid–1980s, equality policies developed unevenly, depending on various factors such as the proportion of women members, the history and culture of the unions, and the dedication of certain leaders (both men and women). The progress made in attracting women both at the base and the top of the organizations conceals threshold effects or even a certain regression in the number of women at the intermediary levels of union structures. In the world of large generalist unions, women have access to power thanks only to quotas, exceptional crisis circumstances, or fundamental transformations within the organization (except in highly feminized federations, in the areas of health and education for example). From this perspective, 'the presence of a woman at the head of an organisation most often corresponds to a moment of transition between two collective identities, a moment when the expectations the organisation has of individuals are relaxed' (Bargel, 2014).

Women often have union careers that are either accelerated or interrupted (Kirton, 2006b). Although the turnover in activists and union leaders is higher in France than in Great Britain, where leaders (including women)

14

last a remarkably long time, women leaders generally have shorter union careers than their male counterparts (Guillaume, 2007). This observation can be explained by their relatively young age when they access positions of responsibility, due to unionization or equality policies, and expected difficulties returning to work after a full-time union role. But women union leaders also talk about difficulties encountered during their union career. Due to a lack of training, or legitimacy (Monney et al, 2013), and because they come to power in difficult roles, these women often suffer from loneliness and a lack of recognition. They seek to redress this by overinvesting, which sometimes leads to burn-out, and often to a desire to leave the union movement. These observations echo research looking into the selective and limited effects of quotas as leverage for the feminization of managerial and executive positions (Kanter, 1977; Cockburn, 1989; Kirsch and Blaschke, 2014).

Union organizations that reproduce inequalities

Although the female workforce, which is clearly overrepresented in the public sector, has contributed to stabilizing union membership rates, women still struggle to progress within the union hierarchy. Common explanatory factors for this situation include the difficulty of articulating union, professional, and family responsibilities for working mothers and/or women working part time (Le Quentrec and Rieu, 2003; Haller, 2017). The question of the historically low representation of unions in certain very feminized sectors, along with the lack of recognition of union rights in different employment contexts, is also a factor explaining this underrepresentation. Women working in the public sector objectively have more access to union leadership positions even though recent research has shown that the demands of 'work' and 'life' hinder women's union participation (Kirton, 2018; Dean and Perrett, 2020; Gavin et al, 2020; Prowse et al, 2020). Low-paid women, often from immigrant backgrounds and/or working on precarious contracts in the private sector and small businesses, have even more difficulty doing unpaid union work in their spare time.

Beyond the characteristics of women's employment, research has underlined how the formal and informal selection processes for future leaders, and the representations associated with defining a 'good activist', all contribute to excluding women from active participation. This perspective emphasizes the role of organizational processes in the underrepresentation of women and responds to the criticism that the field of employment relations is interested only in structures and institutions (Wajcman, 2000). It draws on a theoretical framework that has developed within productive organizations to explain the career differentials between men and women, and the glass ceiling that remains unbroken for many qualified women.

This school of thought developed in 1974 following the critical article by Joan Acker and Donald Van Houten (1974), who encouraged scholars to question the 'neutrality' of organizational rules and norms. In the UK, it developed notably through the work led by Mike Savage and Anne Witz on bureaucracy (1992). Studies in this field (Colgan and Ledwith, 1996; Wajcman, 1998; Halford and Leonard, 2000) have demonstrated the interest of a 'meso approach' focused on the embeddedness of gender inequalities within organizational rules and processes, shedding new light on career differentials between men and women.

Sue Ledwith and Fiona Colgan (Ledwith et al, 1990) thus developed a gendered analysis of union organizations with an initial study conducted on SOGAT,[6] one of the biggest printing unions, in the 1980s. This research adopted a 'union careers' methodology which is now widely used in political sciences (Fillieule and Mayer, 2001; Guillaume and Pochic, 2021), identifying four different stages of union participation – activist, local leadership, branch leadership, elite activism. For each stage, the authors identified both the external factors favourable to women's union activity (or their absence) – family influence, family responsibility, the support of one's partner – and the internal factors linked to the organization of union work as such. For example, the authors highlighted that compulsory union membership in closed shop[7] industries explained the high level of unionization among women there. However, women activists still needed to obtain support from established unionists, who were most often men, to access local leadership positions. They struggled to be identified as legitimate candidates because of the time constraints associated with union activism.

Becoming a union leader involves not only 'biographical availability' (McAdam, 1986) that is incompatible with family constraints, but also long and ongoing experience with union roles. Because of gendered segregation in the workplace (and the fact that this is reflected in the union structure), women activists often represent only women, which is not considered sufficient to be able to represent their male colleagues in a range of different activities. Occupational segregation confines women to a small number of low-paid jobs, which are often isolated and have limited autonomy. Due to the characteristics of their jobs, women tend to only rarely acquire the legitimacy needed to represent a larger constituency, have less access to union training, and are not often able to acquire the broader activist experience needed to construct a career within the union. Similarly, it is often because of the characteristics of their jobs (casual, precarious, part-time, without any prospects for promotion) that women struggle to gain the confidence and skills required to feel legitimate in an activist role and, inversely, to be identified as a potential leader (Cockburn, 1991; Lawrence, 1994; Munro, 1999). Part-time employees (a form of employment that is more common in the UK than in France) have trouble finding the time to get involved in the union, and also express doubts as to the willingness of unions to defend their interests (Tomlinson, 2005). Skilled or semi-skilled professions seem to give women more opportunities to acquire competences that can be transferred to union activities (particularly public speaking and conflict management) and to access autonomous forms of representation (Cobble, 1990).

Pursuing this line of research, the comparative study conducted with Sophie Pochic (Guillaume and Pochic, 2011) in France and Great Britain sought to explore the mechanisms behind the underrepresentation of women by considering the characteristics of different 'internal (union) labour markets' (Doeringer and Piore, 1971) in various union contexts. Like in the political field (Lovenduski and Norris, 1993, 1996; Latté, 2002), this research emphasized the powerful discriminatory effects of the informal mechanisms that make trade union careers possible. It also underlined the persistent vocational definition of the norms associated with a union career, particularly involving long working hours (Franzway, 2000) and a high demand for geographical mobility. The mechanisms by which individuals are designated to be union leaders reveal the informal nature of union recruitment, the role of (male) mentors, the importance of 'time served' as a critical marker of leadership ascendancy, the absence of formal leadership definition and training (Pocock and Brown, 2013), and the importance of 'partisan resources' (Dulong and Lévêque, 2002) in access to formal positions of power. Union organizations are often structured around internal clans or factions that work to exclude outsiders and constrain insiders. Although they have the benefit of creating stable zones of cooperation in an environment subject to the hazards of election and the conjectural effects of internal crises, these factions encourage conformism, closeness, and a preference for in-group members (Melville, 1959; Kanter, 1977). In certain organizations which remain male dominated, women struggle to find their place in a male world they feel excluded from (Buscatto, 2009) or which systematically reduces them to their 'unavoidable sexualisation' (Guillaume, 2007; Monney, 2020).

As the proponents of feminist institutionalism have demonstrated (Krook and Mackay, 2015), institutions contribute to reproducing gender hierarchies. Although both women and men are present in political institutions, it is the 'masculine ideal' that continues to infuse existing structures, practices, discourses, and norms, and which shapes ways of evaluating, acting, and being. Institutions construct gender relations, in connection with other institutional spaces, through the images, symbols, and ideologies they transmit, but also in the framework of everyday interactions. Historians of unionism have, for example, emphasized to what extent unions have played an active role in the mythification of the (white male) trade unionist, the figurehead of the working class (Frader, 1996). Today the gendered representations associated with the fulfilment of a union role have evolved somewhat due to the feminization of the membership, but also the changing structure of the workforce. In the UK today, 50% of union members are women and half of those are in skilled or managerial positions. Union organizations have been transformed, and, with the exception of some sectors that are still heavily male-dominated, gender representations have also evolved.

Evolutions in both demographics and politics have opened up new spaces for women's participation. In France, like in Great Britain, the advancing age of (male) union leaders foreshadows a large number of vacancies in the union structure that will have to be filled in the future. Despite this, the conditions for training and transmission of power are still not necessarily met for the recruitment of workers who are not yet familiar with unionism, particularly in the personal services sector, which is very feminized but not very unionized. The professionalization of union activities (Guillaume and Pochic, 2009a), which can be seen in certain moderate unions, has also opened up opportunities for the identification of women who have professional skills that are potentially useful for the union structure. These organizational needs can incite unions to recruit women at the top (particularly those who are young and qualified) to paid rather than elected positions, even though this does not necessarily help the promotion of women activists at the workplace level. As a result, the latter are often not detected, trained, or given support in accessing leadership positions.

The progress of gender equality

Unions have progressively undertaken a process of selective feminization. But what effects has this had on their internal functioning and the way they represent the interests of working women (and minority groups)? This debate is most often dealt with from the perspective of the connections between descriptive and substantive representation (Pitkin, 1977) and is the subject of a substantial literature in political science. The feminization of the political field is analysed through the integration of women into political institutions together with the inclusion of women's issues on the political agenda (Mackay, 2010). These two questions involve different research topics. The first echoes the discussion described earlier on the reasons for the underrepresentation of women. The second revolves around several other research questions. Does the presence of elected women really make a difference? Are elected women sensitive and reactive in dealing with the issues of the women they represent (Pitkin, 1977)? Do they represent the interests of these women as a 'group' (Phillips, 1995; Lovenduski, 1997), and, if so, how are this group and its interests defined? What are the processes, particularly the democratic processes, that can enable a better substantive representation of women? All these questions have been applied to trade unions, but, unlike the political field, they have been the subject of a much less substantial literature.

Women at the table, women's issues on the table

From the beginning, the feminists who fought for the inclusion of women in unions theorized a supposed connection between internal and external equality (Dickens, 2000a). For Linda Briskin, a feminist perspective on unions goes beyond the simple inclusion of women, 'it is about transforming structures, hierarchies, cultures, and the agenda of demands' (Briskin, 1993). Like in the political field, this objective of transforming union organizations is associated with the increased presence of women in positions of formal power (Childs, 2004) and in decision-making bodies where priority demands are decided. It is through a 'politics of presence' (Phillips, 1995) that women are likely to contribute to improving the democratic functioning of organizations (whether political parties or unions) and to pay greater attention to questions of inequality, focusing on problems that have been undermined by male representatives (Dovi, 2007).

That unions fail to take into account the interests of women workers through the co-production of gender inequality via collective bargaining has also long been attributed to the lack of women at the negotiating table (Dickens, 1997; Ledwith and Munakamwe, 2015; Conley et al, 2019). Studies suggest that women activists bring knowledge and awareness of the problems encountered by women workers that male unionists do not have, and as a result they can influence the course and content of collective bargaining (Heery, 2006a). This premise of common interests shared by women as a result of their gendered social positions and experiences (Young, 2000) is both defended and debated by researchers who also recognize the internal diversity of women as a category and the danger of essentializing their interests (Briskin, 2014), by associating them either with questions traditionally seen as of concern to women (children, family) or with the demands of feminist movements.

Above all, recent research has emphasized the social distance that often separates women members from those who have become leaders (Galt, 2021). The social and professional over-selection of women leaders and those 'elected from diversity' gives rise to questions about their ability to represent all women. In France (Guillaume and Pochic, 2013; Guillaume, 2018a) and Switzerland (Monney, 2020), or in Great Britain (Guillaume and Pochic, 2013), recent research has demonstrated that women who manage to pull themselves up to positions of union leadership have specific characteristics. They tend to have stable employment with allocated union facility time or are employed directly as full-time officers. In both countries, these attributes are more frequent among White women, even though academic success, and access to higher education for young women from immigrant backgrounds, along with the desire to promote young women (and men) from diverse backgrounds, has facilitated access to positions of leadership for some Black, Asian and minority ethnic (BAME) activists.

This observation should not invalidate the fact that unions, often under the impetus of the first female leaders, have contributed to adopting a certain number of measures to promote women and advance gender equality. Since the 1970s, and following the initiative of activists, union confederations have progressively enlarged their demands to include 'women's issues', such as the right to abortion, contraception, childcare, maternity and parental leave, or the fight against violence against women, while also promoting women's right to work and shared domestic labour. In spite of the weakening of second-wave feminism, but thanks to the arrival of left-wing governments in power in France and in the UK, unions have contributed to developing laws to promote gender equality, and also legislation to establish national minimum wages or the improvement of rights for part-time workers, both of which particularly benefit low-paid women workers. Driven by EU doctrine, since the beginning of the 2000s, unions have also contributed to extending antidiscrimination legislation to other groups (lesbians, gays, bisexuals, transsexuals, workers with disabilities, ethnic minorities, and so forth). These policies conducted by union confederations as part of their political lobbying were also transmitted internally through awareness-raising campaigns and activists' training at the workplace level to facilitate collective bargaining on the subject. Specialized roles were also established, such as equality reps in the UK.

However, in both France and Great Britain the ability of women activists to genuinely influence negotiations continues to be an issue, even in a context that is generally less macho than it was in the 1990s (Dorgan and Grieco, 1993; Cunnison and Stageman, 1995). Research has also revealed the difficulty that women leaders have in influencing the agenda of negotiations, due to the highly bureaucratic internal functioning of unions, the segmentation of the collective bargaining process (particularly in Great Britain), and the gendered division of union work. In particular, the implicit assumptions shared by negotiators contribute to aligning employees' interests with the interests of the male negotiators (Dawson, 2014). In France, recent studies have demonstrated that collective bargaining on workplace equality remains secondary and comes up against numerous obstacles (Cristofalo, 2014; Conley et al, 2019; Milner et al, 2019; Pochic and Chappe, 2019; Pochic et al, 2019). Like in other countries, gender equality is often considered secondary or dealt with in a 'standardised' manner (Charpenel et al, 2017), particularly in a context of economic recession and austerity policies. Some studies have established that although unions generally demonstrate a genuine concern for workplace equality, their action against privatization and restructuring policies in the public sector (in Great Britain or Australia for example, see Yates, 1996) displays their short-sightedness as to the detrimental effects of these policies on women workers.

Women as transformational leaders

The other argument in favour of promoting women relates to their supposed ability to transform union culture and facilitate more inclusive functioning for both women and underrepresented groups. This perspective has been the object of an abundant anglophone literature but is less developed in France. Outside feminist spheres, studies on union renewal have given a central place to feminization as a tool for the transformation of repertoires of action and the development of an inclusive culture encouraging internal democracy and rank-and-file participation (Colgan and Ledwith, 2002). In her extensive literature review (2006), Linda Briskin emphasized the convergence between studies conducted in different countries to describe this 'post heroic' leadership (Prowse et al, 2020) which is said to have encouraged the empowerment of women. Recently, Gill Kirton and Geraldine Healy defined this leadership style as 'interpersonally oriented, democratic, collaborative, and transformational' (Kirton and Healy, 2012), as opposed to a more 'transactional' masculine style. However, some authors recognized that this leadership style can nevertheless be adopted by men (Prowse et al, 2020). Women leaders can also (sometimes simultaneously) be involved in 'different combinations of (masculine) status quo and (feminine and feminist) transformative leadership talk' (Kirton and Healy, 2012: 979). As other studies have claimed (Guillaume, 2007), this kind of communal leadership style can be more adequately explained by the type of union role and the length of experience rather than by individuals' gender.

Above all, research on women leaders has investigated the power resources and positions that allow women to promote alternative union practices. There are a certain number of organizational and institutional factors that influence the ability (and desire) of female elected representatives to promote women and prioritize women's issues, and thus also contribute to the transformation of institutional norms and practices. These include belonging to a more or less explicitly feminist organization (Norris, 1986; Norris and Lovenduski, 1995; Lovenduski and Norris, 2003), interference between the defence of gender equality and internal partisan logics giving rise to greater or fewer opportunities to promote a feminist perspective (Healy and Kirton, 2000), and the strength of institutional norms and democratic rules within organizations. Although the increased presence of women at the 'focal job' level (Cohen et al, 1998) improves the probability of seeing other women access it, this causal connection is mainly verified for major organizations in growth periods (Huffman et al, 2010), or unions seeking to become the majority union (Blaschke, 2011). This effect may dwindle over time. Above all, choosing to defend women's issues and declaring oneself a feminist can mean not being identified as a leader with a sufficiently large (and universal) power base to access higher positions. On the contrary, the use of a different repertoire of action and/or a differentialist discourse can be a source of legitimacy for women in a world that is still dominated by an ageing generation of male activists (Guillaume, 2007). But alignment with the dominant style and the 'neutralisation of gender' (Laufer, 1982; Pochic, 2014a) is often seen as a more efficient strategy.

The promises of 'self-organization'

Some British unions have engaged in political reflection as to how best to radically transform 'union democracy' out of a deep belief in feminism, but also out of a fear that 'liberal' equality policies (Jewson and Mason, 1986) to facilitate the individual access of women to leadership positions had proved insufficient. Since the late 1970s, some of these unions have therefore attempted to promote a more inclusive and participative democratic model via 'radical' equality policies (Jewson and Mason, 1986) to counter the organizational mechanisms that (re)produce the glass ceiling. These separate structures can be used in different ways (Briskin, 1993). First, they might be used as a form of ghettoization that keeps women silent and inefficient, communicating only with each other. This strategy can be employed by men to maintain the status quo and marginalize 'women's issues'. Another approach considers these measures as a way to redress the lack of women and help them to gain the confidence needed to become a part of the union's functioning, but without changing dominant rules or norms. A final, more proactive model defines separate structures as a place for feminist awareness raising and as a springboard for 'gendering' the union agenda. Many studies have thus documented the contribution of these structures to the internal democratization of unions (Parker, 2003), the expansion of the pool of future leaders (Healy and Kirton, 2000), the capacity to build external coalitions with other social movements (Briskin, 2002), and also the reformulation of union demands (Hunt and Rayside, 2007; Galt, 2021).

These studies have also emphasized the pragmatism of women activists in implementing these separate structures in a context of significant resistance from their male colleagues (Healy and Kirton, 2000; Parker, 2003; Galt, 2021). As Jill Humphrey (2000) stressed, these structures are caught between the union that authorizes their existence as transitional structures to challenge union traditions, on the one hand, and, on the other, the fact that the goal of the structures themselves is to transgress these norms and become institutionalized. Linda Briskin (1993: 101) argued that women's separate self-organizations 'simultaneously contests gender, power, and organisational structure', and thus encounter significant resistance from male trade unionists. Besides, there are two kinds of problems that emerge with these separate structures. The first is connected to the risk of bureaucratization and detachment from the union structure (Munro, 1999; Galt, 2021). These separate groups may adopt hierarchical and procedural working processes to be able to operate, mirroring the functioning of internal union rules, which contributes to creating a strong distance with the members. Alongside this, the need to produce motions for the annual general conference, which are often scheduled at the end of the conference (Galt, 2021), absorbs most of the energy of the self-organized groups or women's committees, to the detriment of other, more empowering activities such as training. The second difficulty that arises is linked to the danger of essentialism inherent in the definition of the group itself. Thus, each group may refuse members who do not correspond to the strict definition of the group's identity; bisexuals who are excluded from the LGBTI group, for example, or White minorities who are not accepted in the BAME group. This inflexibility prevents the identification of shared problems and can lead to a competition between different spaces of separate representation (Briskin, 2008).

The ability of these structures to adequately represent the diversity of women's issues (Colgan and Ledwith, 2000; Galt, 2021), and those of minority groups, has therefore been widely criticized, as has their ability to contribute to (re)defining union priorities. Having looked at length at the conditions that enable an effective use of these radical measures according to a strategy balancing autonomy and mainstreaming, Linda Briskin (2014) has advocated a reconceptualization of what she calls 'representative justice'. This involves redefining the links between collective bargaining and separate structures – particularly 'women's committees' – to move towards greater formalization or institutionalization.

The permanence of rank-and-file mobilizations

Although it has proved difficult for union representation to incorporate women's issues through traditional avenues, women have continued to promote their rights through their activism, sometimes in mixed groups (Kergoat et al, 1992), but most also in women-only mobilizations. In France, various research has investigated strikes led by women workers in supermarkets (Benquet, 2011), the hotel industry (Puech, 2005), or in the home services sector (Béroud, 2013; Avril, 2014). As Sue Ledwith (2009) argued, British women also have a tradition of organizing women working in small workplaces and marginal jobs, and involving migrant women, such as in the case of the Grunwick or the Gate Gourmet strikes (Sundari et al, 2018). In both countries, these mobilizations are often based on original tactics, the use of autonomous forms of organization, and strained relations with the union structures that are supposed to support them. In her comparison of four strikes led by women workers in the 1970s, Margaret Maruani (1979) revealed the existence of highly variable relations with the unions in place, but also in some cases the emergence of more horizontal forms of participation, which were more attentive to internal democracy and more considerate of the difficulties in articulating paid work, union participation, and family/domestic responsibilities.

These examples emphasize women's abilities to rely on their professional situation and family constraints to question union practices and seek new repertoires of action (Briskin and McDermott, 1993). In her care workers study, Christelle Avril (2014) thus demonstrated how constraints in the very nature of their paid work led women to choose innovative forms of mobilization, outside the usual codes of 'masculine' strikes, particularly through alliances with the elderly people they looked after. Linda Briskin (2011) and Charlotte Yates (2010) also emphasized this ability to build coalitions in the health sector. This search for the support of 'clients' shows that women can mobilize to defend their interests without the support from traditional union structures. The success of these campaigns demonstrates a reframing of the union struggle that incorporates the defence of occupational identities and quality of service (Briskin, 2011), as well as the defence of concerns specific to women (discrimination, equal pay).

These organizing campaigns have challenged the idea that it is difficult to organize women and emphasize just how much unions and employers have internalized a number of misconceptions about women workers (for example, that they are less involved in defending their jobs, more passive, less prone to becoming activists, working in paternalistic small businesses) and therefore are not easy to unionize (Yates, 2006). However, these studies have also emphasized the pitfalls of women-only forms of mobilization which have frequently struggled to gain stability (Perrot, 1974) and have been less successful than male or mixed-gender strikes, not always leading to the creation of a union or a lasting form of representation. The institutionalization and the generalist scope of large unions remains non-conducive to the emergence of rank-and-file groups with their own objectives (Kergoat et al, 1992), which remains easier in craft unions. Therefore, women belonging to general unions have rarely chosen to define their mobilization as a 'women's strike' to avoid their struggle being undervalued or not taken seriously. This strategy also tries to avoid the difficulty of defining what it means to be a 'woman', which can be the subject of controversy even within women-only groups, depending on the unions they belong to (Meuret-Campfort, 2010). Although this gendering of mobilizations has been interpreted by some as being the sign of a duality within unionism, with the emergence of unions that have almost exclusively female members (Milkman, 2007), the definition of women's interests remains complex. Research on domestic workers, a sector that is extremely feminized, has clearly illustrated the demarcations that run through workers' groups depending on prior social and professional trajectories (Avril, 2014), and the difficulty in agreeing on a shared definition of the profession (Béroud, 2013).

All these studies have pointed not only to the need to rethink the relationships between descriptive and substantive representation, but also to the importance of investigating substantive representation as such. Well developed in British political science (Celis et al, 2008), this research perspective has specifically looked at the relationship between representatives and those whom they represent, from the angle of 'claims making' (Saward, 2010). It has investigated the ways by which representatives construct the group that they say they represent and how they formulate its interests. Who are the actors, whether individual or collective, who initiate propositions or implement policies? When do they do this? What are the relationships between them? Do they put forward a homogeneous definition of what representing women and their interests means and covers? Which women do they say they seek to represent? How do they consider the intersections between gender, class, and race? What means and strategies do they implement? With what outcomes?

These concerns reflect questions raised by scholars concerning the implementation of equality and antidiscrimination legislation. After two decades of putting equality on the agenda, the emergence of formal policies, and the affirmation of antidiscrimination rights at the European and national levels, research is now focusing on the analysis of the implementation and the effects of these laws and policies. The role of unions (Dickens, 2000b), which is sometimes obscured by other 'equality entrepreneurs', such as 'femocrats' or diversity professionals (Kirton, 2007; Bereni and Prud'homme, 2019; Kirton and Greene, 2019), is reconsidered in this research, due to the importance of collective bargaining in most European countries. Unions indeed play a critical role as 'legal intermediaries' (Pélisse, 2014, 2019) in both equality and antidiscrimination law, helping to enact legal norms through collective bargaining and bringing cases before the courts (Willemez, 2003; Pélisse, 2007; Guillaume 2015a, 2015b) to promote workers' rights. Studies on the ways by which trade unions can foster the substantive representation of women (and minority groups) have therefore stressed the need to investigate the ways in which unions engage with legal rules to defend women's interests (or not).

A twofold comparative study

Unions, like other institutions, are spaces for both the objectivation and transformation of the social order. They tend to reproduce gender inequalities internally and to limit the field of possibilities in terms of equality policies, but they can also act as 'critical actors' (Childs and Krook, 2009) for the defence of women's and minorities' rights in the workplace and sometimes beyond. This dual position explains why second-wave feminists became active in their union in order to change them from the inside, to transform union culture, and to promote women's rights. Studies have shown that women were often confronted with the inertia common to political organizations but have also found spaces in which to promote their demands and import norms and beliefs able to challenge patriarchal norms. Depending on the institutional context, which may be more or less democratic and porous with other social movements, women seeking to promote equality have had to adapt to the characteristics of their institution in order to promote the cause of women and other minority groups. In the field of industrial relations, comparative research on the ability of unions to confront new issues – unionization (Frege and Kelly, 2003), representation of migrant workers, and so on – has emphasized the importance of considering unions' institutional characteristics so as to understand the variety of their proposed responses. Although the underrepresentation of women in unions has been noted in all international studies (Colgan and Ledwith, 2002), each institutional context produces specific 'inequality regimes'. This concept, as it is defined by Joan Acker, incorporates 'the practices, processes, actions, and representations that produce and maintain class, gender, and race inequalities within organisations' (Acker, 2006). Beyond providing a methodological framework that is useful for describing the organizational production of inequalities in different contexts, this perspective advocates studying the mechanisms by which inequalities based on gender are (re)produced (but also class and race, which are often the subject of separate or only partial analysis). However, other studies have pointed to the need to investigate a multitude of institutional hypotheses at the national level (such as public policies, gender regimes, or industrial relations regimes) to explain the varying successes of feminist policy in different national contexts (Rubery and Fagan, 1995; Mazur, 2003).

Drawing inspiration from these two approaches, this research has opted for a 'case study' methodology (Yin, 2014) that enables the investigation of how and why institutional contexts at different levels (European, national, local) interfere in (Demazière et al, 2013), constrain, or facilitate the development of unions' internal and external equality policies. This approach aims to grasp the variations between unions within countries, as well as the variations between countries. From this perspective, this study investigated two 'contrasting contexts' (Crompton, 2001) to draw out the elements that are shared within the trade union movement in terms of the difficulty of representing women, but also to look at what is specific to each trade union at different periods of time. Several studies have compared two unions within the same country, and only rarely between two countries (Kirton and Healy,

2013a; Kirsch and Blaschke, 2014). The variables frequently used to justify national comparisons include different rates of feminization, work sectors, or lengths of existence, and distinctive ways of framing equality policies in each union. But access to fieldwork is usually also decisive in the choice of the case studies. Many studies have therefore been conducted in the same unions, which are likely to be more open than others to researchers who are often explicitly identified as feminists and who have also sometimes contributed to establishing internal equality policies. However, it is rare to find studies that compare different unions in different countries.

This second chapter presents research that is based on a twofold comparison; it looks at four unions in two countries, the CFDT and Solidaires in France, and GMB and UNISON in Great Britain. These two countries were chosen for their differences in the way equality has been adopted in unions, Great Britain being more advanced in this respect than France. By comparison with French unions (Ardura and Silvera, 2001), there are more tools for promoting equality in the British unions, and gender equality policies there are more stable over time and clearly more voluntarist, particularly in the large unions and above all in UNISON. More generally, these two countries differ in many respects, whether in terms of the 'model of capitalism' (Hall and Soskice, 2001), models of employment relations (more or less centralized and coordinated), or the type of union 'identity' (Hyman, 2001). On the other hand, these countries share a similar situation in terms of union decline as reflected in the drop in union membership, and (in Great Britain) the decline of collective bargaining (see Box 2.3).

Box 2.3: Union presence in France and the UK[8]

The rate of unionization in France is one of the lowest in the OECD (11% in 2016), but after a significant drop in the mid-1970s and early 1980s it has since stabilized. Union membership is higher in the public sector (19%). Although the number of women members in unions has continued to increase, women are less unionized than men (10% compared to 12% in 2016). This low union density is associated with one of the highest levels of collective bargaining coverage in the OECD (93% in 2020). This paradox reflects the particularity of the French model of employment relations in which unions and employers negotiate collective agreements for all employees in the sector and not only for union members. Despite this low union density, French unions are present in many workplaces. By comparison, union density in the UK is much higher, around 23% in 2019, but it has decreased steadily since the 1970s. Women in the UK are more unionized than men (25.9% compared to 21.1% in 2016). These average rates conceal substantial disparities depending on regions and sectors, however. Wales, Northern Ireland, Scotland, and North East England have over 30% union members, but the

South West of England has a rate under 20%. Moreover, only 13.4% of private sector employees are union members, compared to 52.7% of those in the public sector, with a strong concentration of union members in former public services, now privatized (energy, telecoms, mail). Like in France, managers and professionals are more unionized (particularly women professionals in the UK) than low-paid workers. It is also the workers in large companies that are the most unionized, but between 30% and 50% of employees have a union representative at their workplace (with regional differences). However, unlike in France, the rate of coverage by collective bargaining agreements is much lower in the UK; it varies according to regions and sectors (14.9% in the private sector, 59.9% in the public sector). In both countries, workers on stable, full-time contracts are more likely to be members of a union.

These major institutional characteristics at the national level obscure much more diverse realities between unions than the existing comparative studies suggest (see Tables 1.1 and 1.2). The unions in Great Britain were chosen in order to balance out the case of UNISON (which has adopted progressive equality policies and is very feminized) with a union – GMB – that is less often studied, more male-dominated, and also represented in the private sector. In France, the choice of the CFDT was evident because of the long-established policies for the promotion of women and ease of access to the fieldwork. The study of the second French union federation, Solidaires, was more recent and linked to an opportunity to work with other colleagues conducting a long-term research in this union federation (Béroud et al, 2011). This opening provided the opportunity to study a union that describes itself as feminist and is more radical than the CFDT (but which has inherited certain equality policies from the latter). Unlike the other unions in this study, which are all very large, Solidaires, which brings together SUD unions (and other independent unions), is a small union federation and essentially represented in the public sector (Denis, 2001).

The equality policies implemented by the different unions in this study are more or less recent and voluntarist. UNISON is often quoted as an example because of the radical constitutional modifications brought about by feminist leaders, along with the resources dedicated to this policy (Parker, 2003). This very feminized union (78% of its members were women in 2020) is unusual in that it combines three kinds of equality structures (Table 2.1). Firstly, there are measures targeting proportional representation for women and other 'disadvantaged' categories, via seats reserved for them in the democratic bodies of the union (the National Executive Committee, NEC). Secondly, UNISON gave itself 'fair representation' objectives to ensure representation of all its members regardless of age, salary, working hours, activity sector, race, sexual orientation, sexual identity, or disability. This took the form of

Table 2.1: Unison internal equality policies

Number of members	1,375,000
Rate of overall feminization	78% in 2020
Rate of feminization at different levels	*Local/regional level* 55% of stewards in 2016 (50% in 2007) 46% branch chairs in 2016 45% of regional organizers in 2016 (36% in 2005) 46% of regional negotiators and 50% of regional managers in 2016 66% of regional secretaries in 2016 *National level* 61% of NEC (National Executive Council) in 2016 65% of national negotiators in 2016 50% of national service groups (local government, health) in 2016 80% of other national department heads in 2016 63% of full-time national officers in 2020
General Secretary	Woman (elected in 2021)
Equality policies	*Quotas* 42 seats reserved for women out of the 67 members of the NEC 13 seats for low-paid women in the NEC, 4 seats for BAMEs, 1 seat for young and retired members *Other measures* 4 *self-organized groups* (SOG) at the branch, regional and national levels for four groups (women, BAME, disabled and LGBTI) with *paid officers* to assist at the national and regional level An annual national conference for the four groups mentioned 2 *membership groups* for young and retired members *Equality officers* at the branch, regional and national levels Assistance for members and activists with care responsibilities Training reserved for women to encourage new women activists Establishment of a programme to promote staff to officers in 2015 New two-day training programme for young activist women since 2015 and specific training for migrant workers Leadership programmes for *senior national officers* (including mentoring)

seats reserved for low-paid women, BAME members, young people, and retirees in the NEC. The NEC is therefore made up of 67 members with nine general seats, 30 seats for women, 15 seats for men, 12 seats for low-paid or black members, and one seat for members under 27 years old. It is one of the rare unions to have a national leader for each category, including a leader responsible for women. The results of this policy are irrefutable in terms of the elected structure (61% of NEC members are women), but the impact is not so clear in terms of full-time officers' positions.

Finally, the principle of self-organization is the third key measure of UNISON's equality policy, even though it continues to be debated internally (Colgan and Ledwith, 2002). UNISON has established separate structures, called 'self-organized groups' for women, BAME, disabled, and LGBTI members who are integrated into the general functioning of the union according to the following system (see Figure 2.1).

Figure 2.1: Functioning of UNISON self-organized groups

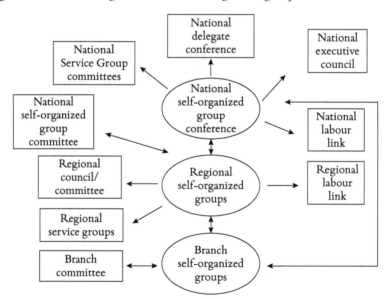

By comparison, the policy of GMB is more integrated and no longer offers measures such as women's groups (Table 2.2), even though they existed in the 1990s (this disappearance is a trend that can also be seen in other unions). GMB is a generalist union that has historically been very embedded in industry and male-dominated sectors, but which has also developed in the public sector and thus has become more feminized (49% in 2013). Its equality policy includes measures aiming for proportional

Table 2.2: GMB internal equality policies

Number of members	620,000
Rate of overall feminization	50% in 2020
Rate of feminization at different levels	*Local/regional level* 30% of stewards in 2013 55% of GMB employees but only 28% of regional officers in 2013 (20% in 2008) No women regional secretaries in 2016 *National level* 40% of CEC (Central Executive Council) in 2012 47% of full-time national officers in 2020
General Secretary	Man
Equality policies	*Quotas* 9 seats reserved for women and 5 for ethnic minorities out of the 56 members of the CEC *Other measures* A *National Equality Forum*, with two representatives for the following groups: women, ethnic minorities, LGBTI, young people, disabled members, and migrant workers A *National Equality Conference* since 2009 *National officer* for equality and diversity *Equality officers* at the branch, regional and national levels *Women-only* training and equal-opportunity training (only since 2007 in certain regions) *National Women's Task Force* at the level of the CEC since 2013 (now dissolved) Formal commitment to zero tolerance of all forms of discrimination for members and employees of GMB Establishment of an *appointment systems review* to make internal recruitment fairer and more transparent. High-level nine-month 'women in leadership' programme for women employees introduced in 2019 Women-only trainings introduced in several regions since 2018

representation for women and other 'disadvantaged' categories in the form of nine seats reserved for women in the Central Executive Council (CEC) and five for ethnic minorities. At the national level there is a single forum for all underrepresented groups and a leader for equality and diversity who is responsible for this policy across categories. In 2007, GMB conducted its first audit on internal equality, which revealed an underrepresentation of women at all levels of the organization, and in particular no women regional secretaries at all, unlike UNISON, in which four of the five Assistant General Secretaries are women. This audit was followed by another study conducted in 2012 that led to the implementation of the National Women's Task Force at the CEC level in 2013. The goal of this task force was to make recommendations to GMB as a union and as an employer, but for the moment there have been no changes made to the statutes. GMB holds national and regional women's and equality conferences and several regions have recently introduced women-only training in an effort to get more women to come forward and participate more fully.

In France, the CFDT is well known for its commitment to the cause of women during the 1970s (Le Brouster, 2006) and for having established equality policies early on, closely linked to its 're-centring' strategy (Defaud, 2009; Guillaume, 2014a). After long debates on the possibilities of establishing quotas, the 1982 Confederal Congress in Metz opted for a 'compromise' which consisted of a 25% quota of women in the national bureau (BN). But, as Pascale Le Brouster (2009) emphasized, the motion in question obtained only 62% of the vote and this feminization went hand in hand with an increase in the number of seats on the BN. In 1985 these measures were inscribed in statutes and the Confederal Congress decided to also enlarge the executive committee in order to increase the number of women on it. In 2001 the National Council set two objectives: representation of women proportional to women members for the federations, and parity for interprofessional and confederation levels. In 2008, the goal of 40% women in elected positions was set for the ballots at the *prud'homale* elections (similar to employment tribunals). A Women's Confederal Commission made up of both men and women has existed since 1964 (15 members elected by the BN every four years – four men in 2016) and a National Women's Officer position has been in place since 1988 (Table 2.3). The organization of the annual women's conference dates back to 1987, and in 1988 the National Council adopted a certain number of decisions related to the establishment of equality charters in CFDT federations. The various structures of the CFDT have implemented negotiation training in gender equality, but since the '*Sessions Travailleuses*' (Women Workers' Sessions) were stopped in 1982, there have been no women-only training programmes. More generally, Pascale Le Brouster has shown how the feminist agenda constructed in connection with certain feminist organizations, such as the French family planning movement, progressively made way for policies focused on internal diversity within the union in the 1980s, with the objective of organizing women and promoting gender equality in the workplace, along with a mainstream approach to equality (Silvera, 2006). In 2012, having noted the stagnation of women's representation in the union structures, as well as significant disparities in equality policy between structures, the Women's Confederal Commission suggested launching a 'diversity action plan' to encourage the different CFDT structures to adopt their own diversity action plan.

Table 2.3: CFDT internal equality policies

Number of members	620,000
Rate of overall feminization	50% in 2020
Rate of feminization at different levels	*Local/regional level* 24% of unions' General Secretaries in 2004 (22% in 2001) 38% of regional executives in 2016 *National level* 37% of executives of the federations in 2016 (32% in 2004) 30% of the National Confederal Council (CNC) in 2016 41% of the National Bureau (BN) in 2016 50% of the Executive Commission (CE) in 2014
General Secretary	Man
Equality policies	*Quotas* Minimum 30% women in the CNC since 1985 Minimum 30% women for the BN since 1985 Minimum 3 women out of 10 on the CE (since 1985) – parity decided by the SG in 2014 but no formal modification of the statutes Objective of proportional diversity for federation, parity for interprofessional and confederation since 2001 Goal of 40% women elected to the arbitration court since 2008 *Other measures* Woman delegates at the national level and network of equality/diversity leaders at the regional and federal level since 1988 Women's Confederal Commission (men and women) since 1964 (15 members elected by the BN every 4 years – 4 men in 2016) Equality/diversity policies for each federation and region, confederal gender diversity action plan since 2013 Women workers training from 1961 to 1982; regular professional equality training since the 1970s Annual conferences, *Actu'Elles*, every 3 years from 1987 to 2004 *Rassemblement de militant-e-* (Meetings of Women Members) every 2 years since 2015

In comparison, and because the union is so much smaller, the equality policy in Solidaires is less well equipped, even though it has inherited certain measures from the CFDT (such as a women's commission) and has maintained a societal and feminist approach to women's rights (Table 2.4). Many of the union leaders responsible for creating SUD unions originally come from the CFDT; Annick Coupé, for example, founded SUD-PTT with other activists in 1988 and led Solidaires from 2001 until 2014. From the

Table 2.4: Solidaires and SUD unions' internal equality policies

Number of members	110,00
Rate of overall feminization	Lack of precise information, but very different depending on unions
Rate of feminization at different levels	*Local/regional level* 30.9% of delegates to the Solidaires Congress in 2011 32.8% of delegates to the SUD-PTT Congress in 2012 42.2% of delegates to the SUD-*Collectivités Territoriales* (local government workers) in 2013 *National level* 4 women out of 12 members in the National Bureau 1/3 women present for national-level meetings (National Bureau or National Committee)
General Secretary	Duo – man and woman
Equality policies	*Quotas* Do not exist in SUD-PTT: 2 seats reserved in the federal bureau (a woman and a regional member) *Other measures* Women's Commissions (men and women) in certain unions (SUD-PTT, SUD-Education, SUD-Santé Social among others) Women's Commission and Gender and Sexuality Commission at the level of *Solidaires* 4 types of training: joint action against inequalities and stereotypes between men and women; joint action between men and women; joint action against sexist violence at work; negotiating professional equality; training for trainers in gender equality

beginning, SUD-PTT implemented a 20% quota for women in the federal bureau and a women's commission. When they were created, many unions did not implement specific programmes to encourage internal equality. Some, like SUD-Rail, did not because there was an overrepresentation of men in the union. Others, like SUD-Santé Social, in the health and social sector, did not because the overwhelming majority of activists in leadership positions were women (Wolf, 2011). Some of these unions, like SUD-Education, established women's commissions later. At the national level, Solidaires has a Women's Commission and a Gender and Sexuality Commission, as well as training session/programmes to fight against stereotypes and violence against women. Since 1997, Solidaires, the FSU, and the CGT have organized the Inter-Union Women's Days, which takes place over two days every year. Like UNISON and unlike the CFDT, Solidaires actively promotes a feminist union approach, but is still reluctant to establish quotas or other voluntarist measures at the national level. The principle of a male–female pair to be the spokespeople for Solidaires was adopted in 2015. The SUD unions do not seem to be favourable to establishing separate spaces for men and women. All the women's commissions at the national or federal level are open to men and women, even though in reality many of them are run only by women.

This research is based on various studies carried out between 2004 and 2014, first as an employee of the CFDT research department and then as an academic. The first study was conducted on the CFDT, based on 40 interviews with women unionists in 2004. This was later completed by interviews in Great Britain with 40 unionists in UNISON and GMB in 2007, of which there were 12 men and 28 women. These two studies were then enriched in 2010 with another study on 'union careers' with 45 unionists in the CDT, 34 men and 11 women (Guillaume and Gayral, 2011). In 2012, 21 additional interviews were conducted with unionists from UNISON, UNITE, and GMB on the struggle for equal pay, using the method of career histories. Finally, in 2014, new research was launched in France with Solidaires, based on 22 interviews with women unionists in the different SUD unions.

These interviews were supplemented by archival research[9] and analysis of union congresses' motions and debates, formal equality policies and campaigns to promote equality in the workplace. Other informative interviews were conducted in both countries, with experts from the TUC, lawyers specializing in antidiscrimination law, and experts from the Equal Opportunity Commission. Observation was conducted during women's conferences at the TUC and the CFDT, women's training sessions conducted at the TUC in 2007, and more recently during debates on the women's motion at the 2014 Solidaires Congress. More generally, working for the CFDT between 2001 and 2005, and then later, participating in many conferences and roundtables organized in that union on the issue of gender equality, helped to accumulate a rich body of empirical material. Other quantitative data come from questionnaires distributed during the CFDT Confederal Congress in 2002 and 2006, the Solidaires Congress in 2014 and the Inter-Union Days for Women organized by Solidaires (the FSU and the CGT) in 2014. This quantitative and historical data help to situate the career histories used in this research within the broader demographic characteristics of union activists and the fluctuations of gender equality policies within each institutional context.

3

The Gendered Making
of Union Careers

Given how different unions are both within a given country and between countries there is a surprising degree of convergence in studies on the underrepresentation of women in the trade union movement. Unions differ in their size, the characteristics of their members, their rates of feminization, and above all in their identity and the scope of their equality policy. So, how can we understand the processes that maintain gender inequalities within unions? What are the policies and measures that facilitate the feminization of different union structures, from the workplace branch to national decision-making bodies?

This chapter intends to answer these questions through the analysis of the 'careers' (Guillaume and Pochic, 2021) of men and women activists, using them to decode the institutional processes that produce and legitimate inequalities, but also the conditions that facilitate the promotion of women and their interests. Using what Rosemary Crompton calls 'biographical matching and comparative analysis' (Crompton, 2001), this research has compared the careers of many unionists, both men and women, in four unions, in France and the UK. As Muriel Darmon emphasizes, the concept of 'career' is particularly useful for the analysis of trajectories inscribed in 'areas where it is not already used as an indigenous term or idea' (Darmon, 2008). Indeed, this term is not only lacking but in fact actively rejected from the unionists' vocabulary, probably because it is usually associated with paid work and part of union work is unpaid and voluntary. Yet, by breaking away from the categories used by trade unionists themselves, which often borrow from the repertoire of 'vocation' (Fillieule et al, 2019), the concept of career explores how union activism is built and maintained in a 'permanent dialectic between individual history and institution, and more generally the contexts' (Fillieule, 2010). This approach allows to explore the institutional processes and norms that produce careers within the union movement, and their effects in terms of discrimination. By shedding light on the ways in which typical stable and ascending union careers are constructed, this comparative analysis implicitly reveals the difficulties some activists (and particularly women) have in accessing leadership roles. Through a dual movement aggregating and comparing individual experiences (Darmon, 2008), with a particular attention to the construction of key stages and sequences in careers, this chapter intends to shed light on the conditions that make union activism possible and sustainable, with a specific focus on gender, context, and period effects.

This 'career' approach (Barley, 1989) is a formidable tool in that it allows researchers to move beyond the pitfalls inherent in comparing (presumably heterogeneous) institutional forms from one country to another. Drawing on previous studies that have explored the different stages of trade union careers (Ledwith et al, 1990; Kaminski and Yakura, 2008) and to resolve problems comparing British and French union structures, I have established 'functional equivalents' that enable a comparison of union roles at different levels. By convention, this distinguishes between three career 'levels': membership and unofficial activism; the first elected roles in the workplace (union rep [délégué du personnel] or shop steward [délégué syndical], member of the work council [élu au comité économique et social [CSE]); intermediary roles within the union (branch officer [secrétaire de syndicat] or regional officer [secrétaire d'union départementale]); and national-level roles (national officer/official or regional officer [responsable fédéral, confédéral ou régional]). Each of these levels reflects different realities in terms of union time (full or part time) and position (paid, elected, seconded). Some unionists are paid by the union, others are on secondment to the union (paid by their employer), and others volunteer in their own time, particularly in Great Britain. One of the specificities of trade unions in Great Britain is that there are unpaid union activists elected at all levels of the union alongside paid officials. These elected representatives are responsible for particular committees (women, BAME, disabled, or LGBTI members) or sit on the National Executive Committee (NEC) that meets three or four times a year, to monitor the activities of paid union officials and ensure that they actually implement the motions passed by Congress. Some paid officials, like the General Secretary or the Deputy General Secretary, who are employed by the union are also elected in Congress. This is the case in France, for example, for the national, federal, and regional secretaries who run the different union structures, but in both countries most paid full-time officers are appointed.

Moreover, particularly in France, unionists often combine several union roles in their workplace, which allows them to take on other positions within professional and interprofessional bodies (departmental or regional structures). This dual dimension – 'pro' and 'inter-pro' – does not exist as such in Great Britain because unions are not represented in other institutions (health, retirement, complementary health, unemployment, social housing, training) in the same way as they are in France. They therefore do not get 'union facility time' for such roles. Moreover, the restriction of union time awarded by employers, including in the public sector, means that most British unionists can rarely be full-time activists unless they are paid by the union. Most of the unionists interviewed in Great Britain are paid officers or paid officials, but they started their careers as lay activists or were recruited from outside the union. Very few of those interviewed remained lay activists elected to the union executive (three in UNISON, and four in GMB).

Unlike other studies focused on union members (Barthélémy et al, 2012) or activists, this research looks at unionists who have a long-term involvement in their union. They have generally had many union roles and been activists for a long time. Out of the 104 people interviewed here, 79 are full-time officers at different levels of the union. Women are overrepresented in the study, particularly in Solidaires where no men were interviewed. The interviews that form the basis of this book are drawn from wide-ranging employment sectors, some of which are more feminized than others (such as local government or health services), but the interviews conducted in Solidaires were intended to specifically address women working in male-dominated sectors (transport, customs, industry). Most of the interviewees work in the public sector, with the exception of some members of the CFDT. Unsurprisingly the average age of these activists is quite high, with very few activists under 35 years old (Table 3.1).

The interviews were analysed using 'biographic tables' that separate the different sequences of work, family, and activism (Guillaume and Pochic, 2021), with specific attention given to 'turning points' (Abbott, 1997), defined as 'an alteration or deflection in a long-term pathway or trajectory that was initiated at an earlier point in time' (Sampson and Laub, 2005: 16). Among other examples, things like getting married, having a child, gaining or losing a job, moving to a new house, experiencing a strike, or taking on a new union role, can constitute turning points that can permanently alter a lifecourse. However, these are not isolated events, they are embedded in social contexts that need to be analysed and understood, especially when it comes to unions' institutional dynamics, including the existence and framing of equality policies. This focus on how social actors' experiences are embedded in multiple worlds is particularly important in understanding the complex interactions of these different life careers over the life cycle, depending on objective and perceived constraints and opportunities in the work, union, and family contexts of individual women (Kirton, 2006b; Guillaume and Pochic, 2013; Lescurieux, 2019). As numerous studies on women unionists have noted, family responsibilities can be a major constraint for women's union participation, but union and feminist convictions can develop hand in hand to progressively lead activists to redefine their representations of gender

Table 3.1: Interviewee profiles

	CFDT		Solidaires		UNISON		GMB	
	Men	Women	Men	Women	Men	Women	Men	Women
Total	10	23	0	22	8	18	7	16
Leadership roles								
National political level (*secrétaire national/* senior national officer/ NEC members)	0	5	0	14	1	7	1	4
National technical level (*secrétaire confédéral/* national paid officer)	0	4	0	0	3	4	1	5
Intermediary level (*secrétaire syndicat/* regional officer)	8	9	0	3	4	7	3	4
Local level (*mandats élus d'entreprise/* shop steward/branch secretary)	2	5	0	5	0	0	2	3
Contract								
Full time	9	19	0	10	8	16	5	12
Union time	1	4	0	12	0	2	2	4
Age range								
Less than 35 years	2	4	0	2	0	3	1	4
35–49 years	3	12	0	11	5	6	0	4
Over 50 years	5	7	0	9	3	9	6	12
Education level								
More than two years post-secondary education	3	9	0	16	3	7	1	6
Two years post-secondary	2	6	0	4	0	3	0	0
Secondary school or less	5	11	0	2	5	8	6	10
Original profession								
Worker/employee	5	7	0	10	6	16	6	11
Intermediary profession/technician	2	7	0	11	0	2	0	2

(continued)

Table 3.1: Interviewee profiles (continued)

	CFDT		Solidaires		UNISON		GMB	
	Men	Women	Men	Women	Men	Women	Men	Women
Manager/senior professional	3	9	0	1	2	1	1	3
Employment sector								
Public	5	16	0	19	8	18	3	12
Private	5	7	0	3	0	0	4	4
Family structure								
Children	7	19	0	17	6	13	5	12
No children	3	4	0	5	2	5	2	4
Ethnic background								
White	9	22	0	20	8	16	7	12
Black, Asian and Minority Ethnic (BAME)	1	1	0	2	0	2	0	4

roles and their involvement in the home. Apart from domestic constraints, job characteristics are decisive in the construction of activist careers, from the perspective both of the formal conditions of participation they allow (job security, union rights) of and the transferable skills they provide. Moreover, although the professionalization of unionism is highly variable between unions, they can provide the possibility of 'alternative' professional careers. Union activism can become a job and sometimes a career. However, unionism can also be a threat to employment because of the impact of labelling and victimization associated with holding a position in the union (Guillaume, 2014b; Kirton, 2018; Chappe et al, 2019). As recent studies have pointed out, it is crucial to examine how the combination of women's paid work, union participation, and family–domestic responsibilities, referred as the 'triple burden' (Kirton, 2018; Gavin et al, 2020), affects women's roles as trade unionists.

Interviews were conducted with both men and women activists, of all different ages, some with technical profiles, others more political. This diversity in career trajectories is important to gain a close understanding of the processes and circumstances that facilitate (or discourage) the pursuit of union activism, in terms both of the formal and informal conditions required for a union career and also of the individual dispositions that make them possible (Becker, 1966). Understanding the different forms of union participation (and their selective logics) implies being able to connect the institutional logics and relationship dynamics that shape the different levels of participation – the company or shop floor/the branch/the region/the executive – and the subjective dispositions toward union participation.

The analysis therefore focuses on the processes and activities that constitute union activism, and an understanding of the subjective dynamics that make the continuation of this involvement possible (or not). It is therefore not so much a question of the meaning of this activism, or the different categories unionists use to negotiate the 'possible worlds' of activism (Demazière and Dubar, 1997), as it is an analysis of the objective and subjective processes that lead to union participation. What activities do members and activists participate in? How do they take on the roles that they are given? What are their constraints and resources in terms of the requirements of their union role? What are the consequences of their activism for other aspects of their lives? The goal here is to explore the elements that bring coherence (or constraint) to the pursuit of a career in the union, and the factors that might lead individuals to reduce their involvement or stop it altogether.

Joining a trade union: the role of individual dispositions

Most studies on the unionization of women, particularly low-paid women, have noted that they are less likely to join the union, due to the characteristics of their jobs. Indeed, these women often work in small, private sector businesses where unions struggle to gain access, and in which the predominantly paternalist social relations do not emphasize the right to organize. Women workers are also more likely to be on insecure or part-time contracts than men, particularly in Great Britain. Often, they also work alone, or atypical hours, and so are not in easy contact with union reps. But women are also heavily represented in the public sector, which provides more stable careers and employment (Box 3.1), and these workplaces are significantly more unionized.

Box 3.1: Characteristics of women's employment in France and the UK[1]

In 2017, in France, 83% of women aged between 25 and 49 years were employed, some 10% less than men of the same age. This figure is lower in the UK (72.5% in 2020) and also lower than the rate for men (80.5%). In both countries women are more likely to work part time than men, but this rate is higher in the UK than in France (40% compared to 28%). In France, low-skilled and menial jobs are more often done by women, representing 27% of female employment, compared to only 15% of male jobs. In both countries, women are present in professional or managerial positions (15% of women) and in public sector management (outside teaching) and administrative or sales management in the private sector. In the UK, more women than men work as professionals (21% women compared to 19% men). In both countries, women are

41

underrepresented in executive roles. In France, only 26% of women are senior executives (*cadres dirigeants*), compared to 33% of women in the UK who are in the highest paid category of 'managers, directors, and senior officials'. Moreover, occupational segregation according to gender remains prevalent in both countries. In France, in 2010–12 there were eight professions in which 90% or more of workers were women: three low-qualified service professions (family day care, home help, domestic services) as well as executive secretaries, hairdressers, beauticians, nurses, and hospital orderlies. In the UK, women are also overrepresented in care, leisure, and other service industries (in which 82% of workers are women), as well as administrative and secretarial work (77%) and sales and customer service (63%). Finally, in both countries, women are exposed to more vulnerable working conditions. In France, 4.7 million women were living under the poverty line in 2010 (less than €964 per month for a single person). The 'working poor' is overwhelmingly made up of women (70%) and the risk of precarity is even higher in single-parent households, where 33% earn under the poverty line. The rate of women workers in unskilled employment is now around 62%, compared to 56% in 1990. Today more than three-quarters of the 1.5 million underemployed are women. In the UK, between 2008 and 2014 the number of women who said they would like to work more hours increased from 1.1 million to 1.55 million; an increase of 41%. Job insecurity affects women particularly badly. The number of women in insecure jobs increased from 773,000 in early 2008, to 892,000 by late 2014.

In Great Britain women's union membership rates have held up better than men's because of their presence in the public sector (see Box 2.3). Increasing unionization of women is also linked to organizing campaigns led by the CFDT, GMB, and UNISON in the private and public sectors (particularly in local government in France and in the privatized public sector in Great Britain). However, the results of these campaigns are highly variable, depending on the sectors and the periods (Simms et al, 2013; Guillaume and Pochic, 2014), due to variations in employment growth, and have had minimal impact on small and very small businesses.

A stable professional situation: the condition for union membership

With a few exceptions, the vast majority of our interviewees joined the union when they were in stable employment, most often in the public sector or in major public or private companies, or sometimes working directly for a union in a technical capacity (without necessarily having been a union member in the past).[2] This characteristic of employees who are long-term union members is not specific to the interview population, which seems fairly representative of union activists in the two countries. The data available for the CFDT (Lescurieux, 2019) and Solidaires confirm that among activists

Table 3.2: CFDT Congress delegates by employment sector

	Grenoble Congress 2006	
	Population	% responses
Private company	333	48%
Public service	231	33%
Public company	75	11%
Other	54	8%
Total	751	100%

Source: Questionnaire distributed during the Confederal Congress in Grenoble in 2006.

there is an overrepresentation of employees with stable, long-term, full-time contracts in major public or private entities. The most recent survey conducted during the CFDT Confederal Conference in Grenoble in 2006 (751 responses, 454 men, 297 women) clearly shows this correlation between union activism and stable employment (see Table 3.2). Although the CFDT has almost the same proportion of members in the public and private sectors (which is quite rare among French unions), it does have a large number of activists in the public sector (44%).

This overrepresentation of public sector workers is even more pronounced in Solidaires. Among the 145 activists who answered the questionnaire distributed during the Inter-Union Women's Days in 2014, only 15% worked in the private sector, and 14% of those worked in a company with more than 500 employees. Moreover, public servants made up 75% of the respondents. These results concord with the data from the survey conducted in 2011 during the Solidaires Congress (270 respondents, 193 men, 77 women). Here there were few private sector workers (26.8% compared to 60.5% public servants), and no female members working for companies with over 500 employees. This concentration of private sector activists in large companies can be found in the CFDT, where only 13.8% of activists work in companies with less than 50 employees (Table 3.3). Although there is no equivalent data for unions in Great Britain, we can safely hypothesize that UNISON members are overrepresented in the public sector (or privatized public sector), while GMB is more present in major companies in the private sector (as well as in the public service).

The CFDT questionnaire did not include questions on the type of work contract, unlike the questionnaire conducted with Solidaires in 2011, which showed that only 2% of activists attending the Congress were on short-term or casual contracts. This figure is particularly low for Solidaires, most likely because SUD unions are active in the public sector. But it may come as a surprise, given the shift in public companies toward a widespread use of casual and insecure contracts. The results of the CFDT survey demonstrate

Table 3.3: Private sector delegates by size of company

	Grenoble Congress 2006	
	Population	% respondents
1 to 10 employees	8	3%
11 to 19 employees	7	2%
20 to 49 employees	22	7%
50 to 99 employees	29	9%
100 to 199 employees	48	15%
200 to 299 employees	26	8%
300 to 499 employees	36	11%
500 to 999 employees	47	15%
1000 employees and more	95	30%
Total	333	100%

Source: Questionnaire distributed during the Confederal Congress in Grenoble in 2006.

the very low number of part-time workers among the Congress delegates (Table 3.4). The number of part-time workers was much higher among the Solidaires activists who attended the Inter-Union Women's Days, where 25% of attendees said they worked part time. This result is even higher than the survey distributed at the Solidaires Congress in 2011, where only 13% of women unionists said they worked part time. This difference can most likely be explained by the overrepresentation of experienced union activists (who have held several roles within the union) among the delegates present at the Congress. Workers on more insecure or part-time contracts (or those who are underemployed) are rarely able to pursue a lasting career within the union because they lack union rights and/or 'biographical availability' (McAdam, 1986; Lescurieux, 2019). These women activists, whose involvement in the union is rarely stable, are underrepresented here.

Another aspect of job security as a condition for union activism can be seen in the number of years' professional experience of the CFDT activists at the Congress, which is associated with an overrepresentation of activists over 40 years old (Table 3.5). This observation is even more visible for Solidaires, as the average age of Congress delegates in 2011 was 48.5 years.

Although we do not have comparable data for British unions, the table of interviewees shows that the majority of UNISON, and above all GMB, activists are over 50 years old (see Table 3.1). Moreover, their career histories show that most of the interviewees from these British unions aged over 45 joined the union with their first job, often as an industrial worker or employee in public services or banking. Given their age at the start of this career (between 16 and 18 for those with the lowest qualifications), these

Table 3.4: CFDT Congress delegates by working hours

	Grenoble Congress 2006	
	Population	% respondents
Full time	617	82%
Part time (less than 35 hours per week)	44	6%
Looking for work	1	0.1%
Retired	66	9%
Other	16	2%
No answer	7	0.9%
Total	751	100%

Source: Questionnaire distributed during the Confederal Congress in Grenoble in 2006.

Table 3.5: CFDT Congress delegates by number of years' professional experience

Years of experience	Population	% respondents
Less than 1 year	1	0.10%
Between 1 and 5 years	3	0.40%
Between 6 and 10 years	22	3%
Between 11 and 15 years	44	6%
Between 16 and 20 years	89	12%
Between 20 and 25 years	138	19%
Between 26 and 30 years	155	22%
Between 31 and 35 years	156	22%
Between 36 and 40 years	77	11%
Over 40 years	22	3%
No answer	44	1.5%
Total	751	100%

Source: Questionnaire distributed during the Confederal Congress in Grenoble in 2006.

women had no children and were working full time on a permanent contract. However, in both countries there are substantial generational differences. Although most of the older activists experienced a stable and continuous career progression, a certain number of younger activists had difficulties accessing their first job or experienced prolonged periods of job insecurity (regardless of their qualifications), even when they later succeeded in joining the public service. The data from the CFDT are once again useful here, although they are difficult to compare because the questionnaires used do not systematically ask the same questions from one Congress to another. Although, on average, 25% of managers present at the Congress in Nantes in 2002 had experienced a period of unemployment, this number increased to 40% for new members in working in management, who had joined since 1995. Exposure to the risk of unemployment remains lower for more qualified groups, however. Among activists in intermediary professions, for example, 36% said they had experienced unemployment. This rate rose to 45% for workers or employees, who constitute a significant portion of new members who have joined the union since 1995.

Even though the job market is different in Great Britain, the same generational differences can be observed there, depending on the periods and type of profile (level of education). The few young women interviewed for this study tended to have higher qualifications. They had occasionally held insecure or temporary jobs during their studies, but rapidly gained job security afterwards by working for a union. These very specific profiles of paid officers employed in specialized positions within the union are also present in the federation, regional, or confederal structures of the CFTD. Solidaires, on the other hand, does not employee paid officials at the national level, but in the SUD unions in the public sector some young women are seconded to national or federation union roles in accordance with union rights. In Great Britain, across all generations, young women with low-level qualifications working as secretaries or assistants also joined the union structure as paid officers and then progressed within the union, particularly in the regions. A clear example of this type of internal promotion is Gill, a very rare case in French unions.

Gill, a secretary who moved up

Gill was born in 1967. Her family was quite "old-fashioned", her mother was a secretary who stopped working to raise her children and later returned to work part time. Gill left school after completing secondary education to attend secretarial school. She did not have academic ambitions because her future as a wife and mother was already mapped out to a certain extent, unlike her older brother, who went to university. "I was brought up in a scenario where it was possible for a woman to work, but as soon as I got married and had children I had to stay at home. I never thought that I could have a career." In 1985, in a period of high unemployment, she was happy to get her first job as a secretary in an insurance company. Then, aged 21, she had her first child and resigned. She stayed at home for a while, but then began looking for work to improve the family finances. She found an advertisement for a secretarial job with the NUPE, without even knowing what a union was. "I saw the advertisement in the newspaper for a job at NUPE. I did not even know what a union was, I had never heard of one.

It was a secretarial job. I went for it and got it." She was sad to leave her child, but her parents looked after him while she worked part time. She quickly grew to love her job and felt that she should have returned to work earlier. She was asked to work with the training manager, becoming his assistant and developing new skills, "things I never thought I was capable of". Following the merger with NALGO and COHSE, many employees took voluntary departure packages, and she immediately replaced the assistant to the Regional Secretary, by-passing other, more experienced assistants. When she divorced in 1991 she moved to full-time work, which allowed her to buy an apartment. Her parents and her ex-sister-in-law helped her with childcare. Her boss encouraged her and advised her to take evening classes at the Open University that he also attended. He was very committed to the women's rights movement. At the time, many women were trapped in administrative roles and could not progress within the union, which had by then become UNISON. When her boss retired, Gill began to work with other leaders on recruitment issues. In 2002 she applied for a position as organizing assistant and was selected over 11 other candidates. She has continued her evening classes and, as soon as she has her degree, she will be able to apply for a real promotion, to regional officer or organizer. She has the full support of her superiors, but promotion will depend on the opportunities available at the time, because she does not want to relocate, and the regional structure is very small.

★★★

Our research, like that of others (Lescurieux, 2019), confirms that the lack of job security is one of the main factors hindering unionization for women (but also for men). Most of the interviewees became union members only once they had a stable job, which was more difficult for young people and which explains generational differences in age at membership for the CFDT activists (Table 3.6). In all the unions studied here, the low numbers of younger members are indicative of the difficulty in organizing this population, particularly because of their trouble in gaining access to the job market. Even in a major public sector union like UNISON, there were only 65,000 members under 27 in 2016, of which 77% were women (which equates to 0.05% of the overall population). This is a clear reminder that union activism, like any other kind of activism, relies on solid social and professional integration.

The issue of part-time work, which is often mentioned in anglophone research, must be relativized in two important ways. This type of contract is less common in France than it is in Great Britain and is often associated with precarious jobs (see Box 3.1). In this case, part-time work, job insecurity, and lack of workplace union representation go hand in hand and make it very difficult for women to join and stay in the union. Conversely, the lower

Table 3.6: CFDT Congress delegates, age at first membership, by period (%)

	Less than 20	20–29 years	30–39 years	40–49 years	Over 50 years	Total	Average age at first membership	% women
Joined before 1974	19	72	7	1	1	100	23 years	29
Joined before 1975–84	6	80	12	1	1	100	25 years	34
Joined before 1985–94	0	39	45	13	1	100	32 years	39
Joined before 1995–2002	0	21	50	26	3	100	35.5 years	51
Total	7	59	24	8	1	100	28 years	37

Note: Of union members who joined before 1974, 19% were less than 20 years old when they joined.

Source: Internal investigation with two thirds of the participants at the CFDT 2002 Congress in Nantes. Original data analysis by Sophie Pochic.

propensity of British part-time workers to join the union may be compensated for by a strong incentive to join – like in traditional closed-shop industries – or simply by the active presence of unions in the workplace and their ability to represent the interests of part-time workers (Walters, 2002; Tomlinson, 2005).

A slower membership process

In the socioeconomic context of the 1970s, young workers were able to rapidly access the labour market, in areas that were often strongly unionized, particularly in traditionally male-dominated sectors such as printing, the postal service, or local public services, or in some female-dominated industries like textiles. These early-career encounters with unions also occurred in France during the same period because of the high levels of unionization in certain union strongholds. This contributed to an early socialization of workers to the union, leading to participation in workplace elections, and sometimes membership. In Great Britain, closed-shop practices were authorized until 1983 and frequent in male-dominated sectors, but also (as is less well known) in some female-dominated sectors like the textile industry. These practices made union membership quasi-compulsory. Many of the male-dominated craft unions have today almost entirely disappeared and merged within large generalist unions, such as UNITE. This category-based (or craft) unionism also exists in France but concerns specific professional groups such as teachers, policemen, or pilots. In Great Britain, and to a lesser extent in France, 'semi-professional' employees (nurses, doctors, social workers) or professionals (engineers, doctors), particularly in the public sector, continue to join specific unions that represent the interest of only their professional group. They may also join general unions that are active in their sector. In this context, union membership is offered in the same way as professional insurance would be and is therefore somewhat seen as a form of protection (Moreau, 2014).

In these professional environments, unions play a major role in managing changes in the profession, identifying information on promotions, changes in pay rates, and questions relating to employment relations more generally (although they also contribute to the identity of the professional group, as Alice discusses later). The question of how early someone joins the union is not necessarily an indicator of how much they will participate (Pignoni, 2017). In this configuration, union activism can remain latent; these unionists do not necessarily take on responsibilities or roles (Haller, 2017). This passive membership is rarely based on a conscious choice resulting from an ideological position and can mean employees choose the majority union without knowledge of what the union world looks like. Beyond the services that unions provide, this form of membership can, however, be an inherent part of occupational identity and a way of defending the profession. Unlike in the 1970s, today this defence seems less political and more focused on improving working and employment conditions, as well as defending professional ethics in a context of organizational restructuring and managerial rationalization.

Alice, doubly committed to the union and to the profession

Alice is the director of a social welfare centre. She joined the union early on, directly after her summer internship, and she considers that "unionism is an integral part of the profession". She became National Secretary of the union after only five years in the profession, at age 29, and was the representative for directors of social and medical–social centres. She had no experience in activism or volunteering as a student (she studied political science, with a master's in administrative law), but she had a genuine desire to work in the public service which she inherited from her mother (a secondary school teacher). During her first internship at the National School for Public Health, she met a key figure, her internship supervisor, who was then the director of a children's home and a unionist with the CFDT, who would later take on responsibilities at the national level of the union (where she still is). Alice was always a member of the union anyway, because of the legal responsibility that directors in social and medical–social care institutions must take on. This profession is highly unionized, and 60%

of union members are in the CFDT. This commitment to the union is also a way for her to make a constructive contribution to reforming public policy to make it more respectful of users: "implementing public policy in the area of child welfare, or assistance for disability or social exclusion means that a director who observes that these policies are insufficient or incoherent has to be able to raise those issues". As the assistant director of a children's home (a position she obtained after her second internship) she found herself unable to concretely apply this concern for users because the director failed to support her when she wanted to sanction a member of staff for mistreatment of children: "I was not able to do my job properly". When her former internship supervisor retired, she had already been elected to the board of the union for two years and it was difficult to refuse the calls for her to go full time. But she considers this transfer to a full-time union position as a "short-term job". She organized to leave in 2006, after five years, but hopes that this experience will not backfire because in this sector appointments depend on local elected representatives (the Mayor or President of the Departmental Council):

'local politicians may be afraid of people who are so closely involved with the union. When you are elected, you like to have directors who are obedient, because not everyone is left wing. Even though the CFDT is seen as a moderate union which does not have a political affiliation, local politicians have their own opinions about unionism.'

★★★

In the 1970s and 1980s, union membership evolved in a context of major strikes led by unions, particularly in Great Britain. These included strikes against wage freezes (for example, the winter of discontent in 1978–79), against industrial restructuring (culminating in the 1984 miners' strike), and also against privatization of the public sector. From 1984, the public utilities sector, along with telecoms, energy, and other public service jobs (such as general services or catering in town halls, for example) started to be privatized through the implementation of a policy called Compulsory Competitive Tendering. This made it compulsory for local public services to open part of their activities up to tender, and therefore externalize jobs in those areas. The unions fought these privatizations (and continue to do so today). Major strikes were also held in France in the 1980s and 1990s to increase wages, reduce working hours in the public sector, or protect pension schemes. For some young women from more conservative backgrounds (sales or agriculture, for example) these strikes, which were often quite fun and convivial, were an avenue for the politicization and liberation that led them to union activism (and sometimes politics), as was the case for Colette:

'This was the second major banking strike, in late 1978. There had already been strikes in 1974 and 1978. And this one was already about purchase power and working hours. In 1974, there had been quite a lot of improvements in the banks in terms of benefits, but in 1978 the strike failed because there were other pressures. It came to an end just when it shouldn't have, because what we got from the bank was nothing at all. We probably got 12 hours knocked off our working hours, that's all. I had been at the bank for a year when the strike started and I had a crazy one on my team – he was far left, extremely nice, he could say anything, he was so enthusiastic. And we were just a bunch of kids who'd been hired a year ago, you know, there was a really great ambience in the group. He managed to get us all to go on strike, but he could say anything, he could have been with FO or the CGT, whatever, it was all the same, we followed him. So, I followed him, I went on strike, and I joined the CFDT by chance.' (Woman, bank employee, age 49, union official, full time, banking sector, CFDT)

Similar stories of participation in major conflicts, like the nurses' strike in 1988 (Kergoat et al, 1992), or localized disputes in certain ministries, are also quite common among activists in SUD unions. From the 1990s, the CFDT progressively shifted towards a more moderate stance and this had an impact on strikes, with the more radical activists continuing to participate in struggles against public service restructuring. They remained a minority within the CFDT until the mid-1990s and then most often moved to a SUD union, which they sometimes helped to set up themselves.

'I was transferred to an area near the Swiss border and that is when the dispute started, the major dispute in '89 over finances, and at the beginning I was a bit lost. I had landed right among the CFDT unionists and they just dragged me along. It concerned the Ministry of Finances as a whole, about pay rates and career prospects. And after this dispute in '89, they revised all the promotion charts, grades, and pay scales, all that kind of thing. It was a dispute that was very long and hard, and widely supported. Even the customs officials were on strike. So, I was just thrown into the mix right away. There was a very strong union culture at the Ministry of Finance, around 82 or 85% participation in union elections. It is the highest rate of all the public service, I think. It is considered a left-wing ministry.' (Woman, customs controller, age 45, union official, SUD-Douanes)

In France, in the private sector, many studies reveal the existence of local disputes following a redundancy plan or restructuring in the industry. This is also the case in other areas of the private sector (Abdelnour et al, 2009), including for qualified workers (Collovald and Mathieu, 2009). The population interviewed in this study is not representative of these casualized and insecure jobs. Employees who join the union in the context of an individual or collective dispute with an employer are often inconsistent members because they are frequently made redundant or move jobs after participating in industrial action (Beaujolin-Bellet and Grima, 2011). Today, unionization is more of an individual process for private sector activists, who are more prevalent among the CFDT interviewees. Many of them joined the union when they were faced with problems at work – unfair dismissal, harassment, or companies not complying with labour laws. They mentioned the impact of the general economic context to justify their membership: deteriorating working conditions, intensifying rhythms, increasing job insecurity, disputes in the workplace, restructuring and redundancy, and so forth. The defence of workers' rights is of utmost importance for workers in the private sector and in small and very small businesses, but it is also present in the public sector, as is the need to block unfair practices and ensure that employers respect labour laws. Although not many interviews were conducted with people working in the most insecure sectors of the economy, this study nevertheless reiterates the fact that women have objectively 'good reasons' to join the union, particularly when they are young and face the deterioration of their working and employment conditions (see Box 3.1). Qualified women workers in all sectors are also vulnerable to the evolutions of the labour market. They are discreetly critical about the management strategies implemented in their companies or in their administration, and often try to defend themselves informally before adopting more formal strategies (Guillaume and Pochic, 2009b). Faced with the desire to feel more supported and protected in these actions, some turn to the union for help. This is the case for Cécile.

Cécile, a union activist 'out of necessity'

With a degree in management from Dauphine University, Cécile was recruited by a software company in 1989 in a management control capacity. After three years she was employed by a large consulting company in an "atypical and multifunction role". She was responsible for management control, human resources, and marketing. The company grew substantially, from 750 to 4,000 people, and after another three years Cécile had been promoted to manager at age 29. She participated in the creation of an internal management control service and was responsible for a team of four people. She was very satisfied with her career evolution, even though integration was difficult. The company was split in two and the consultants (most of whom were male graduates from elite universities) did not mix with the administrative staff (often women with less prestigious educational backgrounds). The situation got worse in 1995 because the company's revenue declined. A new manager arrived to "clean things up". Cécile's direct superior was fired, but she kept her job because they needed her to oversee the transition and manage the team. She faced a lot of pressure and felt like she was being pushed to make mistakes. She then refused to testify against a co-worker whom the new manager wanted to fire. "I didn't want to be part of that, and that's when the poor evaluations began." Progressively she had her work taken from her. "When I walked by the financial director, he would turn his head away, and because it was a big open space, everyone saw." She thought she would either end up depressed or would have to quit. But in the end, she decided to learn about employment law. She ran for the workplace elections and was elected to the works council without a union affiliation. She had always been interested in unions and it "all came back". She had initially been offended by the very "fussy and procedural" approach of a fellow council member affiliated with the CFE-CGC, whom she did not know, but she rapidly came to understand that was the necessary approach. Several council members had left the company and the group of newly elected members pushed her to run for council secretary. She realized that members of this work council got "walked all over by management" and decided, with another member, to join the CFDT in 2000. This choice was driven partly out of respect for Nicole Notat, then the female General Secretary of the CFDT, and the values of the organization, and partly by elimination of other unions. In the meantime, Cécile found a decent position within the company, at the head of a team of six. She also had three children in close succession. She therefore had to "juggle full-time work, union responsibilities, and family". In 2003, she negotiated a union agreement with the company and became a full-time union representative with a part-time role in the company and part-time as the union treasurer. It became impossible for her to combine everything, as neither the objectives nor the responsibilities of her new professional role had been revised. She was no longer attracted by career progression because that would have "forced [her] to associate with top managers whom [she did] not like". Although she was a member of a moderate union, she became increasingly seen as a "radical unionist" within the company.

★★★

Aside from these cases of 'circumstantial' unionism and in a context where joining the union has become a relatively rare initiative (in France), even in the public sector or major private companies, becoming a union activist is often described as a highly personalized and progressive process. Participation in the union is constructed over interactions with one or several people also involved within the workplace (a representative, an activist, or a group) or in an external union structure called on for support (branch, local union, region). Sometimes employees do not know these people are members of the union, but this relationship not only helps to normalize and demystify unionism, it also makes it more familiar and tangible. New members need to be supported in this initial phase of involvement. These union contacts need to be good listeners, accessible, patient, available, realistic, and able to support new members (Dean and Perrett, 2020). Mentoring and support from older members (often men) is central. The presence and number of women in union groups is also one of the factors that facilitates the recruitment of other women. The principle of resemblance is key to the unionization of women, young people, or workers from immigrant backgrounds, and is at the heart of organizing strategies in the United States (Fairbrother and Yates, 2003; Milkman and Voss, 2004), and to a lesser extent in Great Britain (Simms et al, 2013). Without being expressed in these terms, this principle has also been used by the CFDT in its organizing campaigns, with actions targeting women, young people, and small business employees (Guillaume and Pochic, 2014). For Nathalie, an activist with SUD-Culture in a major museum, the feminization of the union branch has been an important factor in increasing women's membership:

> 'well, there is something, like a kind of imitation. ... Like when I arrived at SUD-Culture there were already women members. ... Even unconsciously, it made certain things possible. And so, I joined and then there were other women who followed me, and there you go. And what's funny is that we've always had more women than men as members of this branch.' (Woman, museum attendant, age 35, national official, SUD-Culture)

How open certain branches are to subjects like LGBTI issues can also attract new members who will identify with the activist group, like Carole at SUD-PTT:

> 'You have to know that when the SUD-PTT union was founded in 1989, one of the founders of SUD-Poste Paris, one of the most important activists, who would become departmental secretary and incredibly important in the 1990s, was bisexual, HIV-positive, and open about it. When I arrived in the job in 1997, very young, SUD was clearly a hideout for dykes and gays basically. People who came to SUD, came for its openness. I mean lots of members and future members were also people who had been in the CGT and been kicked out because of their sexuality. Some of the founders of SUD had also been through the CGT as well. And there were some who came from the CFDT because the CFDT offered greater possibilities.' (Woman, employee, age 45, national official, Solidaires)

Political socialization and activism

Although participation in the union can be assisted by a strong union presence in the workplace, it is generally associated with a desire to defend rights, working conditions, and occupational identities. This is facilitated by a pre-existing sensitivity to fighting against injustice that generally stems from forms of political and/or religious socialization transmitted in the family environment or through experiences predating union membership (Fillieule et al, 2019). Many unionists interviewed who joined in the 1970s mentioned their intense politicization as members or sympathizers of left-wing political parties. Particularly in Great Britain, many of the UNISON activists were involved in feminist and/or Trotskyist/Communist groups or were members of the Labour Party. Within GMB, which covers less-qualified workers, many of those interviewed – men and women – mention their working-class background in the North of England and a family culture of unionism as factors in their activism (Pochic, 2014a). In France, these forms of political socialization are more frequent among Solidaires activists, including younger ones, than they are in the CFDT. Older CFDT activists with leftist political leanings generally left the CFDT or were behind the creation of SUD unions in the 1980s. This was the case for Jacqueline.

Jacqueline, active in politics and the union

Jacqueline trained as a teacher but quickly wanted to shift into a manual job and work in a factory. She was an activist with the Communist Revolutionary League in 1981 and decided to participate in the 'workers shift' and studied to become a fitter and turner. She was hired by a big company, Thompson, joined the CGT, and became the workers' rep. She was proud of having succeeded in this job and had the chance to work with men who did everything to help her integrate. "I was almost like their mascot, it was the first time they saw a girl in their workshop, but it was a bit paternalistic. Their vision of me changed when I became the CGT delegate." In 1988 she was fired after participating in

> 'three weeks of total strike, occupying the factory and everything. It was intense, I had lots of things to experience. It was a very, very, very tough strike, and so when I saw that it was not going anywhere, I thought I absolutely have to find a new job and so I sat the first exam that came along, at France Telecom.'

She was hired on the information team (known as the '12', the then number for information) and once again joined the CGT. But she found the ambience much more bureaucratic than what she had experienced at Thompson: "we could talk, we could argue, even quite violently. At the time, in the CGT there were people linked to the Communist Party, there was me in the League, and comrades from *Lutte Ouvrière*." So, she joined SUD-PTT, which had just been set up, as a simple activist. She decided to quit France Telecom because she hated her job, "I just could not deal with. It was a completely mind-numbing job. I had the impression that I was becoming stupid. Unionism is not enough when the job itself is tedious to that extent." Because she had an undergraduate degree in law, she was able to sit the exam to become a job counsellor with the unemployment office (ANPE). She arrived just as SUD-ANPE was being set up, "it was a great opportunity, everything was yet to be created. We had meetings at night because we did not have any union rights. We had to fight for them! It was a wonderful project." Jacqueline is now approaching the end of her career. She chose never to have children, a decision that was made conjointly with her partner, also an activist, "because between union activism and the meetings every evening for the League, it was really a frenetic kind of activist life".

★★★

By way of contrast, many of the CFDT activists interviewed mention participation in non-profit or community associations (Table 3.7), with notably less partisan political socialization. This evolution can be explained by the shift within the CFDT itself and the departure of more politicized activists, particularly toward the SUD unions. However, this involvement with multiple associations remains higher in this group than in the general population (Pignoni, 2017) across all education levels. By comparison, the study conducted at the Solidaires Congress in 2011 (with 278 attendees) shows that 21% of the respondents were members of a political party and 15.5% were members of an anti-globalization movement. Involvement in more politicized issues, such as the defence of refugees and asylum seekers, and housing rights is thus an important distinction between the activists with SUD and those with the CFDT.

Combining political and union activism is also quite frequent among older British unionists, particularly because of the historic links between the Labour Party and trade unions. This correlation is no longer systematic for younger generations of activists (Moore, 2011), with the exception of some of the qualified female paid officers interviewed at GMB and UNISON. These young women started working directly for the union and often studied political science, and were involved in other movements and sometimes in student unionism. Some of them were also involved in the Labour Party, as is the case for Scarlett.

Scarlett, unionism as a 'normal outcome' of an interest in politics.

Scarlett was born in 1977. She does not come from a typical working-class northern family, but went to university in York, where she studied political

Table 3.7: Participation of CFDT delegates in associations

	Management		Intermediary profession		Working classes		Total	
	Population	%	Population	%	Population	%	Population	%
Member of an association	137	66%	212	60%	153	47%	502	54%
Family, cultural, sporting associations	66	32%	117	33%	79	24%	262	28%
Humanitarian action	61	29%	47	13%	66	20%	174	19%
Parent–Teachers Association	44	21%	83	23%	51	16%	178	19%
Insertion, fight against social exclusion	20	10%	30	8%	24	7%	74	8%
Environment	20	10%	21	6%	17	5%	58	6%
Local development	15	7%	24	7%	19	6%	58	6%
Religious associations	12	6%	21	6%	9	3%	42	5%
Secular associations	9	4%	7	2%	10	3%	26	3%
Other groups	24	11%	35	10%	20	6%	79	9%
Political party membership	43	21%	46	13%	40	12%	129	14%
Local politics	4	2%	19	5%	20	6%	43	5%
Population	209		355		328		929	

Note: Among the managers present at the Congress, 66% are also members of an association.

Source: Internal investigation with two thirds of the participants at the CFDT 2002 Congress in Nantes. Data analysis by Sophie Pochic.

science and philosophy. Her parents were not in the union, but her mother joined when she got a job in the probation service as a secretary, encouraged by Scarlett's brother, but also by the strong union culture there. During her studies Scarlet was active in the youth branch of the Labour Party and she has remained a member. In 2003 she found an ad in the newspaper for a job in the research department of the telecommunications union, the CWU, in London. She stayed there five years but wanted to broaden her experiences to other sectors in the public and private spheres. She described the union's way of operating as not very strategic or political, and above all focused on "reactive responses". "Their way of operating is strange. I suppose it is linked to the fact that they are not an economic organization with quantifiable objectives. It is often difficult to understand what their strategic stakes are in the medium term, beyond the immediate desire to help members improve working conditions." She was then hired as a human resources (HR) officer with GMB. This job was more to her liking even though she was not a specialist in HR. Above all she could not see many possibilities for career progression within the union. For young experts, the question of career evolution within union structures remains an issue. There are not many internal training programmes and most of the high-ranking positions are awarded to people elected by the regions. Scarlett nevertheless considers that unions are good employers that give workers a chance even when they are not already qualified for the job. However, she predicts that the rest of her career will take her elsewhere, probably into the non-profit sector.

***

In terms of socialization, a certain number of activists also mentioned direct or indirect family heritage that legitimizes their union activism and at least partly explains why they chose a particular union. In France, many of the interviewees from Solidaires, but also from the CFDT, mentioned their father's or sometimes both their parents' membership in CGT or the Communist Party. This affiliation with the CGT was sometimes presented as a counter model, considered too rigid or too masculine, associated with an environment that is macho, full of aggressive, loud-mouthed male individuals. That being said, as Julian Mischi (2016) shows in his investigation of a CGT railway workers' local union, many (younger) activists have no union or political affiliation, which is also the case for some of the French interviewees, including in Solidaires. Despite declining unionization rates in both countries, the interviewees we spoke to for this research work in sectors where unions are recognized, even though membership and active participation are increasingly rare, particularly in France. In fact, it is this union presence that allows workers to challenge their assumptions, having never encountered unionism in their workplace before. This was the case for Carole:

'In the summer of 1995 I worked for the Post Office up until September. When my contract finished, I went to work at the Grand

Rex, a very well-known movie theatre in Paris. During the strikes in December that year, when I was working at the Rex, I did not go on strike. There wasn't a union, so I wasn't unionized. In fact, I never met an activist. During the Christmas school holidays I was rehired at the Post Office, on a long-term contract. I had got a permanent position and that's when I got to know the local union and the remarkable female activists, whom I had previously seen from a distance.' (Woman, employee, age 45, national official, Solidaires)

In both countries, unionization of young workers is now often delayed. Aside from instances of individual workplace disputes or very strong political socialization (which was more common among ultra-politicized activists of the 1970s, like Jacqueline), union membership is usually dependent on the encouragement of union organizations present in the workplace. In France, in unionized sectors where union rights are generous, it often happens that sympathizers are not called on to formally join the union. In this respect, organizing practices are very different between the two countries. In France, recruiting members is not necessarily seen as a priority, even for the CFDT, which had a very active organizing policy in the 1990s and 2000s (Guillaume and Pochic, 2009a). Obtaining large votes at the work council elections is now more important than recruiting members, as it has become the main criterion of union representativeness, in terms both of bargaining rights and of access to financial resources (Box 3.2).

Box 3.2: The 2008 law on union representativeness

Since the enactment of the 2008 law on union representativeness, in order to be considered representative, a union organization must henceforth satisfy a range of cumulative criteria. It must:

- have been established for at least two years (from the date of the formal lodging of statutes) in the geographical and professional area of the company;
- have sufficient membership and dues;
- have obtained at least 10% of votes at the first round of work council elections. Thus, the only organizations considered representative are those who obtained 10% of votes cast (excluding blank and invalid votes) in the first round of the most recent elections for members of the work council or employee representative body, or, when necessary, staff representatives, regardless of the number of voters;
- respect republican values to ensure freedom of opinion, political philosophy, and religion, and refuse any form of discrimination, fundamentalism, or intolerance;
- be independent of the employer;

- be financially responsible and transparent: this new criterion is guaranteed by rules on certifying and publishing the financial records of confederations, federations, and regional unions, as well as any union with resources over a certain threshold, established by law.

In Great Britain, unions rely on membership dues for their resources and consequently put a lot of effort into recruiting new members. It is therefore more unusual to meet activists who were not directly asked to join. Although in certain sectors the extent of the union's presence means it is more likely that one will encounter unionism in the workplace, joining nevertheless implies an affinity with the existing group of activists on issues to do with gender, race, and class. For most of the female activists interviewed, the presence of women and sexual or ethnic minorities (less common in our sample) in the union branch was critical in their decision to join. The desire to organize women (or other minority groups) can be supported by top-down unionization policies with support from specialized organizers, but the success of these membership campaigns is heavily dependent on the goodwill of local leaders (Voss and Sherman, 2000) and the number of women workers in the sector. As we have shown elsewhere (Guillaume and Pochic, 2014), some male-dominated federations of the CFDT, like the mines and metalwork federation (FGMM), never identified women as a specific target for their organizing policies.

In both countries, despite the various ways members join, they all share a retrospective view of their union participation as 'self-evident'. The interviewees described their involvement as 'natural', rooted in their history because of predispositions linked to their character, personality, or family background. For these established activists, union membership is presented less as a form of 'self-transformation' (Darmon, 2008) than as a way to create coherence between one's values and dispositions. Regardless of generation, union membership is informed by instrumental objectives (Klandersman, 2004) – fighting against workplace injustice, standing up to bosses – but it is also driven by a desire to promote social justice (Yu, 2014). Yet today it is less associated with other elements of political socialization, like Communist Party membership in France, or Labour Party membership in Great Britain. This political affiliation is more common among British interviewees, however, because of their age, but also because of the type of roles they have within the union, generally as paid officers/officials. As we will see, membership in or proximity to the Labour Party remains a benefit for paid officers, but this is less the case for activists elected in the workplace, as the study by Sian Moore (2011) showed. Although union membership enables a certain form of ideological individual coherence, today it is less associated with strong beliefs in the importance of unions or their role in society (Klandersman, 2004), especially in France. Membership needs to be facilitated by a colleague who is recognized as legitimate both personally and professionally, preferably in a workplace context where the value of unionism and social partnerships are recognized (high levels of participation in workplace elections, old and established union presence, existence of social partnership). As Julian Mischi (2016) reiterates, one of the main roles of full-time activists is precisely to oversee unionization and generational renewal. In all unions, these are the figures who progressively encourage 'sympathizers' to take the plunge and join the union, by continuing to construct a feeling of belonging to the militant group and a local branch identity, sometimes in tension with the agenda and ideological orientations of the national union they belong to.

Getting involved in the union: building legitimacy

The unionists interviewed in both countries tended to rapidly take on union roles in the workplace, especially creating branches, as was the case for many of the SUD unions, or in workplaces with high numbers of women workers and union rights, like the public sector. It is worth remembering that one of the explanations for the higher rates of women members in the UK is the fact that their public sector jobs are still relatively stable, with more union rights than in the private sector, although the situation is changing. Since their return to power in 2010, the Conservative government has intensified the privatization process begun under Margaret Thatcher and sought to dramatically decrease the means awarded to unions, particularly in terms of facility time. British unions already have less resources than their French equivalents, and this decrease will undoubtedly accentuate the gender disparities in terms of union participation – particularly for young women with children who already have trouble reconciling professional, family, and union responsibilities.

A lack of candidates and the role of local leaders

In both countries, there was a lack of candidates for local union roles among the generation that joined the union in the 1990s and 2000s, which was a by-product of declining membership and frequent union victimization (Chappe et al, 2019). Employees identified as potential workplace representatives were most often directly contacted by one or several established activists who suggested they put their names on the electoral list or become a rep. Identifying new activists relies on interpersonal relationships and the detection of certain activist skills or professional knowledge that could be useful in a union role. It is also sometimes part of a specific strategy that seeks to identify new candidates able to represent a given category of workers. That is why sometimes individuals who spontaneously volunteer can be dissuaded from running or other 'more representative' candidates can be positioned to compete against them in their workplace.

'There was someone else who felt able to run, it was someone who was a middle manager [*category B*], who did not have the recognition, who did not get a consensus when we asked around management, administration, directors, etc. And that person took it very badly because she wanted to be the branch secretary and she did not have the recognition in the workplace. So that was complicated. And in the end, she didn't run. Here, most workers are senior managers [*category A*], so you can understand why a middle manager might not suit all of them. And it is true that if you are not recognized by the managers. ... For example, if you are defending a worker and you as the union rep, you aren't recognized as legitimate by management, it is very difficult, you won't be able to get things from management.' (Woman, manager, age 40, branch secretary, CFDT)

The identification of future reps is also a question of pragmatism because of the rarity of union vocations. Julie, for example found herself the front runner in a union election because her colleagues were not available enough to ensure the union presence in the workplace. However, like for other women in this situation, the fact that Julie had management skills was not unrelated to her position on the work council, where she quickly took on the role of treasurer. Women are often selected because they are assumed to have transferable or 'naturalized' skills in certain union roles (Guillaume, 2007), which are often quite technical or relational (from organizing social activities in the work council to managing the union finances).

'At the beginning we needed a name for the top of the list. My two colleagues lived far from work, one was on shifts, and the other was in the lab with time constraints, so I was the most available. It's easy to answer the telephone when you work in the documentation centre. So, naturally, it was me who put my name down, but not because I wanted to be at the top, just because I was there to answer the phone.' (Woman, technician, age 50, union convenor, CFDT)

In workplaces where there is little or no union presence, it is often pressure from workmates following disputes with management that pushes people to act, sometimes by changing unions. This was the case for Karen, who worked in a council in South London and was a member of UNISON, along with her 40 colleagues. She was disappointed with the lack of support from her union and turned to GMB.

'I was working for a council and my team had a security problem with aggressive clients. We were union members, but the union had not supported our demand to work behind glass barriers to avoid this kind of situation. GMB came to see us and offered to help. I was elected shop steward, and a month later branch secretary for the council. There was no one else, GMB wasn't very represented in the council. I took office for three years, on part-time secondment, and then I applied for a paid position at the regional level.' (Woman, council worker, age 31, regional organizer, GMB)

This dissatisfaction with the way women's interests are defended is common in Great Britain. It was particularly visible in the 1970s and 1980s, when unions were still very male-dominated and there was clear professional segregation. Older women activists clearly evoked their discontent with unions as the driving force behind their involvement in the union and the need for them to make their way in male-dominated groups. These women were sometimes supported by a male unionist mentor who helped them express their demands, like in the famous example of the women's strike at the Ford factory in Dagenham in 1968, where one of the male shop stewards supported the women's claims against the union leaders (Cohen, 2013).

Louise, a pioneer confronted with male hostility

Louise comes from a working-class district in North London. In the early 1950s she completed a secretarial training course. It was not her choice; she came from a "very poor background". She began working as an "under-secretary of the secretary" for a car manufacturer. She was earning more than her father but decided to change jobs because of harassment from her boss. She got a job in the printing industry, which, at the time, was a closed shop. "You couldn't work there if you didn't have the support of the union. My uncle recommended me." She was unionized with NATSOPA, which she describes as "very patriarchal". She got married in 1958 and had her first child in 1959. She stopped working for 15 years and had three other children during that time, in 1960, 1962, and 1966. When her youngest son was eight, in 1974, she decided to go back to work. "I wasn't any use there anymore. He didn't want me to take him to school, and I was just twiddling my thumbs at home." Rather than return to office work, she became a welfare assistant in a nursery school, so she could spend the school holidays with her children and look after them. She was a member of NALGO because she was assimilated to white collar teaching staff, as opposed to administrative or manual staff who were in a different union, the NUPE. There were only four of them in this type of role and they were mistreated by the teachers, who gave them the most difficult students. She worked part time, 30 hours a week, and only during term time. When she had a problem with one of her administrative co-workers, her union told her she was overreacting. So, along with her colleagues they decided they needed a union rep. She was elected because she was the most articulate and had the best writing skills. She contacted the union again and was invited to attend the meeting at the town hall in the evening. She was the only woman, did not understand the debates, and was rebuffed whenever she asked a question.

'It was not at all "woman-friendly". These after-work meetings continued at the pub. I was the only woman in the big Town Hall meeting room with lots of men who all knew each other and didn't bother with introductions. I didn't understand the debates, so I started asking questions. Their reaction was terrible. They put down their pens and crossed their arms. The union president just said someone would explain after the meeting.'

After that first meeting she went home mortified, but her daughter encouraged her to go back. Which she did. "I asked my questions again, and after a few months things got less aggressive." When the women's conference came around, the men asked her to "deal with it" and they kept all the other activities for themselves. She asked for training and was rebuffed, but an older man backed her up. "He gave me moral support and helped me with lots of things. He taught me everything. He was a great help." Then another woman arrived, and they joined forces against the "big boys". She then participated in the big strikes in the 1980s and progressively earned the respect of her male colleagues. "Katie and I managed to make a place for ourselves in this patriarchal system." She then continued her involvement, contributing to the creation of UNISON in 1993 and participating in many commissions – recruitment, training, women – at the local and then national levels, but always as an elected official so she maintained her freedom, continued her work, and looked after her family.

★★★

In France, the activists interviewed often mentioned one or more mentors, but above all emphasized the characteristics of the branch. An existing group of activists that is open and welcoming, and horizontal relations in the group, all make it easier for individuals to get involved. Democratic practices within the branch are also appreciated by new women members, like Anne, but this observation is also true for young men (Mischi, 2016).

'So, when I arrived at this production site, there was the CGT, the CFDT, and the CGC. I worked with people who were members of

64

the CGT. Pretty soon I was given little brochures on what unionism is, why it's good to unionize. I thought I'd join, but that I'd wait a bit and see. In 2002, some CFDT members who were annoyed by the fact that their union was signing agreements with the employer too easily left the CFDT and set up a SUD-Chimie branch. I followed that from a distance. And then I think it was two years later, they made a "join us" leaflet, a little flyer to join up and pay dues with them. So, I called them. I went to lunch with the old guard of the union, Jacques and Pierre, who had already made a good impression on me when we participated in walkouts or strikes. We'd gone on strike for a few different things, so I'd been in contact with activists. The minutes of the council meetings were sent out, the questions of the staff reps, and the minutes of the health and safety committee (CHSCT) as well. These two colleagues from SUD-Chimie made a good impression. The first question they asked me was "do you want to be on our electoral list? We have to submit it in two weeks." So that's how I became a member. We are consulted. There is always a general assembly once a year, and we are sent regular e-mail alerts. That's the democratic aspect that I like a lot, so the next elections I am well placed to be elected.' (Woman, technician, age 40, union rep, SUD-Chimie)

Although this participative aspect is present in other unions, the interviews conducted with SUD activists all emphasized this difference in union democracy practices. The creation of a SUD branch/union often involves an alternative form of internal organization directly opposed to the perceived traditional bureaucratic failings of other unions. From this perspective, new members (especially women) are sometimes not so much attracted by the radical social transformation agenda of SUD unions (and Solidaires) as by the prospect of internal democracy and the practice of consensus, as well as the small numbers of paid staff taking turns in union roles.

'Why did female membership increase? It was really to do with the way the union operates, which allows this feminization, especially the rule of consensus. We can have arguments, but we go and have a coffee, we don't try to force a majority. At SUD-Culture, when we do something, it begins with unanimous agreement. If there is one person, one branch that says, "no, there's a problem with this", if it is well argued, then we go back and look at it. So, it is not just, "I want to impose my way of seeing things", but rather "we discuss it". This is not a majority system. It is not 50+1 that counts.' (Woman, museum attendant, age 46, union official, SUD-Culture)

On the other hand, some characteristics of union organizations can be not favourable to union participation, whether because activists are isolated, or because there is disagreement within the branch, or because union work is segmented. Increasing specialization of union roles, combined with the restriction of local branches, and also sometimes the inexperience of new activists, can lead those with more experience to rationalize union work. This results in further specialization of skills and a concentration of union roles in the hands of a few seasoned unionists. The interviews revealed the case of isolated (women) union members dealing with conflict situations, or who were left in the cold by established unionists who controlled the branch and restricted the participation of members in the union's activities as well as access to union leadership roles in the workplace. Most of the interviews in France mentioned the fact that branches are now centred on a small core of activists who sometimes do not want to let go of their roles and are therefore not concerned with generational renewal. In very male-dominated sectors, such as GMB (Monaghan, 2020), this seizure of power by experienced male activists goes together with bullying, misogyny, cronyism, and sexual harassment, which can reflect workplace practices. This can be discouraging for some women, as Elizabeth in SUD-Rail recounts.

Elizabeth, enduring twofold discrimination

After a few years of struggling in personal services and in sales, Elizabeth applied for a job as a train driver at the French railways, the SNCF, somewhat by chance "because you needed to have done science at high school, and I had". She was hired while she was pregnant, which earned her the disapproval of her colleagues and her superiors, and she had to wait two years for training. In 2001, when she finally attended train driving training, she decided to join the union because, "at the SNCF there is a real union culture, there are lots of unionists and especially there was one guy in the CGT who had always been nice to me. He'd always said the most important thing in life was family and that I should not be ashamed of my pregnancy." She acted as union rep for the CGT for seven years and was elected onto the health and safety committee (CHSCT). Then her office was restructured, and she did not like the new union branch she had been mixed in with. "They were the old guard, very tough, very hierarchical." She worked a lot with activists from SUD-Rail on the CHSCT, and she decided to join them for several reasons. During a picket line she was sexually assaulted by a colleague and none of the CGT activists present tried to defend her. She was also an anti-nuclear activist and found it "schizophrenic" to be in a union in which the position was "more than dubious on the nuclear subject". Like other unions more generally, the CGT did not defend women's interests in the workplace; they were a tiny minority and subject to all kinds of discrimination. They had no work clothes in their sizes, there were no women's toilets, and they had to deal with constant sexual harassment from colleagues, which was further accentuated by night shifts and rest conditions in the train depots. Initially, things went well at SUD-Rail, "it was quite democratic, their way of doing things. Well, there weren't any women, but in any case, I had always been the only woman activist, so I was used to it." In 2010 she was offered a seat on the CHSCT (Health and Safety Committee), which she had asked for. "It was okay for the first year, but then they decided I was taking up too much room, because I did things to the max, and there were significant restructuring projects in the company." Her branch began to organize meetings on Wednesdays, when she did not work because she was looking after her three children. The branch organizer, whom she described as misogynist, told her she "would have to learn to make sacrifices as a union rep". He never supported her in her struggle to improve the situation of women, arguing that "we are not going to waste time on that when there are only 150 girls out of 16,000 train drivers in France! We don't have much union time. We have to work for a real fight that affects everyone!" She decided to give up her role with the CHSCT and, in her absence, the branch decided to send her to the local Solidaires union every Thursday. This was a breath of fresh air for her. "I thought it was incredible, but in fact they were just normal, they respected women's voices." She made the most of this time to complete training, particularly on gender stereotypes. She realized that "I was a man. Often when I talk about myself, I say I am train driver [she uses the male form *conducteur*, rather than the feminine form *conductrice*], I talked about 'the boys', I had denied all my femininity." During this period, her branch was still meeting on Wednesdays and she could not go. In fact, she never returned. According to her, the problem came from the management of the paid union staff at the SNCF, a system that was also approved by SUD-Rail.

'I really believed that at SUD, our values and our rules meant we were sort of protected from this kind of professionalization of the union, and that we really fought to defend workers' rights. And in fact, what I saw – at least in my local branch – were people who fought to keep their place in the union, so they did not have to work. Because train drivers work in tough conditions, they work nights, weekends. And so, what these guys wanted was to remain full-time union staff. So, there are loads of union reps who only work once or twice a month to keep all the advantages of the night shifts. They get the same hardship pay rates. When I was discriminated against, and they realized, they did not defend me.'

The national union level did not support her either, because they promoted branch autonomy. After a year, Elizabeth decided to throw in the towel and retire – after a 15-year-long career and three children – while that retirement option was still possible. She plans to go and live abroad with her partner. They have had difficulties in recent years which, according to her, are linked to her previous working conditions. She realized only afterwards the extent of the constant pressure she was under.

★★★

This example demonstrates how intermediary structures within the union (branches, local unions) are free to implement (or not) the policies that their union has theoretically adopted, whether in terms of internal democracy or gender equality. From this perspective, the significant decentralization and autonomy of SUD unions are both tools for feminization – because the political decision to increase women members can be promoted by the rank and file – but also a possible hindrance because of the principle by which national structures and policies do not intervene in local branches. But in certain highly feminized unions, like SUD-Pôle Emploi (job centres), the feminization of roles took place through deliberate actions by certain women to challenge the omnipresence of men in the branches. The fact that SUD unions were often created by seasoned activists from other unions (often men) meant that women unionists had to declare themselves feminists in order to challenge existing forms of male patriarchy. This was the case for Hélène (helped by Jacqueline, as we saw earlier).

'At the beginning I was just a member. I went to the meetings. I saw the union evolve and little by little I began to attend training sessions and committees, things like that. So that's when I realized that it was going to be a real fight, because when it was founded, there were a few of us women, some already politicized, who were looking for their role in this union that was just starting out. At the beginning I was not in the spotlight. I just watched and listened and then at one point I said to myself "why is it always the same guys talking?" When Jacqueline arrived, it shook things up a bit because she was not going to be pushed around. At the beginning we had a strategy for counting speaking time, counting the number of women who spoke. And that's how we managed to regulate the time men were speaking. And then, little by little, there were more and more female members who took on leadership roles. But it was still a struggle. And it was a constant worry because it is easier for men to speak publicly. And there are some enormous egos. Sometimes at the federation level there were quite important disagreements with some people, particularly men, who were a bit invasive, omnipresent, experts in everything.' (Woman, employment counsellor, age 42, union official, SUD- Pole Emploi)

The same thing can be said for the CFDT and the British unions; it is extremely difficult for equality policy to be adopted in intermediary structures without the support and drive from local leaders. 'Radical' measures like quotas or seats reserved for women only concern the elected positions within the national bodies for the CFDT (Executive Commission, National Board), or the federation level for some SUD unions (SUD-PTT for example), and the representative bodies for lay members in British unions (Regional Committee, National Executive Committee, self-organized groups). There are no quotas or reserved seats at all for shop stewards or branch chairs, or for elected union roles at the workplace level. New legal provisions (the Rebsamen law[3]) introduced in France in 2015 have changed the rules for the representation of men and women within employee representative bodies, requiring that the lists of candidates must include a number of women/ men corresponding to the proportion of women/men in the company. This provision should improve women's participation at the workplace level. Nothing like this exists in the UK. Even in a very feminized union like UNISON (more than 78% female members), the underrepresentation of women begins with these initial union roles (Table 3.8), along with a concentration of women in roles with the least amount of union facility time and more traditionally 'feminine' responsibilities (training, welfare, equality).

In addition, weak union rights in Great Britain, which allow only a small number of seconded union reps in a company, mean that activists tend to want to hold on to their roles for several years. This is exacerbated by the fact that there are often very few guarantees as to the conditions of their return to work, and employment contexts in which their relationship with their employers are often strained, notably in the public sector, after successive restructuration or privatization projects (Kirton, 2018). There is also a low turnover in France for workplace union reps, especially those who are appointed by their federation (central or group shop stewards/work council secretaries) and/or those who hold multiple union roles at the workplace, branch, federal, and national levels.

Table 3.8: Gender division of union roles within UNISON

Role	Women	Men	Total
Branch Secretary	450	446	896
Branch Chair	376	433	810
Stewards	3303	2692	6002
Branch Education Coordinator	307	185	492
Branch Welfare Officer	460	175	635
Branch Equality Coordinator	346	213	559
Total	5242	4144	9394

Source: Data from UNISON membership files, 2016.

Specialization and acceleration of union careers

Except for activists who set up their own union or branch, and become the chair or convenor, activists' first union roles in France are generally as union rep (*délégué de personnel*), elected member to the work council (*Comité social et économique* – CSE), or the health and safety committee (CHSCT). This has changed slightly since the implementation of the Macron *ordonnances* in 2017.[4] In Great Britain, first union roles are generally as union rep (equality or learning rep) or shop steward. One of the specificities of British unions is the existence of equality reps, who are responsible for promoting equality in the workplace (Bacon and Hoque, 2012), but without facility time. In UNISON, for example, these positions were introduced when the union was set up in 2009. Within the union structure there are also self-organized groups for women, BAME members, LGBTI, and disabled members (see Table 2.1), which members can join (and sometimes chair). Although not much facility time is associated with these roles, new areas of responsibility have enabled unions to attract different members – women, BAME workers, disabled workers, and sexual minorities – and these forms of participation can lead to more traditional union roles. This was Tonia's experience, a transition from a role as a BAME activist to branch secretary. However, the different studies conducted on BAME reps emphasize how difficult it is for this group of workers to move up the union hierarchy, which is reflected in some of the interviews conducted here.

> 'I was transferred to another council, closer to home. At the time, I was in a relationship with a UNISON activist who started showing me information about the union's equality policy. He also suggested I come with him to the National Black Member's Conference. I went as a guest and I found it extremely interesting. When I returned to work in Northampton, I started talking with unionists from UNISON, and I quickly became a steward and then equality rep with one day a week facility time. I was also elected to the Regional Women's Committee. I was active and I began to understand how the union works. A few years later I was elected branch secretary for the council.' (Woman, admin worker, age 40, regional officer, UNISON)

At the time of this research, the proliferation of union roles in companies and the 'generosity' of union rights in France meant that new members could rapidly move into roles as staff reps, or elected members of the work council, or health and safety council if they wished to.[5] The dearth of candidates and the unpredictability facing union branches, whether because of internal crises (conflicts, political discord, malpractice) or individual upheavals (departure of an official, interpersonal conflict, redundancy, illness), all meant that new members could quickly take on responsibilities. Given that the pool of activists who are willing and considered able to take on more responsibility is limited, sometimes staff reps or work council members (or their surrogates) are encouraged to take a position as shop steward or secretary of the work council when it becomes vacant. At the CFDT, and consequently also at Solidaires, this career acceleration took place in a climate of high tension, partly due to the departure of many former CFDT activists in the 1990s and 2000s who left to set up SUD unions (joined other unions or left the union movement). The members who remained at the CFDT saw their union participation increase and found themselves in leadership roles, which was a test for their commitment and loyalty to the union. For Solidaires, this split from the CFDT was the impetus for the creation of several SUD unions that had to start from scratch to gain legal representativity within their company or administration. In some cases, this led to a break in union participation, as was the case for Valerie:

'We left the CDFT with nothing, and afterwards we had to set up a new union. So, we created SUD-Douanes, with new statutes and regulations. There were fewer than 20 of us. We tried to run for the first workplace elections. I managed to set up a full list for the elections, in all general categories. But unfortunately, the administration refused our ticket. We appealed to the administrative court, but we lost on a formality, because the person who had lodged it was apparently not authorized to do so. So, we could not be elected as representatives. So, I spent the next ten years in the desert, a closet unionist! Because, of course, the members turned towards institutionalized unions that were able to have elected reps and union rights to defend their members. It is not really worth being a member of the union when you know that they don't have the right to defend you.' (Woman, customs control agent, age 45, union official, SUD-Douanes)

However, these internal political tensions also helped women to access leadership positions in both unions. At the CFDT many women with less experience were called on to replace older male leaders who had left to join the CGT or create SUD unions. Their loyalty to the organization was an objective factor in their promotion. In Solidaires, the small size of the pool of available activists facilitated women's access to leadership positions. However, women activists were also sometimes stuck in union rep roles within the work council or other consultative roles because SUD unions were small and not very representative (see Box 2.3). More generally, in France, women remain overrepresented in union rep positions and are less present in roles involving negotiation and bargaining (Breda, 2016) or works council secretary (Hege et al, 2001; Contrepois, 2006). One explanation for this is that there are more vacancies in representative roles, and the fact that they are elected makes it easier for women to access them (where some central shop steward positions are appointed by the union hierarchy and exempt from the Rebsamen proportionality rules). An alternative explanation lies in the advantages to be had from the stewardship or work council secretary roles (or secretary of other workplace representative bodies at the group or European level), which are more prestigious and involve greater resources, particularly in terms of facility time. In France, cumulating workplace union roles is one of the main ways to become a full-time union convenor, but this situation may change dramatically with the introduction of the new Social and Economic Committee (*Comité Economique et Social*), which has more limited resources and sets a limit on union roles.[6] Moreover, as we have demonstrated elsewhere (Chappe et al, 2019) stewards and convenors (as well as full-time union staff more generally) are more protected from discrimination than workplace representatives, who are less covered by the collective agreements negotiated. This was the case for Paul, whose career narrative emphasizes significant existing union rights in the company, which is a factor of its size and the quality of employment relations, but also the degree of representativity of the union he represents. This type of 'moonlighter' career cumulating different roles is easier to organize with the CFDT or other very representative unions that it is with SUD unions. In the best of cases, the representativeness of SUD unions may reach 20% but it is often much less, whereas the CFDT often achieves scores of 40% in professional elections. This cumulative career is also more common in large private or public companies than it is in the public service because of the range of different representative bodies at the local, group, national, European, and sometimes world levels.

Paul, a union career 'in the shadow of union rights'

Paul comes from working-class background. He finished his high school diploma in automobile mechanics while working as an apprentice in the automobile factory where his father worked. In 1996 he was hired on a permanent contract in the cable service, which shut down after three years. He was then transferred to another service, maintenance in general technical services, which was outsourced; then he moved to central equipment services. These repeated shifts did not help his career. With each transfer he had to prove himself once again. "Anything was a good excuse to not give the job to me." However, when he was 20, "he was not too concerned about that kind of thing". His father has never been a union member. Then Paul got married and his wife fell pregnant. "I began to see life differently. I thought, hang on, I have been in the company for three years and I still haven't had a promotion because I am young." He knew of the unions because of their posters. One day he was talking with a colleague who was a member of the CFDT about his department being closed, because he was offered another transfer as part of another reorganization. "Management was offering me a position below the one I had, leaving maintenance to go into production. I'm not criticizing those in production, but I've studied, I have experience in the company, it's not so I can go backward." So, he joined the union to be defended by the CFDT, which he thought was "the union that tried to find the best balance between workers' and employers' interests". The branch rapidly suggested he become the health and safety rep (CHSCT). He accepted because his colleague reassured him that his career would still progress. "In 2002, we'd already signed a union rights agreement that guaranteed that unionists would have the same wage progression on average as the rest of their colleagues." He was promised that he would receive assistance and union training and that the branch leaders would "go and see my direct superior, the factory manager, and then the site manager, to say 'we have a new activist in this section, he'd better not be shot down'".

'My factory director was very understanding; he reassured me and didn't set up extra obstacles. They didn't try to dupe me because I was just starting out in health and safety and, you know, you have to know certain rules, legislation too. They even included me in the working group with other unions so that I knew what I was talking about. On the other side, the branch did the same, I had training.'

Two years later Paul became a member of the union branch executive, and also steward at his workplace. In 2007, at age 32, he was appointed central shop steward, after completing a training programme organized by the union federation. Three people were sent for in-house training for three weeks. After that, they had to write a short essay, and the Federation called Paul to say, "you are the one we want as shop steward". He hesitated a little because he was a new father and his partner had returned to work, but he ended up accepting and became a full-time paid official. At the time of the interview, he was waiting for the results of the 2012 workplace elections to know whether the CFDT would still be representative; if not, he was ready to return to the factory, particularly as he had been promoted to a position of technician.

★★★

In Great Britain, there is an even greater risk of women being stuck in specific roles. Because of gender segregation in employment and the existence of different bargaining units, women activists have often represented their female colleagues only in specific departments and therefore have had trouble gaining broader union legitimacy. However, the separate bargaining bodies for different professional groups were progressively abandoned over the course of the 1990s. In the public sector, two new national agreements were signed in the 2000s. These aimed to achieve a harmonization of job categories across the National Health Service[7] and in local government,[8] and helped to attenuate the gender segregation that had developed in unions as a reflection of the employment structure. However, the low turnover among shop stewards or convenors (often male) continues to make feminization more difficult in general representative or negotiating union roles, especially in male-dominated industries. So, women may tend to choose to be the equality rep or equality officer, which can mean they are seen as less suited to more general union roles, as Geraldine describes in the next quote. She managed to become a union official, but partly by developing other skills.

'I became an activist very young. I was a full-time paid officer at 27, which is not unusual today, but it was then. Men tended to go full time around age 40. I was very lucky. Right when I became a paid officer, the equality policy was set up and I played a role in its development. That helped my legitimacy in the union, even though I've remained very involved in my role in representation and negotiation. I was never considered a key person in terms of equality policy. I was just a full-time union officer who happened to be a woman. I do not know how I would have been seen if I had been passionate about equality issues. My extensive negotiating experience gave me a broader legitimacy and helped me get elected.' (Woman, blue-collar worker, age 47, national official, GMB)

Learning skills and techniques

These initial union roles are essential for unionists to develop legitimacy and gain support from their constituency – a pool of employees or members who support their candidacy – and to acquire basic knowledge and skills (Kaminski and Yakura, 2008). In both France and Great Britain, the ability to 'serve' members (that is, to respond to their demands and support them in difficult situations and provide services) is decisive in winning elected roles and gaining union legitimacy in the workplace. The women activists interviewed here (but also the new male activists with the CFDT) particularly emphasize the importance of being useful for employees and members. This research, like others (Dean and Perret, 2020), confirms that being seen as a good rep is associated with different relational competencies: being accessible, concrete, available, concerned about other people, and having good listening and dialogue skills. These interpersonal skills are valued by unions in both countries, but even more in France since the 2008 law that made workplace elections the central mechanism for union representativity. In Solidaires, this focus put on workplace unionism has a more ideological basis. It is considered the condition and essence of union legitimacy, by opposition with delegative and professionalized forms of unionism relying on paid full-time officers caught up in institutional logics (and thus removed from the problems of ordinary workers).

'In our statutes, there are no full-time union reps. It is a struggle to maintain this principle. It is true that there are times when it is a bit complicated to not have any full-time union staff at all. So, some are full time, but for a limited period, like three years. But not for life. There is a concern about not losing touch with what is happening on the shop floor because then you are too far from the reality your colleagues are going through, and that is an element of the union values we want to establish.' (Woman, employment counsellor, age 62, national official, SUD-Pôle Emploi)

In Great Britain, UNISON also cultivates a rank-and-file culture, partly due to the legacy of NALGO, with a large network of strong branches, and GMB has apparently intended to return to organizing campaigns and practices since the introduction of the *GMB At Work* programme in 2006, having focused on employer agreements during the 1990s and 2000s. In both countries, providing services and effective workplace representation remains a central tool for recruiting and keeping members. In this context, women (but also men) who demonstrate supposedly 'feminine' qualities – listening skills, availability, emotional support – may have an advantage in accessing workplace union roles (Dean and Perret, 2020). However, trade unions have seen an increase in technical roles (elected to the CSE or CHSCT in France, or as health and safety rep in Great Britain) and have supported the development of social partnership practices that require skills and competencies that are less naturalized and seen as more professional. In France, in particular, the decentralization and extension of collective bargaining (large numbers of negotiations on wide-ranging subjects) and the multitude of consultative bodies in which union reps have to participate have contributed to the promotion of a professional framing of union work.

'I find my union role useful professionally. Thinking about an angle, an objective, a result to attain, thinking about methods and strategies. It involves an interesting intellectual process. Then there are the operational aspects, the implementation of the agreements we negotiate. The whole process is interesting and helps develop skills. And then there is the negotiating process itself, where you sit around the table and there is management, the other unions, and you have to take a stance in all that, understand the interactions between actors, their interests.' (Woman, financial controller, age 41, shop steward and union officer, financial services union, CFDT)

In this context, charisma and heroic forms of leadership seem challenged by other forms of legitimacy that appear less gendered, but which can incorporate other discriminatory biases. Certain behavioural traits are still listed as important in identifying future union leaders, such as the ability to stand up to the employer, express oneself in public, and more generally 'defend a position'. However, the requirements for being a capable union rep/officer seem to have broadened, incorporating new managerial and technical skills, as one of the CFDT interviewees explained: "we have gone from a paid officer whose legitimacy came from struggle and the ability to manage a dispute, to a paid officer who is professional, pedagogical, rigorous, competent, has technical mastery of the issues, is credible, open, and has good listening skills". This transformation is not disconnected from the promotion of social dialogue, which is defended by some unions, notably the CFDT. In SUD unions, the qualities associated with the exercise of a union rep role are less technical and more focused on maintaining a *rapport de force* (power struggle) with the employer. It is interesting to note that a virile and heroic approach to union leadership is sometimes endorsed and promoted by (older) women activists, who may discourage young women 'for their own good', as Sophie says:

'At the Louvre, it's a bit different. We take a lot of tough actions, sometimes illegal. At first, I was side-lined by the union Chair in those kinds of actions, because I had kids. She did not want me to get arrested. I ended up participating, but it's true that at the beginning it was hard. The female union leaders didn't have kids. I was a mother so I couldn't be in danger, because of them. Little by little, I got involved in all the forms of action.' (Woman, museum security guard, age 45, national official, SUD-Culture)

That being said, the high degree of institutionalization in workplace relations in the companies or administrations where SUD unions are set up means that activists must also engage with the technical and institutional aspects of their union roles. Even when they resist this on principle, trade unionists are drawn into a logic of professionalization that can be seen as detrimental to generational renewal (Guillaume and Pochic, 2009a), but which they might find stimulating on a personal level. In Great Britain, women unionists seem less inclined to mention their personality and leadership skills as elements contributing to their legitimacy in their role as shop steward or convener. Far from mobilizing a kind of 'feminine leadership', the female interviewees who have become leaders in UNISON or GMB instead tend to emphasize the need to adopt a form of 'virile' legitimacy (Heery and Kelly, 1989). Some mention acquiring legal knowledge or negotiating skills, but most emphasize the ability to be persistent, to take a stance, and be self-confident.

This is particularly true at GMB, a union in which many female unionists also have had to deal with sexism and sexual harassment (Monaghan, 2020).

Do you know why you were elected?

'Mainly because of my "vocal skills" and the fact that I am not afraid of saying what I think. I've had these personal skills my whole life and they have helped me a lot in the union. Today people are afraid of my honesty, like the employer used to be. But that's who I am.' (Woman, home help, age 42, national officer, GMB)

The fact that union activity at the workplace level appears less technical in British unions can be at least partly explained by the existing division of work between workplace reps and paid officers who are responsible for more specialized tasks involving negotiation or expertise (which varies depending on the union culture). However, in both countries the question of public speaking in union branches and decision-making bodies (general assemblies or congresses and so on), appears to be a challenge for some women, even in unions with strong female membership (Kirton, 2018). As Raphaëlle points out, the importance of consensus within Solidaires does not necessarily entail equal distribution of speaking time, and women's voices are often drowned out.

'There's having a voice, that's the first thing, but even once you have the opportunity to speak, that doesn't mean that you are heard and listened to. So that is the second struggle, and then it is being able to be listened to without some guy coming after. Because I have experienced that as a political activist as well. Some guy speaks after you, he didn't hear what you said, he says exactly the same thing, and that time it gets heard.' (Woman, mid-level manager, age 45, union officer, Solidaires)

These problems with self-confidence and self-affirmation experienced by women activists are at the heart of British unions' reflections on their internal equality policies. NALGO (later UNISON) set up training for women (Kirton, 2006a), as well as self-organized groups that were specifically conceived as spaces for women to develop their capabilities for individual expression and collective action as an 'oppressed group'. In the 1970s, French unions trialled workplace women's groups (Maruani, 1979), but they were not echoed by separate union structures for women members. The women's commissions that exist today in some SUD unions or at the confederal level of the CFDT are run by experienced women unionists who have other roles within the union structure, and they are open to men as well (at least in theory). At the workplace level, awareness of the difficulties that women (particularly low-paid women) face in participating in union life, and the desire to address these issues, depend on how sensitive existing union leaders are to gender equality. Informal and individual mentoring programmes for new unionists – men or women – do exist, but neither the CFDT nor SUD unions have envisaged establishing formal separate programmes.

Skills required for workplace union roles are varied and not always formalized, despite existing training. Although this variety allows for a range of interpretations, it also conveys gendered representations that may discourage women (and some men) from volunteering for certain roles (known for being theatrical) or taking on roles in direct contact with the employer, particularly in a difficult economic climate. These hesitations can recede through the progressive learning of techniques and developing a taste for the effects of the actions conducted (Becker, 1966). Almost all the interviewees mentioned disputes or negotiations that produced concrete results (bonuses, positive agreements, successful elections, or workers' representation). Conducting these actions is an integral part of learning to become a trade unionist; they constitute a series of successive challenges, with the associated failures and frustrations, but also successes. Above all, these initial experiences help to change activists' perspectives, so they sustain their union participation. Their first successes help to confirm them in their union role and shape the dispositions required for sustained union participation – even if that is interrupted when they change employer, as was the case for Isabelle.

Isabelle, a 'serial' unionist

Isabelle trained as a network administrator and was hired by a major computer assistance company in 2000. The CFDT soon sought her out to become a member, and then she was elected to several bodies, for her temperament and skill in representing workers.

> 'I opened my mouth, you know. I already had a strong personality, I already had character. I defended my colleagues even before I was a unionist. Then there was a union that asked me to join, because they said, "we want people like you, because at least you speak up, you're there for the workers". And that's how I came to be the union rep.'

Isabelle was the only woman in her service, but there were other women in sales, and the union branch was open to both men and women. She did not feel like there were gender issues in the company. She then decided to train to be a plumber, something she had wanted to do since she was a child, but that her parents had forbidden. She also had a vocational certificate in secretarial work and an undergraduate degree in law, which she only alluded to. She completed her training as a plumber, where she was the only woman among 29 male students. She struggled with some of them, as well as with the teacher, who was sexist and graded her badly, but she stood up to them and came head of the class in the final exams. She was then hired by a company to do maintenance on hot water boilers, as a pipe technician. Once again, she was the only woman in the team. She was surprised that there were not any union posters in the company, even though there were over a thousand workers, and after her boss began to "make life difficult" she decided to join a union. But she had to go to the head of her agency to have the list of unions. She went to the CGT to ask for a membership form, but she never received it. The CFDT told her that the union leader would have to see her work before accepting her membership – which she found strange, given her previous union experience. By chance she saw a 'call for members' leaflet to try and set up a SUD union in the company. She called the SUD activist, who agreed to put her name on the list in the second election round. SUD got only 9.5% of the vote, which is not enough to obtain union rights. She could therefore participate in the work council only as an observer, but she "gave the other unionists a headache". "I made them extremely uncomfortable; I refused to let them push me down, and when workers needed me, I was there." The CGT is the majority union, but the reps are too close to management for her liking. She therefore embarked upon an open conflict with the leadership of the CGT. She was the only SUD member in the work council but had a lot of support from her union. She was stuck in the company and knew her career could not progress "because SUD bothers people", but she does not want to be promoted; her goal is to have SUD expand further within the company and obtain full legal recognition.

★★★

For Isabelle, like for many other activists in Solidaires, the union is a space for acquiring new skills or using skills developed through their education, which they cannot always use in the workplace. Isabelle chose to become a plumber, but many women activists find themselves in non-managerial positions even though they have university degrees. This situation applies to many unionists in Solidaires, as evidenced by the quantitative study conducted at the 2011 Congress (Béroud et al, 2011), which showed that a third of SUD unionists were working in jobs that are below their educational level. But young women activists (well represented in this study) are particularly exposed to the risk of 'professional downgrading', defined here as the 'situation of any individual whose primary education exceeds that normally required for the position he or she occupies' (Peugny, 2009). Some of these young graduates choose to sit the public service exams or enter public corporations as a refuge (Kopel, 2005) in a context of repeated conjunctural employment crises, but this comes at the cost of downgrading. Many of these interviewees under 45 are in this situation. Unionism therefore appears to be a way to use the skills acquired through education – knowledge of the law, writing and argumentation skills, use of figures and economic data, and so forth. Moreover, the trade union movement can provide a space for attainable career conversion (or professional and social promotion), at least in the initial workplace roles, for employees with medium- or low-level qualifications.

The constraints of union professionalization

Most interviewees described unionism as a 'greedy institution' (Franzway, 2000) that requires considerable investment in terms of time and energy. In Great Britain, commitment to the union essentially relies on volunteering because of weaker union rights. Whether it means being a shop steward or participating in the branch or being elected to democratic decision-making bodies in the workplace, all these roles are at least partly conducted outside working hours. Obtaining facility time or means (car, telephone, BlackBerry) for union work is dependent on the number of union members in the company and the agreements negotiated with the employer, which are increasingly meagre. In France, where unionists have greater means at their disposal, the question of balancing paid work with union activism also comes up, but it becomes a more biting issue for those with greater levels of involvement. At some point in their union career, unionists are often obliged to choose between taking on more responsibilities (going full time or becoming paid officials) and taking a back seat (withdrawing from union life or focusing on workplace-level roles).

The career narratives of French unionists reveal the processes that lead them to become more involved in their union roles, generally because the unions ask them to and also because they progressively come into conflict with their hierarchy (and sometimes colleagues) who do not accept their repeated absences for union work. They also do not progress professionally because they miss out on professional training sessions and/or feel progressively overwhelmed by new technologies. Once they reach a certain degree of participation in the union, activists have trouble concealing this 'shameful difference' (Goffman, 1963) and end up not only at odds with the cultural norms at work but also in conflict with their managers and their colleagues. Many unionists, particularly those in low-paid jobs, express a feeling of guilt because they benefit from a working regime that allows them to be absent from work and avoid some of the time constraints their fellow workers are subject to, and which are often exacerbated by their absences. This feeling of guilt weighs particularly heavily on women working in the care sector or in education who do not want to penalize their clients by their absence (Cunningham and James, 2010), knowing that they will not be replaced during their union time. Moreover, many union reps are subject to discrimination for their activism because their careers are essentially capped, without progression, and they are sometimes threatened with dismissal. The reality of union discrimination is noted by some of the women members of the CFDT, but SUD activists are even more open about this, often refusing to benefit from compensation measures put in place for unionists, as Maïwenn explained.

Maïwenn, refusing the 'privilege' of a normal career

Although she was "rather brilliant at school", Maïwenn dropped her studies early. She did not enjoy the first year of medicine, which was "too individualistic", and decided to move in with her boyfriend. She gave birth to her first daughter when she was 20 and made a living from doing odd jobs. She eventually sat the exam to join the postal service in the mid-1990s and joined SUD-PTT the following year, when she had a permanent position. At the beginning, she worked in the sorting room, where she had to do "lots of overtime because obviously, at the beginning when you start to work, you don't know the rounds, it takes you longer than your colleagues who have been doing the rounds for years and years". Her boss refused to pay the overtime. She came from a background close to the CGT, but she remembered how that union had failed to support her mother, a local council worker, when she had had trouble with her supervisor, and it had left her with a bad feeling. So, she called the SUD-PTT union and joined up in the middle of a strike related to the implementation of the 35-hour working week. "We won, and that is how I became an activist, among other things." She began to attend the union branch, "but I was really focused on my workplace, because I was not very self-confident". She was transferred to another office and began to get involved again. "I had a little bit of experience with activism, and there were problems, we had to intervene, you know. And then they asked me to come to the union branch exec meeting once a month, and after two years I got facility time. I was part-time with the union." She broke up with her partner, with whom she had had a second child, and moved to a different region and started in a new office.

'I was not full-time right away; it took more than three years. They offered me a role on the consultative reps committee, and then I was on the departmental health and safety committee [CHSCT]. At the time, in this area, we really wanted to get more women in the union structure. There were almost as many female members as male members.'

In 2007 she was employed full time by the union. "I was the first woman to be a full-time paid union member since the union's creation in 1989. There'd never been another woman." In 2009, the union General Secretary suggested that she join the federation national committee full time. There were three other women there. "It was just men, all big mouths too, so we had to carve out a place, you had to have the nerve, it wasn't easy." When the General Secretary left, she was offered the position, but she refused because of her family situation – she was raising three children on her own, after separating from her partner. She also did not want to be chosen because she was a woman, and she did not want to serve as an alibi for the low feminization of the federation executive. She was almost at the end of her second term, and she felt she had to return to work, so that she would not become too disconnected. She was still on the same pay grade as when she began working at the Post Office because SUD refused "to apply the promotion quotas allocated by the employer to trade unionists to avoid wage discrimination. We are the only union to refuse it. We subscribe to the principle of no benefits, no discrimination." She said she could not imagine herself becoming a manager, unlike activists in other unions. Instead, she thinks that she might retrain to become a social worker.

★★★

By contrast, CFDT activists do not see any incompatibility between union roles and career progression and are quick to ensure that they benefit from the measures guaranteeing the progression of pay rates and recognition of skills gained in the union. But their ability to reconcile union involvement and career progression is largely due to the nature of their jobs. As we have seen elsewhere (Guillaume and Pochic, 2009b), the public sector (and to a lesser extent public companies) allows the cumulation of union duties and professional activities, because trade union affiliation is less stigmatized and union rights are more protected than in the private sector. There is usually the possibility of adapting working hours, and no danger in taking facility time. The public servants present at the CFDT Nantes Congress were often on secondment to varying degrees, depending on their level of qualification. Of those present, 66% of mid-level public servants (*catégorie B*) were on secondment, and this proportion was 58% for low-level public servants (*catégorie C*), and 40% for senior public servants (*catégorie A*) (Table 3.9).

But even in these contexts, the 'biographical availability' (McAdam, 1986) and geographical mobility required to fulfil several concurrent roles mean that managers tend to consider their union involvement as intermittent, leaving their position temporarily to work for the union full time (or more rarely part time) and then returning. For private sector workers, the cumulation of these two roles is difficult and workers see this as an alternative – a union career *or* a professional career – rather than a possible combination. Some prioritize their professional career and try to stay in their job by keeping the same number of hours (working nights and weekends) and limiting union activities to what can be done in a volunteer capacity (outside working hours), which often leads them to refuse promotions within the union hierarchy.

Table 3.9: Congress delegates by forms of union activism

	Delegates on secondment	Union staff paid by the CFDT	Volunteer full time	Volunteer more than part time	Volunteer less than part time	Population
Management	36%	10%	6%	23%	22%	209
Manager, engineer	34%	19%	8%	18%	20%	91
Senior manager	27%	13%	7%	20%	33%	15
Senior public servant (A)	40%	2%	5%	29%	21%	103
Intermediary professions	44%	12%	5%	17%	21%	355
Supervisor	35%	21%	7%	14%	22%	100
Technician	30%	14%	5%	21%	27%	132
Mid-level public servant (B)	66%	2%	3%	15%	13%	123
Workers/employees	33%	16%	4%	18%	27%	328
Skilled worker	27%	24%	3%	17%	27%	104
Unskilled worker	19%	25%	0%	31%	19%	16
Employee	28%	14%	3%	21%	31%	144
Low-level public servant (C)	58%	3%	8%	9%	22%	64
No answer	11%	3%	0%	14%	57%	37
Total	37%	12%	5%	19%	25%	929

Note: Among the managers present at the Congress, 36% were on secondment to the CFDT (paid by their employer).

Source: Internal investigation with two thirds of the participants at the CFDT 2002 Congress in Nantes. Original analysis by Sophie Pochic.

Union activism, even when it is limited by what can be done as a volunteer, nevertheless clashes with the long-hours model which is necessary for a management career in the private sector and can therefore hinder any chances of promotion. Fulfilling these two roles (manager and unionist) is thus a delicate balancing act, whether because of access to strategic information (a financial controller in the context of downsizing or redundancy plans), management procedures (for example, being a superior in the context of a dismissal), but above all because of the lack of everyday availability (and repeated and visible absences). Because of this, unionists in management positions are often in the same situation as women managers working part time. They are pushed into expert or non-managerial positions and their career progression is often compromised – if not completely obstructed – in terms of promotion or salary. Thus, where leadership positions come with secondment or work contracts, the union might seem like a space in which to construct an alternative career for people who have 'explored all options' in their occupation or profession. This strategy is most often seen among managers midway through their careers, or in untenable work contexts, for whom a union career may seem like a new beginning.

The costs of unionism, the difficulties in maintaining commitments, and the impact on other spheres of life all depend on the profile of the unionist in question, but it is objectively harder for women with children to succeed on all fronts. Previous research has shown that women's union careers are often horizontal and discontinuous (Kirton, 2006b), pointing to the need for women to balance multiple parallel careers which can come into conflict with each other, while at other times being mutually supporting (Kirton, 2006b; Lescurieux, 2019). In Great Britain, frequent career interruptions for women workers (particularly low-skilled workers) who stop to raise children have an impact on their progression within the union, as was the case for Louise, quoted earlier. In France, family constraints influence the continuation of activism, but it is also the difficulties in balancing union and professional life that raise issues. At both the CFDT and in British unions, these tensions are often resolved by moving into a paid union position. UNISON and GMB are generally described as good employers, attentive to family constraints (flexible working hours, possibility to go part time or work from home, or take parental leave). This complete dedication to the union institution is less common in SUD unions because of the smaller number of paid staff and the desire to avoid full-time secondments (Guillaume, 2018a). Performing union duties therefore appears to be a kind of sacrifice, even though this framing is criticized as being one of the difficulties in attracting young people to leadership positions.

'Because the job is a job that's already very demanding and means you're not available. It's extremely tiring, emotionally exhausting. I understand that colleagues don't want to add to that by working impossible hours. Because it's true that when you're in the union for the day, you arrive at 9am but you don't finish at 5pm. And sometimes a union day is more exhausting than a normal work day. So, there's that difficulty. There are lots of people who make personal choices to not get involved, who are members but not activists, and it always comes back to the same ones in the end, and they eventually get worn out. So, it's true that we need to recruit more people, but that also requires time and energy. And it ends up being never ending, we can't escape from it, it's always the same people running the union.' (Woman, job counsellor, age 62, union official, SUD-Pôle Emploi)

Although this research is based on interviews with women activists who have a lasting involvement in the union movement, often as paid officers, there are also many who do not make this choice, and who try to keep up their involvement alongside their careers (Kirton, 2006b). Strikingly, more than 70% of women activists we spoke to during the Inter-Union Women's Days in 2014 did not want to take on more responsibility within the union, and their forms of involvement fell into two categories. On the one hand there were very active women (more than ten hours' a week involvement with the union), and on the other hand there were much less active ones (who worked less than two hours a week for the union), who were much more frequent among the workers aged under 40. The survey also showed that the difficulty in reconciling professional life and personal life, and how much time and energy was required, were the two major obstacles identified by the respondents when it came to moving into leadership positions, followed closely by a dislike of power struggles. These observations confirm that women union leaders need suitable family structures and support, like other 'exceptional' women who have managed to break into professions designed for men, such as politics.

Becoming a union leader: relying on the institution

In both countries, taking on a position as a union leader, which is generally associated with becoming a paid official, is a decisive step in a union career. However, the concrete modalities of this shift differ according to the national context.

Two parallel paths to union leadership in Great Britain

In Great Britain, paid union officials are most often employed by regional or national structures because of limited union rights in companies. It is rare to find activists who are seconded at the branch level. Some of these positions are subject to election by governing bodies of the union made up of lay members – such as the positions of Regional Secretary, or General Secretary. But for the other positions, standard recruitment practice applies. These rare paid positions are therefore highly sought after because they are not subject to election, and up until recently were generally occupied by White men with low-level qualifications, nearing retirement (especially at GMB). These union jobs are objectively less attractive for more qualified activists, for whom they would mean a pay cut and a loss of future retirement benefits.

'Many lay members who are active in the union apply for jobs as paid officials, for two reasons. It means they can continue their union work at a different level, and when they become paid staff, they don't need to worry about being re-elected every year. There are more women than there used to be, but vacancies are rare, and employees tend not to move. They stay in their jobs.' (Woman, IT worker, age 53, senior regional officer, UNISON)

However, privatization and increasing job insecurity in the public sector have meant these positions are now more attractive, appealing to younger and more qualified men (particularly at UNISON) who may feel penalized by the policies promoting women and the intense competition for positions. In the two British unions studied here, access to paid positions at the regional and national levels is limited due to the low turnover of unionists in place. Progression within the union structures is also very slow and there is a long waiting list that can be dissuasive to younger activists, some of whom are women. Traditionally recruited at the branch level for their skills in a particular area, regional officers coexist with other, more specialized roles focused on recruitment, organizing, but also equality officer positions, which are much more feminized[9] but also more insecure, with short-term or temporary contracts. These positions are sometimes filled by rank-and-file activists, but also by people from outside the union movement, Labour activists, or young graduates. These technical positions also exist within national structures. Specialists in education, human resources, research, or communication work alongside elected or co-opted paid officials responsible for one or several industries/sectors (health, local government, and so on). The distinction between political and technical positions is very clear here.

'This is a very hierarchical organization. Most unions are. There are two sorts of positions. There are elected activists who were shop stewards and who become regional or national officials. These are elected positions defined in the statutes of the union. And then there are people like us staff, who are hired on work contracts. We have different grades and pay levels. There is a strong hierarchy between elected officials and staff, a very clear hierarchy. Well, when you get to the top of the staff hierarchy, relationships are more egalitarian with the officials, but we're not equal.' (Woman, secretary, age 50, senior research officer, GMB)

It is therefore unusual that technical union staff move into more general (often elected) roles that allow for greater career progression, unless they apply from within the union. Equally, competition is tough for lay members who want to become paid officers, but that does not prevent them moving into elected positions. There are thus two parallel career paths in British unions, one paidand the other unpaid. The volunteer path is less well known but includes different kinds of regional and national roles and culminates in a seat on the National Executive Committee, responsible for overseeing the governing decisions of the union. Maxine took this second path.

Maxine, top lay member

Maxine was born with a disability. She attended special schools, learned to be a shorthand typist, and started work in 1976, at age 19. She regrets that she was unable to go to university but says "I did not have much choice. I was not university material." She was lucky and found a job quickly in her local town council. She passed the test and was hired. She worked in a team of typists for 13 years. She did not join the union right away, but eventually joined the TGWU in 1987 because one of her colleagues was not very nice to her. "I thought I should join the union, to protect myself, I didn't know exactly from what, but it seemed a good idea. And then my colleagues also joined." Her parents were both workers and union members "but they were not active, and we did not discuss it at home". She then applied for an administrative position in child welfare services. Her superior was not immensely helpful, and she asked for a transfer to social services. She also became more involved in the union and took the position of shop steward "to equip myself" and to be sure that she would know how to act if she ever faced harassment. In 1994 she decided to change unions and joined UNISON, who organized a strike for a wage increase that the TGWU did not support. She was also attracted to UNISON's equality policy, which took her disability into account and provided her with braille documents, which the TGWU had never done. She rapidly became shop steward and disability officer. She had seven hours' facility time per week for her union roles and was also asked to sit on the branch committee, and then the Regional Disabled Members' Committee. There were several committees at the regional level. Soon afterwards, she joined the Women's Committee and became very involved in that. In 2006, she was asked if she would like to run for the National Executive Committee. "It was a much bigger challenge. I had to write a campaign statement, which was sent to all the branches in the London region. I had my colleagues help me." She was elected to one of the seats reserved for women. She also sat on the National Disabled Members Committee. She still has the same amount of facility time as before, one day a week, which she uses for the local, regional, or national levels depending on what needs to be done. She also uses her holiday time. She is single and lives with her parents. The context is not very favourable to negotiating more time with her employer, even though she works for a left-wing council, because she supports the chair of her branch, who has been fired. She is very satisfied with her work for the union. These cumulative experiences have given her enough self-confidence to feel ready to sit on the NEC. The union has been supportive, has encouraged her to take leadership roles, and has funded all her travel and the assistance she requires. She has never applied for a paid position within the union because she likes her work and her elected roles. "I am at the top of the union hierarchy, at the NEC, we manage the union and decide what its policies should be." She hopes to be re-elected in two years' time.

★★★

Unlike the paid career path, the elected one has been the subject of significant debate in terms of fair representation. At UNISON in particular, all the radical measures like reserved seats or self-organized groups are for this kind of elected role (see Table 2.1). The means associated with these equality policies, and the fact that they have been in place for several years, mean that increasing numbers of women and minority groups have been able to access these elected positions, although this hasn't had a mechanical knock-on effect for paid staff positions. This focus on the 'democratic deficit' and the representation of women in elected structures has most likely contributed to downplaying the question of women's access to management (paid) roles within the union structures. When UNISON was created, this policy was driven by the perspective of a compromise between two organizational cultures (Terry, 2000): an officer-led model at NUPE, and a model that allowed greater autonomy to branches at NALGO. The isolation of equality structures, whether in the form of equality officers or self-organized groups, and the lack of union legitimacy of the female activists elected to these different structures (little experience of negotiation in the workplace) did not allow systematic integration into 'mainstream' union careers leading to more generalist elected or paid roles, such as that of branch chair or paid officer.

In France, a cumulative model

In France, paid union positions exist in the regional, federation, or national structures, particularly within the CFDT. This is less true for SUD unions and Solidaires, who have fewer paid staff (aside from the handful of staff who are on secondment from their workplace, on union rights). In the 1990s the number of paid staff increased significantly at the CFDT out of a desire to

Table 3.10: Accumulating union roles and responsibilities, by primary position in the union (averages)

	General Secretary	Deputy Secretary	Treasurer	All positions
Women	5.3	3.8	3.7	4.1
Men	5.1	4.2	4.0	4.5
Total	5.2	4.0	3.9	4.3

Note: Each unionist was asked to specify their primary role within the CFDT, no combinations were possible. Respondents were asked to indicate their primary (one only) and any additional roles. Each role counted for 1, regardless of what kind of role it was.[10]

Source: Internal investigation with two thirds of the participants at the CFDT 2002 Congress in Nantes; 929 individuals. Original data analysis by Sophie Pochic.

professionalize union structures, particularly by hiring young graduates to join the Confederation. Like in Great Britain, many activists were selected for their ability to recruit other members and were hired by the union as organizers. But the most common path to a full-time (paid) union position in France consists of holding concurrent union roles (Breda, 2016). Once again, the statistics from the CFDT speak for themselves (Lescurieux, 2019); for all positions, and for men and women alike, trade unionists combine on average four different union roles or responsibilities (Table 3.10). The General Secretaries at different levels (branch, federation, region) accumulate even more roles, fulfilling an average of five union roles simultaneously. Gender differences do not appear to be particularly significant in this practice.

In French trade unions, paid staff careers are constructed in a range of different ways, combining workplace trade union rights and financial resources available to the union structures. Although the amount of facility time authorized per union role is set by law, arrangements are frequently made with employers, to the point where some activists are entirely seconded to the union. The fact that in France there are more extensive union rights and fewer activists seems to suggest that it is easier to become a full-time unionist there than it is in Great Britain, particularly in major companies, as was the case for Paul, quoted earlier. For the CFDT it is relatively easy to access leadership positions in developing sectors[11] (or services) where the union is newly present (and thus creating positions) and there is a high turnover. Although they usually disagree with the principle of full-time union staff, some SUD unions also benefit from union rights because they are representative in some workplaces, and therefore also employ a few union staff members. Here the major difference between the CFDT and SUD is the latter's commitment to the principle of turnover in union roles, which theoretically forces officials to give up their position after two or three terms – although this is sometimes difficult to enforce.

Moreover, some SUD unions have chosen not to allow full-time secondment for union duties, like at SUD-Education, which puts additional constraints on activist groups. Although the Solidaires structures at the national level allow local activists to become involved in different commissions – immigration, international, or women's commissions, for example – depending on their interests, SUD unions struggle to mobilize activists who are already busy with their local branch and/or the local Solidaires union. Unlike in Great Britain, the existence of 'interprofessional' structures at the local level (counties), which can attract activists interested in more societal or political issues (housing, social security, immigration, equality), leads to competition between professional and territorial structures in attracting participants, as is the case for Chloé. This over-solicitation is particularly pronounced in small unions which cannot offer much facility time.

Chloé, an activist with limited time

Chloé is a history and geography teacher in a high school on the outskirts of Paris. She set up a SUD-Education branch in her school as soon as she was made permanent. She says that it was "obvious" that she would join SUD,

> 'there wasn't a SUD branch at all. We started with nothing. Well, there was a girl at the SNES (FSU) who was there, she was the epitome of the kind of girl I can't stand, like "I am the one who knows, and I am going to explain it to you, I am the one who puts in union time and talks for an hour".'

The year she joined, she had the opportunity to see how SUD functioned differently. During the strikes she had contacted SUD activists who were organizing the general assemblies. She realized that "if you are motivated and want to get things done, there is room, it's not like you have to prove yourself for ten years". The following year she obtained enough facility time to do union work part time. She participated in the local branch and also in the different commissions within Solidaires, as well as in the campaign for the defence of undocumented migrants. She did things she found interesting. In 2012, she accepted a role within the union executive, which was made up of three women and six men. According to her, feminization is difficult at this level both because men do not want to give up their positions in elected roles, and also because women limit themselves. She said she personally came up against this problem and had to push herself to get past it. "At that moment I realized I was conditioned. I thought about trying to get over that whole reasoning that makes girls say, 'I won't do it because there must be a guy who will'. In other words, voluntarily stepping back without realizing we'd do it as well as the guy." The other problem for women is work–life balance issues. At the time of the interview, Chloé had just had her first child. While she was pregnant she worked through a lot of questions and wondered if she was going to be able to keep her union role. "There were friends who teased me, saying 'Did you get the union's approval?'" She decided to continue. Living in Paris makes things easier for her, unlike her colleagues who must travel to the city every week to attend various meetings. As a secondary school teacher, it is also easier to manage her union role than for her primary teacher colleagues who feel guilty about leaving their classes for one or two days a week. Her involvement meant she had fewer classes. She has only one year left to do because SUD-Education imposes limits on the number of terms unionists can hold.

> 'Now, I am in my seventh year of work, so my fifth year with facility time. I have one year left to do. The number of terms is limited at SUD-Education. We can have between three and eight periods of time off. And after eight years you have to have a two-year break.'

So, she plans to take a break from her union roles for two years and then see what she does afterwards.

★★★

As we have seen here, union rights have recently been revised in France, following the enactment of the Macron *ordonnances* in 2017, resulting in the restriction of the number of staff representatives and the reorganization of work councils, which will likely deprive unions of some of their resources. There is little doubt that these new restrictions will not benefit women.

Partisan resources and co-optation processes

Moreover, although French unions provide more possibilities for new members to become full-time unionists than British ones do, in both countries access to leadership roles remains subject to informal recruitment processes that are often unfavourable to women and minorities. In GMB, for example, when a paid officer position becomes vacant, the union structure controls the circulation of recruitment information internally to benefit preselected candidates, or spreads the information through branch meetings in which women participate less. Some interviewees, like Cheryl in the next section, spoke of the obstacle course they had to get through in order to make a place for themselves in this male-dominated world where men are still used to co-opting each other within structures primarily made up of men (regional structures in particular, as the recent report of Karon Monaghan (2020) showed). Her narrative also emphasizes the role of the TUC as a space for encouraging and valuing female activists who struggle to find support within their unions.

Cheryl, overcoming obstacles in a male-dominated world

Cheryl was born in 1948 in the North of England. When she left school she got a place at university but did not really know what she wanted to do and began to work in the purchasing department at the Ministry of Defence, where she realized that she was paid half as much as her older (male) colleagues. She spoke about it to her manager, who responded that she would not be the one to change the situation. She then moved to a bicycle company in 1969 as a trainee and rose up in the hierarchy until she became the deputy head of the purchasing department, having returned to university in the meantime. She stopped working for a while to raise her son as a single mother. Then she met her first husband and was hired as a purchasing manager in a toy company. In 1982 she was pregnant with her first daughter and left her job after almost having a miscarriage, during which her employer was not very helpful. "Purchasing is a man's world," she said. She then had two other daughters and stopped working for five years. But her husband accumulated gambling debts and she returned to work in the bike factory before divorcing him. Although she is very organized, it was difficult to juggle her family and her work, and she ended up selling her house because her ex-husband did not pay the children maintenance. She then decided to stop working and became involved in the local section of the Labour Party. She participated in several campaigns and was elected to different local committees of the party. She was also a volunteer in the 1996 electoral campaign, and was eventually hired by an MP. She worked for him for a year and a half but had trouble with his arrogance and the fact that he spent his time in Westminster rather than looking after his constituency. So, she applied for a job as a recruiter for GMB. "I did not know much about GMB, its culture. And it was a huge shock for me. My integration was very difficult." The objectives she was set were huge. She had to recruit 1,200 new members in the first year, and then more after that. After three months an organizer position became vacant, and she applied but was not successful.

> 'I sat an interview for a position in the team responsible for the north of the region. My interview went very well. I should have got the job, but I didn't get it. It was the Regional Committee that interviewed me, 17 people. They're elected union members. I was the only woman in the room, so I know I didn't get it because I'm a woman. I was angry because I knew that my interview had gone well and that I could do the job.'

The manager of the region set up a culture of fear and her workload was much too heavy. After three years of this she took six months' sick leave for depression. No one called to support her during that time. When she decided to return to work, her boss explained to her that she had been transferred to a rural Conservative town 40 miles away to do the same job. "That was my punishment, being sent to the sticks." She was forced to sell her house and move. Her new husband was unemployed. She decided to make this "punishment" a success. "To succeed, you need to be tough, resistant, have confidence in what you do. You constantly have to show them that they are wrong. You have to be brave." She became involved in the issue of undocumented migrants and managed to get funding for a dedicated assistance programme, with the help of two migrant women workers, one Polish and one Lithuanian. Her project was recognized as the TUC's project of the year. After the region was restructured into three areas, she applied for a job as senior organizer in one of the areas but was not selected because there was a local candidate. The following year she was appointed to the same job for the southern part of the region, replacing another woman who became a European MP. She heads a team of 200 people. She has six years before retirement and would like to continue to progress within GMB but is considering a career change to become a consultant. She considers feminization to be a "major problem for the union". "All the leaders are men; they have their own little kingdom. The culture is just 'I'll scratch your back, you scratch mine, we've been friends for a long time, the next job is yours'."

★★★

Since the National Women's Task Force was set up in 2013, made up of women on the paid staff or in elected roles, GMB appears to be directly targeting these non-transparent and nepotistic recruiting practices (see Box 3.3). One of the main areas of the action plan concerns the recruitment of new officers, as well as senior officers including regional secretaries, with a greater role given to elected officials, national officers, and human resources. However, as the recent independent investigation led by Karon Monaghan showed, the GBM remains 'institutionally sexist'. The General Secretaries and all regional secretaries are, and always have been, men. They hold disproportionate power, as exemplified by Cheryl's experience outlined in this section, which they use to manipulate members of lay bodies. Besides, 'bullying, misogyny, cronyism and sexual harassment are endemic with the GMB' (Monaghan, 2020).

Although this organizational inertia is less pronounced in French unions, with more frequent renewals of union branches, the independence of the various structures in implementing equality policies remains the major obstacle to greater feminization. The continued existence of a typical union career moving through a series of key positions within the workplace and then in intermediary union structures (branch, region) is a source of discrimination for young female recruits who are hired because of their skills (directly into paid positions) and for women stuck in specialized

---

Box 3.3: Recommendations for change[12]

The task force recommend that the appointments process should:

- be robust and one in which faith, trust, and confidence can be placed by those who seek employment in those whose role it is to appoint and promote employees;
- be compliant with relevant equality legislation and ensure that the best candidate is selected based on merit and capability;
- be implemented consistently across the Union for senior appointments;
- include profiling as well as a relevant task-based evaluation exercises;
- always be conducted in a fair, transparent, and accountable manner.

The task force recommends that the appointments panel should:

- all receive regular and appropriate training to ensure compliance with current equality legislation;
- be suitably qualified and have good knowledge of the post;
- be made up of an equal balance of CEC lay members, Regional, or Section Committee members with appropriate industrial knowledge;
- include the National President/Vice President or Regional President determined by the type of post being interviewed.

National HR Department:

- will support regional and national appointments as outlined in the proposals;
- determine whether any other person be required without voting rights in order to authenticate candidates' claims or conduct or provide information for the use of the panel in their deliberation (that is, ex-officio);
- act in a responsible and transparent manner ensuring that there is no predetermination and no informal contact with the interviewee outside of the process.

---

roles (particularly related to questions of equality or union organizing) or everyday representation activities in the workplace. In this context, the role of mentors and proactive measures to promote women, such as quotas, are central in accessing leadership roles. Within UNISON, many low-paid women, sometimes employed in administrative roles in the regions (like Gill, quoted earlier) or as branch secretaries, have benefited from the support of one or several local leaders who persuaded them to take on a position as an officer and gave them confidence in their abilities. This was the case for Lisa:

'I was branch secretary for a few years. People told me that I would make a good regional officer. I said no, I wasn't interested. Why? Because I wasn't ambitious. I worked for two reasons, to pay my bills and to have a social life. It was only when they explained that being an officer meant doing the same work as a branch secretary but for several branches that I accepted. I understood that my skills were transferable. When I got the job, I said, well I can't say no because there aren't many jobs available and it's a privilege to have got it.' (Woman, office worker, age 42, regional officer, UNISON)

This observation echoes others on the making of management careers, for both men and women, in the private sector (Guillaume and Pochic, 2007). The more well placed this mentor is, the more influence he has. The increasing number of women among national leaders in UNISON has thus been broadly attributed to the strategy of the former General Secretary, Dave Prentis.

'Our General Secretary was involved in setting up a plan for succession, with a view to getting more women into positions of national officers and regional officers. I never talked about that directly with him, but I know he was very aware of the fact that the union was made up of two-thirds women. He thought that it wouldn't send a good message if there were only men at the top. He liked that the public image of UNISON was often embodied by a woman.' (Woman, employee, age 51, senior national officer, UNISON)

At the CFDT, the situation is identical. The General Secretary, Laurent Berger, enforced parity on his team in 2014, and the same is true in Solidaires, where a man–woman duo replaced Annick Coupé at the head of the union in 2015. This strategic action by leaders is emphasized among the 'seven key factors for success' in the CFDT's equality plan (Box 3.4).

For some women therefore, a rise to leadership positions sometimes takes place in tandem with an experienced male activist who takes on the political role. There are many duos like this – a male General Secretary and a female Deputy Secretary – that have given women access to political positions via certain shortcuts. This special relationship can be an element of weakness in women's careers because it means their success as the 'protégée' is subordinate to that of their mentor. This limitation is further accentuated for women who do not maintain their own broader personal support and internal networks. Previous study of women political leaders' careers has shown the importance of 'partisan resources' (Dulong and Lévêque, 2002) in access to formal positions of power. It is the ability to make oneself visible and maintain a large power base that confers lasting power on leaders. Being able to maintain oneself

---

Box 3.4: The seven key factors for success[13]

- responsible and committed leaders;
- General Secretaries who take initiatives, referent activists, and groups that get involved;
- an incentive approach promoted by the Confederal Women's Commission, respectful of the role of each organization within the CFDT;
- a knowledge of how to analyse obstacles, to better overcome them;
- a 'reflexive culture', by challenging gender stereotypes, promoting action that changes everyday reality over the long term;
- ongoing concrete action in stages that goes beyond symbolic gestures;
- a dynamic that operates at all levels of the organization, permeating our functioning and union practices.

---

in the space of union structures means being sufficiently socialized and integrated into the 'deviant group' (Guillaume, 2014b) to be able to maintain relationships of mutual obligation with peers who can provide support in certain positions. The acquisition of this 'militant capital' can be partly compensated for by individual academic or professional resources but remains essential for less qualified activists who have no other choice but to rely on the organization, and increasingly so as they rise up the hierarchy. In both France and Great Britain this relational aspect of the career is often criticized by women activists (and by some men). Because they are often restricted to technical and/or specialized roles (gender equality, training, organizing) or hold elected positions in the workplace, women have fewer opportunities to construct their influence within the organization. Many of these women activists, but also more rarely the men who find themselves in these technical positions, feel like they are stuck in their career. When they are young, they imagine they will change careers and leave the union movement, like Scarlett quoted earlier. Otherwise, like John, they tend to remain.

John, rank-and-file activist

John was born in 1953. He left school at age 15 without graduating. He played football semi-professionally in Scotland and moved to England in the late 1960s to work in a factory. "There were several of us who immigrated, there wasn't much work in Glasgow at the time." He worked in the construction industry, where working conditions were disastrous. "We were treated very badly." After a few years in the sector, he looked for a more stable job because he was now married with two children. He got a job with the Postal Service in Basingstoke and joined the CWU. "It was natural for me, and the late-1970s was a very interesting time in Great Britain, with major political change. Working conditions had deteriorated dramatically, even in the public service." He quickly became shop steward and branch secretary and fought against the paid officers who were not democratic enough and above all not radical enough for his liking. As a far-left activist, he participated in several strikes and organized mass meetings, even though it was illegal. In 1983 he was fired; the members of his union supported him, but the leaders did not. He spent two years unemployed, with two young children and a wife at home. So he decided to go back to school and he enrolled at the London School of Economics, while working nights in a disco to supplement his scholarship. In 1989 he got a degree in sociology and industrial relations. He was then employed as an educator in a TUC centre in Southampton. He also taught at the Open University. In 1997 he became the manager of the training centre and completely overhauled the CWU training programme. He was also giving lectures in political economics for TGWU activists. At the time, he was a member of the NASUWT, a teachers' union. He was fired after opposing a major restructuring of the training institute. He continued to work for some unions, including the GMB. In 2003 he was recruited as an education officer for the GMB. The position was advertised in the newspaper "but it's very rare that this kind of job goes to someone from outside". "I was a good applicant, with lots of experience, a long history in the union, and I knew all the training institutes well." Along with a Polish colleague, he set up a new training programme for migrants and for women. At the time of the interview, he said he feels like he is in sync with the project defended by the General Secretary Paul Kenny, elected in 2006. He hopes that he can stay in this kind of role until he retires, and he does not have the skills or desire to progress further in the union hierarchy. John does not appreciate the union bureaucracy; he enjoys his work identifying and encouraging new activists to "reinvigorate the rank and file".

★★★

The introduction of quotas in the national structures of the CFDT (Executive Commission) or in certain Solidaires unions (SUD-PTT for example) has allowed some women to be selected even without the activist experience required. But this also means they run the risk of being perceived as token or symbolic appointments (Monney et al, 2013). Increasing the number of women in the union and the legitimacy of the equality policy, as was the case in UNISON, can have a negative impact on women. Certain candidates found themselves accused of having built their career on their gender with the support of their feminist networks. For example, one woman, who was candidate for General Secretary of UNISON in 2015, faced these accusations even though she was the only woman running against three men. A letter in support of her candidacy was signed by several women academics,[14] which

---

Box 3.5: Message from an ex-branch secretary with UNISON, on the CRITICAL-LABOUR-STUDIES@jiscmail.ac.uk mailing list

'In the union movement there is a certain shared position that the election of a leader is a matter for members. External attempts to influence the leader's election are considered inappropriate. I was therefore surprised when a group of women describing themselves as "female activists, academics and trade unionists" chose to write to the *Guardian*, citing their academic credentials, to campaign on behalf of a candidate for the position of Secretary General. I have worked with some of these women, whom I have admired for many years, but this time I believe they have taken the wrong approach. They advocate supporting a candidate because they say they have confidence in her, but they also say their main argument to justify this support is that it is time that a union made up of three quarters women is led by a woman. The question of the feminization of union leaders is central, but in this particular case they chose to ignore the fact that their candidate did not receive the support of even one of the women sitting on the National Executive Council. They could have supported their argument with proof of their candidate's commitment to the fight against wage inequalities for low-skilled women in the public sector. [...] Some of us are old enough to remember the argument that it would be good for the country to have a female leader and we got Thatcher. Not that I'm comparing this particular candidate to Thatcher, but I am emphasizing the importance of politics and actions over gender.'

---

was interpreted as a form of 'gendered factionalism' (Healy and Kirton, 2000), and this sparked a debate among some female lay members who questioned the interference of people from outside the union in the running of the election, but also the female candidate's supposed track record in defending women (Box 3.5). Several women in elected positions contested her application, favouring a male candidate who was perceived as more left wing and therefore considered more likely to defend the interests of low-paid women, particularly those affected by job losses and privatization in the public sector.

Internal political struggles remain important within some unions, including UNISON, and can interfere with the implementation of equality policies. They can be a hindrance or an impetus to increasing numbers of women in the union. Thus, in the 1990s and 2000s the departure of certain CFDT branches and the creation of SUD unions created opportunities for certain women. But accessing leadership roles in these circumstances can be an additional hardship for women leaders, particularly when they have skipped critical steps in their career. Because of the difficulty of the position and issues they are given to deal with, women are described as sitting on a 'glass cliff' (Ryan and Haslam, 2005), which is not conducive to a long-term career. The high visibility or complexity of the issues they are responsible for and the atypical nature of their career (often accelerated or based on specific skills) can explain the high turnover among women leaders, particularly at the CFDT, even though these activists have the professional skills which have become essential to fulfilling leadership roles. From this perspective, taking on the equality issue is not necessarily the most strategic choice for women leaders, even if they often end up with it. The quick succession of women's officers at the CFDT over the years is a sign that equality continues to be controversial within the organization and that the women responsible for this issue still have limited possibilities for action. This was the case for Geneviève.

Geneviève, a whirlwind passage on a controversial subject

Geneviève is one of those women who discovered politics and feminism during the 1968 countercultural movement, even though she comes from a traditional Catholic family. She initially trained in prosthetics, but then rapidly moved into the field of adult education, and in 1977 she joined a service associated with the Prime Minister's Office, alongside the Commission for Women's Rights. She has been a member of the Communist Revolutionary League since 1973, under the influence of her older brother, and she decided to create a union branch because the ambience in her workplace was "nice but we had the feeling that it was not transparent. Our supervisors did what they liked." Although she was in a relationship with a CGT activist, she agreed to go along with her colleagues and set up a CFDT branch. She fought against job insecurity, along with her colleagues working on short-term contracts. She was also a feminist activist and involved in the struggle for abortion rights, but for her "that is not a union struggle" even though the CFDT was involved in this mobilization at the time. For years she was a branch activist, taking on different representative roles in her ministry and changing jobs quite often. She had two children, in 1979 and 1984. She managed to combine all these activities partly because her various superiors were trade union sympathizers. In the 1990s she met a young colleague who was later recruited to the CFDT and who recommended her for a role as a paid officer at the Confederation to deal with employment integration issues in 2002. Geneviève was 52 and she felt like she could "leave the ministry, it was now or never, there wasn't too much at stake". She accepted the position because these were issues she had worked on previously, but she quickly became bored. After a few months she was offered a position as the National Women's Officer; she was not expecting it but was very pleased. The position had been an ordeal for her predecessor, who had issues dealing with "the ambient machismo". Geneviève decided to learn some lessons from that.

"It quickly became obvious that there were some macho big shots in the Confederation, and I thought I'd put my feminism aside for a bit, so they'd like me. I'm quite likable, I like to go for drinks and mix with people." She knew that the women's issue had been around for a long time at the CFDT but that it had always been held at arm's length by certain women. She adored her job and worked hard at it. Her children were grown up, but she still had trouble making space for her private life, even though her husband was supportive. She was forced to abandon some of her charity activities. She managed to set up joint actions with other federations, organizing the *Actuelles* meeting in 2004 with 1,500 activists, without much logistical support. She also set up a partnership with the feminist organization '*Ni Putes Ni Soumises*'. Her relationship with her female superior was terrible, but she felt supported by the General Secretary, "who was not a feminist but saw what it could bring to his image". Her action was highly criticized internally by other activists working on other discrimination issues who did not like the partnership with '*Ni Putes Ni Soumises*', an organization that was seen as too radical and as encouraging the stigmatization of BAME men. The relationship with her hierarchy became more and more tense, until she opposed one of her superior's decisions and was dismissed. She returned to her job at the ministry but remains bitter and frustrated at the amount of energy she invested in her mission within the union, only to get caught up in internal conflicts between 'clans' and the inability of the organization to establish a clear position on equality and diversity issues.

★★★

Geneviève's case is a reminder that paid staff positions can be impacted upon by internal and political fighting as much as elected positions are. Besides, depending on the union and the periods, equality policies are subject to multiple, competing, and evolving definitions which can be detrimental to the careers of women's officers, an aspect little studied by the literature.

Constraints and selectivity of managerial roles

Beyond the ability to evolve in these highly politicized spheres (which are also often in the media spotlight), union leadership positions at the regional, federation, or national level require managerial and organizational skills to manage both activists (who are often male and politicized) and employees. This is the case in UNISON.

'Historically, we have promoted people who were good negotiators, but not managers. Now that we have become a big organization, we are much more careful about regional secretaries being good managers. I am lucky, it is an area I am quite good at, even without being trained in it. I manage 85 staff. The other very important management skill in this position is more political, with the elected regional members. The London region is old fashioned. The elected members have been there since the 1970s. They want to strike at the drop of a hat, they're very politicized.' (Woman, laboratory technician, age 52, regional secretary, UNISON)

At this level, union work is also more individualized and requires more formal writing, communication, and management skills. Training programmes are rare (Pocock and Brown, 2013), and activists sometimes get worn out trying to understand and operate the structures that they manage, or in which they participate, without assistance. Activists often pay a high price, particularly when they are female and have low-level initial qualifications or have not progressed much in their career. They appreciate the more expressive and relational aspects of union work and have sometimes hesitated before taking on a role as a paid official. Union officials who come from low-paid jobs frequently express a feeling of illegitimacy in their interactions with employers (or politicians and senior civil servants when they hold national official positions), and concerns about their ability to manage union staff. They also struggle to deal with the autonomy that is expected of them in their role. Having a higher level of education, whether self-taught or from school, helps trade unionists adjust more easily to this requirement for autonomy and discretion (Lenzi, 2009), and also to adapt to the deliberative practices that are formally organized in union structures (union board, departmental union council) which are highly political.

The sometimes-brutal nature of the interactions between union officers/officials is also often mentioned as being dissuasive to the participation of women, even though union culture seems to be changing with feminization. Frances, who is today a UNISON Regional Secretary, explained that "the work culture was very aggressive in the union, with lots of conflicts. It changed a lot when women moved into leadership positions. We plan more, we work together to build our strategy, we talk about problems and we look for solutions together. It is a much nicer environment for women today." We might wonder whether this cultural change is linked to the presence of women or whether it is the increasing qualifications of leaders (some of whom are women), which led to a greater professionalization of union work. The interviews studied here were conducted with people who remained active in the union, but we can hypothesize that many activists (women and men) may have left out of a real and symbolic 'fear of incompetence'. Some activists interviewed in fact preferred to not be involved in the elected bodies of the organization and refused certain political roles, like Martine, who asked to return to a non-elected position after having had a role in the Executive Commission of the federation.

Martine, a spectacular rise ultimately hindered by social background

Martine was a miner's daughter and began working at age 14 in an industrial dye factory, in 1972. She then did various jobs in the sales and service sectors before becoming the concierge of an apartment building in order to raise her children, because they could not live on her husband's salary alone. She had this job for 17 years and describes herself as "a little bit privileged" because she had comfortable accommodation in the apartments and a large separate lodge, as well as being employed by a large company with a work council. She was not in the union, but one day she received a flyer from the CFDT that made her laugh, and which she thought hit the mark. "Without thinking about joining" she decided to meet the author of the flyer. She came to see her in her lodge and it "made a huge impact on me". She agreed to be on a list as the deputy staff rep (*suppléant DP*) in 1996. Shortly afterwards she was called to a meeting of the union and "everything took off at high speed". Although she was reluctant to attend the meeting, because she "was not interested", she found herself in the middle of a violent dispute between the branch chair and the representatives of the Federation that led to the resignation of the whole branch. The paid officials of the Federation then suggested that she become the chair, because they said, "you did not say much but we thought you managed it well". She said "sorry, I don't have a degree and I don't know how to use a computer". They advised her to think about it, and in talking about it with her husband she decided to try, because "I am no dumber than anyone else". In one year, her branch went from 30 to 500 members. Six months later she was asked to become a national paid official at the Federation level. Although she had been chosen as a "representative" of low-paid professions in the executive committee, she felt undervalued compared to her colleagues. Often, she had to ask people to explain things on "very politicized and crosscutting debates". She was surreptitiously supported by the General Secretary, who had low-level qualifications himself. Because she felt "a little ashamed", she took night classes for a year to catch up, but did not tell anyone. Ultimately, she carried out only one term in this role and then asked to be moved to a more technical position as federation secretary, with branch-level negotiation roles. When she is in the field, negotiating with employers at the workplace level, she feels good. "I can use my professional knowledge and experience." Today, ten years later, aged 50, with the benefit of the experience she has acquired, she says she would do things differently but feels "good where I am".

★★★

Other recent studies have emphasized that some activists, often those with low-level qualifications, choose to moderate their ambitions and restrict themselves to workplace unionism, among the activists they know in their workplace. As Julien Mischi (2016) demonstrated, in France, low-paid workers often choose to get involved at the workplace level rather than in union structures. They feel their union legitimacy comes from being rooted in the professional community. It is rare for them to aspire to roles at the regional or national level. Certain women activists may make these same choices if believe they can accomplish more – particularly in terms of the defence of women's rights – at the workplace level than in the union structure.

A lack of initial formal qualifications may be partly compensated for by further training, but unions vary in their provision of education programmes, depending on their size and resources. At the CFDT, for example, the offer of training for union leaders within the structure began to run out in the late 1990s (Guillaume, 2011) at a moment when many leaders went into retirement. Certain federations or regions have tried to set up longer-term training that to mitigate against the fact that it is now the activists with higher-level qualifications who seem to be able to take on their union roles most easily (Defaud, 2009), but union education is unevenly distributed among sectors and regions. From this point of view, education has provided leverage (Guillaume and Pochic, 2013; Lescurieux, 2019) that has enabled women to make a place for themselves within unions, sometimes recruited 'from above' into specialized roles, or up 'from below' from their place of work where they were professionals or managers. We have already seen that women activists in SUD unions have high levels of qualifications, and this is also true for most of the female union officials at the national level of the CFDT. The process is less striking in Great Britain, because there is less generational renewal of union elites (men and women), even though the educational level among permanent staff has increased steadily in recent years (Heery, 2006b). Moreover, training is more developed in large British unions like GMB and UNISON, where there are also specific training programmes for leaders, and sometimes for women (Kirton, 2006a). Most of the women activists interviewed here have returned to study at some stage (for example, through distance learning or the Open University) or made good use of existing union education provisions. Many did this through the intermediary of the TUC, which organizes 'women's-only schools' (among other things) to motivate women to take on leadership roles and remain in the union movement. Like UNISON, the TUC has set up training or mentoring programmes for union leaders with the help of senior managers, often women but also from minority groups (BAME, LGBTI). Marc, a regional officer with UNISON, argues that "there are many role models today in the organization, not only for women, but also BAME, and gays too. Moreover, UNISON has a good career review system if people want to go into a career in the union. It is a matter of experience and acquiring skills." In both countries, this kind of training is particularly important for low-paid women who often lack self-confidence.

The other specificity of full-time paid union work in both countries is the increase in time constraints (Kirton and Healy, 2013b). In spite of the family-friendly policies adopted by British unions (shorter working days, holidays, paid maternity and parental leave), which above all benefit administrative staff who are mostly women, the work culture among union leaders is still described as 'a long hours culture' (Watson, 1988). Taking on union leadership positions requires a work pattern that follows managerial norms. This means at the very least accepting putting in office hours similar to those of a manager. For some employees who were used to having staggered or shorter hours in their 'normal job', this reorganization has significant repercussions on their family and private lives. Constraints on geographical mobility are also significant, including for the lay members elected to national bodies. They are linked either to the type of union role that may require frequent travel to London or to the need to be mobile to have a career in the union movement. The low turnover among leaders, the fact that national-level positions are concentrated in London, and the intense competition for access to higher leadership levels often force candidates to accept roles in another region (sometimes even in another union) while waiting for their desired position to become available. Recently, certain unions, like GMB, have reduced the requirement for geographical mobility for national leaders, which allows them to continue living in their original region while working in London during the week.

Similarly, in France, the centralization of unions (confederations and federations), also means significant geographical mobility and frequent travel to Paris. Unionists encounter major difficulties reconciling their family and professional responsibilities with the demands for 'biographical availability' (McAdam, 1986) that are essential for a union career. In this context, the age of one's children and the support of one's partner and family in managing everyday life are all essential criteria in accepting union responsibilities, particularly for women (Le Quentrec and Rieu, 2003; Haller, 2017). Although some of the interviews with women unionists in France mention an encounter with a (future) partner who was also an activist in the same branch, and his support for her union activism, this shared union practice in the same workplace is much less frequent in Great Britain. Probably because of the greater gender segregation in employment there, this kind of support from one's partner was rarely mentioned among British interviewees. Instead, they often described their partner's lack of interest, and/or frequent separations, but some, like Charlotte, had their husband's unwavering support.

Charlotte: a long career at the top of the organization

Charlotte was born in a poor working-class district in Glasgow. She left school at 16 because she needed to work, and joined the Communist Party after attending a political rally as part of the 1972 dockers' strike. She worked for years as a tax officer, and then in the financial department of a supermarket chain. She joined USDAW and became a shop steward but said she was not regularly active. At age 22 she returned to study, along with her husband, and obtained a degree in English and history. She was then hired by a town council, working in social housing department. She was not passionate about her work. She became involved in a union defending the interests of people on welfare benefits. She began to study law. In 1982 she applied for a position as the wage counsellor for GMB after seeing an ad in the newspaper. The same year, she left the Communist Party, which she considered too divided. "I always thought that working for the union movement could be interesting." There were many Communists working at GMB. There was a lot to do in this position and she was very stressed. Around this time many distilleries were closing down and she had to advise the workers who had been laid off. In 1985 she applied for a job in the legal service at the London office of GMB, because she had no possibility of career progression at the regional level, and no way of moving into negotiating roles, which were "reserved for men". She moved to London and her husband followed her. Progressively she began to work on wage inequality and feminization in the union, which were hot topics at the time. She worked with one of the rare women national officers who had managed to break into the very male-only world of national negotiators and who encouraged her to participate in the TUC Women's Conference, as well as the conference organized by the Labour Party (which she ended up joining). "Pat really supported me and gave me the opportunity to do so much." When her mentor retired, she applied for a position as women's officer with NALGO. Despite the large number of women in the union, she had limited means and had to do everything alone, assisting the development of self-organized groups who did not get along and did not appreciate the union staff. "At the time, there was really a rank-and-file culture, anti-staff." In 1990 she finally got the position she wanted, as a national officer, after having run against external candidates. She stayed in this position for around 12 years and had two children during that time. Her husband supported her because she often had to travel and work late. "It's important to have a helpful husband. He was probably more involved in our children's education than I was, to be honest. He worked full time but he worked shorter hours to be able to look after the children." She also had financial support from UNISON for childcare. She applied for a job as senior national officer so her career would progress. The competition was tough. There were only four positions of this kind in the union. It was a big change for her, particularly as she had to restructure the service, which involved managerial skills that she did not fully have. In 2003 she took a training course for union leaders at the TUC, 'Leading Change', which she found fascinating. She says she does not aspire to becoming General Secretary, because "the position is too exposed", but perhaps deputy. At 51 years old she does not plan to leave

UNISON, because professional reconversion would be too difficult. "It is sometimes difficult to tell which are transferable skills." In 2010 she accepted horizontal transfer and transferred to her colleague's position.

★★★

This biography also illustrates how paid union staff, particularly those who are elected, can become dependent on their organization, and try to maintain their position out of fear of not being able to transfer somewhere else, or out of attachment to a job that is meaningful for them. The difficulty full-time union activists have in reintegrating into the labour market is well known (Pochic, 2014b; Simonpoli, 2020), as is the detrimental impact this issue has on equality/diversity policies. Yet, for women to have access to leadership positions, the men currently occupying those positions have to give them up, which they do with more goodwill when they perceive the possibility of a positive professional reconversion. The analysis of the most recent data on the composition of CFDT federation boards confirms the existence of a persistent glass ceiling in the organization (also observed elsewhere, Guillaume and Pochic, 2007). Women have access to lower levels of leadership, but not to higher levels (Table 3.11), largely because of the low turnover in those roles. Given that trade unionists arrive in these executive positions aged 50 or more, it is rare that they consider leaving them before retirement, to return to their roles in the workplace or to their initial professions (particularly if they come from the private sector and are on secondment to the union).

Exceptional women?

To build a lasting career in the trade union movement and gain access to full-time roles, women still have to conform to the dominant norms of

Table 3.11: Gendered make-up of CFDT Federation executive boards

	Women		Men	
	Distribution	Percentage	Distribution	Percentage
President		0%	1	100%
General Secretary	5	28%	13	72%
Deputy General Secretary	4	25%	12	75%
Treasurer	5	28%	13	72%
Deputy Treasurer	2	40%	3	60%
Other roles	36	45%	44	55%
Overall total	52	38%	86	62%

Source: Confederal data 2016.

male careers. From this perspective, some of the internal equality measures are clearly designed to facilitate individual empowerment, enabling a small number of over-selected women to access leadership positions. These 'liberal' equality policies (individual mentoring and training, for example) have developed in recent years, including in the more feminist unions, but they are particularly visible in the CFDT. In this confederation, gender inequalities have been reframed as a 'diversity' issue (*mixité*), signalling a clear de-politicization of the equality policy as compared to the 1970s (Le Brouster, 2014). In contrast with other unions, women in leadership positions in the CFDT rarely define themselves as feminists (or as socialists), the CFDT having long abandoned any reference to class unionism. Instead, like Laure, women leaders choose to 'neutralise their gender' (Pochic, 2014a), rather than promote their difference.

Laure, a feminine leader

Laure trained as a secondary teacher and joined the union during teachers' college in 1992, where she represented her fellow trainee teachers on the governing board. She was headhunted by the teachers' union, the FEN, who suggested that, once she became a rep, she should be responsible for recruiting young teachers. She put strategies in place to do this, but they did not go very well with the local branch. "I was young, had a different approach, I wanted to do new things." She thought about quitting, because "for us women it is not about power, but the possibility of setting up new things". She instead decided to run for a position in the national office, hoping "to get some air". She was elected and went part time at school. "Again, there were lots of conflicts. Being a young woman in a world of men, there was the whole seduction thing and I had never had political responsibilities before." She quickly asserted herself in her role and took on more responsibility. She set up projects for young people and on the European issue. When the FEN participated in the creation of UNSA in 1994, Laure began working towards a rapprochement with the CFDT, which did not come to fruition but which did open the doors of the CFDT to her. She joined them as Confederal Secretary in 2002, at the request of Nicole Notat. She rapidly decided that this should be more than just a technical position and got involved with other groups and went out into the field, holding debates in the regions. She spoke in many places and sought to acquire a political profile. The rank and file began sending signals to the Confederation that it would be good to have a new Nicole Notat on the Executive Commission. But, apart from being tall and blond, she did not really have the profile, she came from UNSA, and her popularity made others in the organization jealous, particularly other women. "There was a lot of bitterness from women who had struggled and who didn't understand why things went faster for me." She was headhunted to "sit on the Executive Commission" in 2006 but first spent a year assisting one of the male officials. "That helped me, because he positioned me not as an assistant but in a political role." In 2006, aged 40, she was elected National Secretary responsible for several issues, including diversity. She believes that it is her personality and her ability to be noticed that make her visible and credible for election within this select group of national officials, "even if I didn't do that to get elected" She has no children and a supportive partner, and she thinks she can provide the immense investment of time and energy the job requires. However, she refuses to subscribe to the masculine methods of her colleagues (but feels "constantly pushed to"), and refuses to let go of her femininity like most of her female colleagues who "are real bitches". Although she does not describe herself as a feminist, she intends to give a social dimension to the women's issue in the union, particularly on violence against women, inspired by Spanish trade unions. She was re-elected in 2010, taking charge of other issues like the public service. She decided to resign in 2013 to move into the political women's rights arena and joined a ministerial cabinet.

★★★

Most of the CFDT women unionists interviewed said they wanted to be considered the same as men, and did not emphasize their differences. They were also generally not concerned about the promotion of other women, with a few exceptions in the youngest generation (age 30–40), who had sometimes benefited from policies to promote young activists. For these women, diversity and generational renewal go hand in hand. Although an 'egalitarian conscience' could be detected among these young leaders (including some men), it was rarely expressed as an explicit feminist identification, and only very exceptionally associated with an awareness of class and race inequalities. Much like women managers who are not particularly interested in low-paid women, these women activists rely on individual strategies to make a place for themselves in the still very male-dominated world of union leadership. Although most of them have experienced the difficulty of being a woman in a world of men, they tend to choose assimilationist strategies or specialized careers that are less exposed to political and electoral logics. The connection between 'victimisation' and 'agency' theorized by Linda Briskin (2006) therefore plays out on an individual level here. Moreover, by comparison with their British counterparts, they rarely see themselves pursuing a long-term union career. Although the CFDT encourages this as part of their policy for paid officers' turnover, women leaders also leave their roles more quickly than men because they underestimate, but then encounter, the full force of the glass ceiling. They are also often halfway through their career when they arrive in these leadership positions and therefore wonder how they can maintain their position within the union structure up to retirement, and/or what might be the possibilities for reconversion after their union term is over. Many studies have emphasized the strategies for reconversion that run through activist careers (Siméant, 2001; Agrikoliansky, 2002), with individuals moving from one organization or one sector to another (politics, NGOs, unions), or sometimes combining different commitments or converting union experience into professional spheres (or political spheres, like the CGT activists elected to local government studied by Julian Mischi in 2016). However, the reality is that reconversion remains difficult for many union activists (Pochic, 2014a; Simonpoli, 2020).

In the other three unions, women appear to have less-individualistic strategies, even though they are still obliged to conform to 'neutral' career norms defined by men in order to access positions of leadership. The women pioneers involved in founding the first SUD unions generally brought feminist awareness and demands into their unions, but they also endorsed a form of 'sacrificial activism', either choosing not to have children or juggling family responsibilities with the help of an activist partner. This is also true for UNISON and GMB for the current generation of leaders (who were for the most part shaped by the 1970s counterculture), but it is also strikingly true for younger leaders who most often do have children but manage to find solutions to meet the time requirements for their union roles. Many of them complain about the personal sacrifices their union duties demand of them, but career norms are slow to evolve, particularly because of the intense workload that weighs on a small number of full-time unionists. The generally accepted vocational framing of union activism (even when it is paid) clearly remains an obstacle for changing the gendered norms associated with union careers (as for clergywomen, see Greene and Robbins, 2015), which can double that of feminized occupations and make it very difficult for women to participate (Dean and Greene, 2017).

By contrast with their CFDT counterparts, most of the women activists in UNISON and Solidaires described themselves as feminists, took on mentoring roles (Kirton and Healy, 2012), and were involved in developing internal equality policy without necessarily benefiting from it themselves. Like other recent studies conducted with British union leaders (Kirton and Healy, 2013b; Pochic 2014a), the interviews collected here demonstrate that feminist identity can be correlated with union activism (Kirton, 1999), but that it is rarely openly expressed in the union context and is sometimes relegated to other activist or political spheres. Even within Solidaires, which associates itself with a societal feminism quite close to that promoted by the CFDT in the 1970s, the expression of a feminist stance is sometimes misunderstood, even by fellow female unionists (Guillaume, 2018a), as Jacqueline explains.

Do you feel comfortable being seen as a feminist?

'Absolutely, in fact the opposite, it is such a deep conviction that it gives you strength, you shout it loud and proud. And to the first person who says, "you're such a feminist", I say, "yes, of course, and more than ever". It is easier to be a feminist at Solidaires than at the CGT, but I can't say it is something that is shared 100%, far from it, even among my girlfriends. Some of them you might even wonder if they aren't anti-feminist, like if you mention it too often it bothers them, or other friends in the younger generation who think that all the struggles have been won.' (Woman, unemployment counsellor, age 62, union official, Solidaires)

At UNISON, depending on the generation, some women take on a more overtly feminist stance, particularly if they act as women's officer or are elected to a reserved seat, but it is rare that they pursue a feminist career within the union movement. The GMB activists from the 1970s generation who rose to positions of responsibility in the union rejected the feminist label (because they felt it would disqualify them as trade unionists) and aspired to mainstream union legitimacy. Many consider it a benefit to not be seen as too politicized or too feminist, because elected officials with profiles that are 'socialist-feminist' or 'feminist-socialist' have been accused of neglecting class inequalities in favour of gender differences and have sometimes been fired for it. Maybe because of the persistent sexist culture (Monaghan, 2020), few of the young women interviewed (who were generally White and with high-level qualifications) describe themselves as feminists even when they are responsible for aspects of the equality programme, which they consider as secondary and sometimes difficult to manage (particularly as concerns LGBTI rights). Some of the BAME women unionists seem to have a more developed 'equality conscience', but their perspective is more inclusive and less politicized, in keeping with the way equality has been framed in public policy since the early 2000s (Breitenbach et al, 2002). Moreover, in these three unions, the dominant framing of union action in class terms – facilitated by the established leadership in GMB and UNISON, and massively supported by the new generation of activists in Solidaires (Denis and Thibault, 2015) – contributes to having women's issues attached to the more general defence of low-paid workers' interests. This approach may help raise awareness for women's issues among leaders when there are a lot of women among low-paid workers, but it does not solve the problem of their underrepresentation, as Florence, a labour inspector, explains:

'There are often debates about the make-up of the governing body of the union, and they're always the same. We realize that even on the National Board there are many more inspectors than controllers, and very few low-level public servants. Generally, at the lower levels, secretarial, admin, it is 90% women in the ministry. The trouble for secretarial workers is public speaking, standing up against other people who might be more educated, and who are more comfortable speaking in public. We don't know how to resolve this question. We would like to have more employees in the governing body, and we are not managing to. There are one or two out of 35 members on the National Board. And sometimes they don't come. They just give up.' (Woman, labour inspector, age 36, union official, SUD-Travail)

The centrality of the class framing within Solidaires has a clear impact on the way equality issues are defined, and in particular the strong focus on the representation of the interests of low-paid workers. However, unlike in British unions, union activism is rarely envisaged as a career here. The fact that SUD unions have scant financial resources at their disposal, along with their rules on rotating union roles, also undoubtedly restrict women activists' opportunities. At UNISON, the relationships between gender, class, and race inequalities were laid out in the creation of the union following the merger in 1993, which saw educated women in NALGO in the same union as women with low-paid jobs who were represented by NUPE and COHSE. This intersectional perspective remains a complicated issue, however. There have been many efforts to identify BAME activists in low-paid jobs and help them to take on leadership roles in the union, and most of the union leaders interviewed are aware of the risks and pitfalls of this underrepresentation. Some have in fact benefited from these mentoring and training programmes and are themselves from ethnic minorities (and sometimes LGBTI) and in low-paid jobs. In this union, maintaining radical measures to promote the emancipation of minority groups and to broaden the scope of equality policies to other kinds of discrimination (such as age or sexual orientation) has helped to maintain a collective framing of equality that is attentive to gender, race, and class, alongside individual empowerment programmes. This framing of equality is highly unusual, and a reminder that equality and diversity policies can be subject to very diverse social constructions (Berrey, 2015).

However, British women unionists, and also those in Solidaires, have a tendency to 'neutralise their gender in order to better represent their class' (Pochic, 2014a), or the class they are supposed to represent in the name of the fight for social justice (Healy and Kirton, 2013b). Unlike women leaders in other professions (Boussard, 2016), they do not want to be 'exceptional', and defend the existence of policies promoting greater diversity even though, as we have seen, they may not benefit much from them themselves. They may, however, have very decided opinions on existing policies. The British interviewees defended the existence of separate groups to give women and other minorities confidence and help them to participate actively, most likely because they are more used to the existence of such groups. But they were more ambivalent when it came to the usefulness of these groups as a path to national leadership. Several leaders said they would not want to run for a seat reserved for women, fearing that it would sap their legitimacy. These hesitations are even more pronounced for Solidaires activists, even though the feminist stance of the union is clearly expressed in its statutes. The quantitative survey conducted at the Inter-Union Women's Days in 2014 showed that although 78% of activists present said they were feminists and 72% supported measures aimed at increasing the number of women in the union, only 45% supported the idea of women-only measures. This reticence is often justified by the idea that such measures would meet resistance from men, and by the anticipated difficulties of implementing them in a context where resources are lacking. This also reveals the impact of the republican 'universal' framing of equality in the French context. However, several interviewees wondered whether these radical measures might not be necessary to reach (and pass) the threshold of 30% women leaders. To compensate for the lack of or limitations of radical measures, some women union leaders have also tried to 'lift as they rise' (Kirton and Healy, 2012), opening career opportunities for other women as they progress up the union hierarchy. This can be seen through the different biographies, but it remains easier in (feminized) British trade unions where established trade unionists (both men and women) can project themselves in their union roles over the long term.

Conclusion

This comparative analysis of union careers in these four unions has revealed the diversity in their 'inequality regimes' (Acker, 2006), depending on organizational and institutional characteristics. It has also identified key lessons from the challenges faced by equality policies, depending on the way they are framed and the tools they involve.

The number of women members has increased across all unions, reaching 50% in the CFDT and GMB, and 78% at UNISON. However, the representation of women in elected or paid union roles is not proportional to this increase in feminization. In Great Britain, union data reveal a dual segregation – both vertical and horizontal – from the first elected roles in the workplace. In UNISON only 55% of shop stewards are women and only 46% of branch chairs are women. This is as low as 30% for stewards at GMB. Women are also more represented in certain roles – particularly education, welfare, and equality. Although equivalent figures are lacking for the French cases, the fact that women are restricted to certain representative roles, such as staff rep or work council member, and certain activities (social activities or the work council treasurer, for example) is clearly corroborated by various studies. This dual segregation has since been accentuated in permanent staff roles in both countries, where quota policies and reserved seats do not apply. The feminization of governing roles – at the regional, federation, or confederal level – is slow and seems to have plateaued, particularly at the CFDT and Solidaires. In these two organizations, it seems to be difficult to get beyond the threshold of 30% women leaders, and the CFDT is struggling to fulfil its 1982 targets of a minimum of 30% women in its two governing bodies, the National Board (BN) and the Confederal National Council (CNC), which are made up of union officials at the federation and regional levels. Although the higher proportion of female members increases the probability of being able to promote women to leadership positions (Cohen et al, 1998), this is by no means automatic (Table 3.12).

The example of these CFDT federations shows that although some, such as Health and Social Services, are highly feminized and have an almost proportional representation of women in their executive body, as well as a female General Secretary, others, like the SGEN (education) or the PSTE (welfare services), lag far behind. Furthermore, even in federations with women on executive bodies (Services, FCC), women struggle to obtain the position of General Secretary. Inversely, in some male-dominated federations, like the FGMM (Metalwork), proportional representation has been achieved, but represents only a very small number of people (two). As Gill Kirton (2015) noted, it is easier to reach proportional representation in male-dominated unions because it means finding fewer women. The large rate of feminization among senior national officers at UNISON should not overshadow the very small number of women involved and the fact that they have been there for a long time. Moreover, the larger the executive bodies are, the more women objectively have a chance of a seat. As other studies have shown (Huffman et al, 2010), feminization is facilitated by the size and growth of organizations, which can be a problem for unions that struggle to expand, like SUD unions, or that show stable growth, like the other three.

This research had also drawn attention to the way inequalities can be produced through the formal and informal processes that enable union participation, and in particular the demands in terms of mobility and time associated with leadership positions. Because of their family responsibilities, women generally struggle more than men to meet these requirements, although some of them have the support of their partners and family and can move house when a position comes vacant. These constraints are well known within unions, which have long tried to implement childcare assistance or promote family-friendly meeting times. As we have shown, the difficulties in combining union and professional life are exacerbated today by the context of staff reductions, management pressures, and union victimization (Kirton, 2015; Prowse et al, 2020), and this makes union activism even more complicated. This is particularly true for women working in the care sector who feel guilty about having to leave their professional responsibilities to perform union duties. The overrepresentation of low-paid women in these professions therefore aggravates previously mentioned class inequalities.

Table 3.12: Feminization of leadership in CFDT federations

	Percentage of women members	Percentage of women in executive positions	Number of women	General Secretary
General Federation of Farming and Agriculture (*Agroalimentaire*)	40%	28%	2 of 7	Male
National Federation for Timber and Construction (*Fédération Nationale Construction Bois*)	15%	0%	0 of 6	Male
General Metalwork and Mining Federation (*Fédération Générale de la Métallurgie et des Mines*)	19%	25%	2 of 8	Male
Services Federation (*Fédération des Services*)	53%	57%	4 of 7	Male
Federation for Training and Private Education (*Fédération Formation et Enseignement Privés*)	73%	50%	5 of 10	Male
National Local Government Federation (*Fédération Nationale Interco*)	60%	33%	3 of 9	Female
Federation for Defence Services (*Fédération des Etablissements et Arsenaux de l'Etat*)	36%	33%	2 of 6	Female
Federation for Finances and Economic Affairs (*Fédération Finances et Affaires Economiques*)	52%	20%	1 of 5	Male
Federation of General National Education Unions (*Fédération des Syndicats Généraux de l'Education Nationale*)	66%	22%	2 of 9	Male
Federation for Health and Social Services (*Fédération des Services de Santé et des Services Sociaux*)	79%	67%	6 of 9	Female
General Federation for Transport and Equipment (*Fédération Générale des Transports-Equipements*)	20%	14%	1 of 7	Male

Table 3.12: Feminization of leadership in CFDT federations (continued)

	Percentage of women members	Percentage of women in executive positions	Number of women	General Secretary
Banking and Insurance Federation (*Fédération Banques et Assurances*)	59%	44%	4 of 9	Male
Welfare, work, and employment Federation (*Fédération Protection Sociale, Travail, Emploi*)	71%	44%	4 of 9	Male
Chemistry and Energy Federation (*Fédération de la Chimie et de l'Energie*)	30%	29%	2 of 7	Male
Communication, Consulting, Culture (*Fédération CFDT Communication, Conseil, Culture*)	48%	44%	4 of 9	Male
Confederal Union of Management (*Union Confédérale des Cadres*)	43%	42%	3 of 7	Male

Source: Confederal data, 2016.

Access to union leadership positions also means having or being able to acquire technical and managerial skills. Depending on the country and the union, union roles are more or less professionalized (with an increasing number of technical roles within the union structures). We might consider that this form of legitimacy challenges charismatic or heroic definitions of leadership, which are often described as being unfavourable to women (Dean and Perret, 2020). But in a context where union education is declining, this kind of legitimacy is more difficult to attain for low-paid workers, of whom many are women. However, formal qualifications provide important leverage for women, particularly when they work in the public sector or major companies with union rights, even though choosing to pursue a union career often means giving up on a stimulating professional career. But it is also because of their perceived 'natural' or professional skills that women can get stuck in specific union roles, particularly those dedicated to implementing equality policy, and why they may have difficulty in accessing the partisan resources and activist experiences required to enter into leadership positions.

In addition to these constraints related to the organization and content of union work, one of the obstacles to equality policies is linked to the informal selection processes for union staff, whether they are appointed or recruited. The autonomy that union branches have in the choice of their reps may be an asset for equality, due to a genuine desire to improve diversity, but it may also consolidate the advantages of activists in place who do not want to give up their seats. From this perspective, the French Rebsamen law, which forces unions to respect proportional gender diversity among their candidates for professional elections, represents a new constraint for union branches (which sometimes simply struggle to get voting lists together for want of candidates). That being said, because this constraint affects only elected positions (*Comité Economique et Social*), in which women are already better represented than in union-appointed positions (central shop stewards), this legal constraint will probably have only a minor effect, except perhaps in very male-dominated sectors. Its effects may even be neutralized by the implementation of the new work council (CSE), which contributes to the re-centralization of employment relations (and therefore accentuates the professionalization of union work) and also weakens workplace unionism.

The lack of transparency in recruitment procedures is associated with another problem which is just as detrimental to the renewal of activists: the stability of the unionists in place. This is particularly striking in the British case (as is the reduction in the number of these positions in the case of merger, cf McBride and Waddington, 2009). Because of the attractivity of these positions for low-paid workers, and the difficulties in moving back into the labour market after a union career, UNISON and GMB both have very low turnover in their regional and national structures. These problems also exist in France to a certain extent, at the CFDT or Solidaires, particularly among workplace shop stewards and in certain regional or federal structures, but union careers are more exposed to electoral logics here. At the CFDT, there is more turnover among members on the NEC, and also in certain federation or regional executive bodies, than there is in the equivalent structures in British unions. In French unions, quotas apply to certain leadership positions (such as in the Executive Commission of the CFDT Confederation), whereas reserved seats concern only lay members in British unions. Although they aim for a transition towards a participative and deliberative democratic model, these measures to promote feminization in decision-making bodies and the creation of separate women's groups have not succeeded in bringing large numbers of women into mainstream (managerial) union roles. This is a blind spot in equality policies, but one that is sometimes compensated for by 'liberal' measures[15] supporting individual women on the union staff to take on additional responsibilities (training, mentoring, networks, secondments). This managerial aspect of equality is more selective; it does not tackle the systemic mechanisms that produce gender and race inequalities and tends to accentuate class inequality.

Although the question of equality has been around for a long time in these four unions, one of the difficulties it involves, as Joan Acker (2006) has argued, is the (relative) invisibility of class inequalities in accessing women's representation (Guillaume and Pochic, 2009c). This is something of a paradox for activist organizations that generally frame their action in terms of social class (Guillaume, 2018a) – particularly at Solidaires – and whose members are largely from the working classes (this is also true, at least partly, for the CFDT). The underrepresentation of low-paid women can be understood as a reflection of the 'masculine-neutral' definition of the concept of class, which effectively tends to render women's gender and class invisible (Dean, 2015). This ideological framing is widely present in male-dominated unions, but it can also exist in feminized sectors, like culture and entertainment (Dean, 2015). Ruth Milkman (1990) provided a comprehensive analysis of this institutional inertia, and shed light on why the evolution of structures and policies is insufficient to transform the dominant representations and hierarchies of gender, race, and class, even when unions have adopted radical equality policies and an intersectionality perspective, as in the case of UNISON. Moreover, although union cultures are today less marked by obvious sexism or machismo, three of the unions studied here emphasize the importance of deconstructing gender stereotypes in the workplace and in unionism through specific training programmes, like those proposed by Solidaires or the CFDT. They therefore promote the idea that it is necessary to 'pay attention to the language, symbols, and visual representation of the union, so that they evolve'.[16]

Finally, the question of control is at the heart of considerations on equality policy. This study, like others, has emphasized the importance of how organizations function in women's empowerment. Although decentralized decision-making can help the feminization of branches, it can also have a negative impact (Kelly and Heery, 1994) when specific structures (women's commissions or women's groups) do not exist or when national structures decide not to intervene to force the implementation of equality policies, as we have seen in Solidaires or GMB, because they consider their intermediary structures to be fully independent (which can lead them to hold disproportionate power, as in the case of GMB, cf Monaghan, 2020). As has been shown in studies on union organizing (Voss and Sherman, 2000), feminization is also often facilitated by the existence of a centralized policy defended by the leaders themselves. In these four unions, the General Secretaries in place clearly support equality policies. They have promoted women and have even imposed parity in their governing bodies, like the CFDT in 2014. These voluntarist approaches sometimes put the women selected in difficult positions and only some of them (with exceptional personal and professional resources) can build lasting legitimacy in the union.

In unions with large numbers of women members, like UNISON, or in certain feminized federations of the CFDT, male leaders can have the feeling that they are now the ones being discriminated against, leading to 'oblique' forms of resistance (Smolović Jones et al, 2020). Certain leaders (some of whom are women) may also be concerned that their teams will be more fragile if additional equality restrictions are implemented, as they might be unable to find women to fill the quotas. Whether or not there is a pool of women to recruit is a sign of the difficulty of 'top-down' feminization, where mechanisms of discrimination remain entrenched in the combined functioning of the labour market and the union, which are often mirror images of each other. Although women union leaders, unlike their counterparts in the economic and political spheres, are more involved in collective strategies to promote (other) women, and are sometimes attentive to class relations, their own careers are in themselves a tribute to an 'elitist' equality (Jacquemart et al, 2016) that supposes significant capacities for individual empowerment. From this point of view, their success contributes to shifting gender hierarchies within the world of trade unions (as we can see in the selective evolution of feminization) but may also overshadow other forms of discrimination. This observation implicitly emphasizes the need to maintain radical equality measures that enable a genuine promotion of women to the top of union organizations, using quotas in elected and governing bodies, but also by constructing or expressing forms of 'sisterhood' (Le Quentrec, 2013, 2014) articulating gender, class, and race, through separate women's organizations (Galt, 2021).

4

Legal Mobilizations by Unions to Promote Equal Pay in Great Britain

The feminization of unions is underway. It is selective and incomplete, but it is progressing. Many women union leaders describe themselves as feminists and actively defend internal equality policy. But what impact does this feminization have on the way women's interests are represented in the workplace? Is having women unionists defending 'women's rights' enough to actually advance gender equality? Research in political science has long considered that a 'politics of presence' (Phillips, 1995) was necessary to ensure that the concerns of women (as a group) were put on the political agenda. However, the supposed connection between descriptive and substantive representation (Pitkin, 1977) has been the subject of an extensive literature outlining the pitfalls of such an assumption (Campbell et al, 2010). Critics have pointed out the risk of naturalizing and unifying the definition of what constitutes 'women's interests' as such. Scholars have also drawn attention to the distinct social characteristics of women in elected positions, their uneven propensity to formulate and represent the interests of (other) women, and the variations of this representation, depending on the institutional context (Mackay, 2010). Fiona Mackay (2010) contended that the relationship between descriptive representation of women and a better representation of women's interests and preferences is not straightforward but would be better defined as 'probabilistic', complex, institutionally constructed, and variable, depending on the problem treated and the political context.

Substantive representation has therefore progressively become a research question, investigating a larger number of representatives acting in the name of women and looking into 'critical actors' (Childs and Krook, 2009). These include men (Celis, 2008), but also women outside the parliamentary arena (Squire, 2008), like 'feminist insiders' within public administration (Banaszak, 2010) or in equality agencies. The analysis of the representation process itself has been enriched by this literature, moving beyond the idea of 'a binary relationship between representative and represented that exists prior to the act of representation' (Dutoya and Hayat, 2016). Scholars have argued that it is the 'claims making' process (Saward, 2010) that needs to be investigated, that is, the way in which representatives construct the group that they purport to represent and formulate its interests. Far from assuming a single or mechanical relation, this perspective encourages the analysis of the interactions between multiple actors all claiming to define and defend the interests of those they claim to represent, and of the legitimacy issues they may face in doing so. Beyond the question of who these actors are, research needs to investigate the spaces, circumstances, forms, and processes in which the representation and interests of represented groups are expressed and defended (Celis et al, 2008).

This approach has rarely been applied to the study of union representation, particularly as concerns women and their interests. Yet it can be used to interpret the intense and rather unexpected legal action undertaken by British unions to defend equal pay. Since the 1960s, they have indeed been involved in various forms of legal mobilizations, in different ways depending on the period and the union (Guillaume, 2013). This adversarial use of the law to obtain legislation and take cases before the courts may seem surprising within a union tradition often described as hostile to the use of the law, particularly in terms of equality policy (Conley, 2014), and criticized for its propensity to undervalue women's work through discriminatory bargaining practices.

To understand how the justice system has become a legitimate space in which unions have defended the interests of low-paid women, often members of male-dominated or mixed unions, this chapter analyses the role of some 'critical actors' (Childs and Krook, 2009), and in particular the first 'feminist insiders' (Banaszak, 2010) who managed to break into the union hierarchy and fought to promote equal pay. It explores the strategies and alliances mobilized over different periods and contexts by these internal actors in conjunction with other actors in the 'space of women's rights' (Bereni, 2007), such as feminist lawyers and experts at the TUC and the Equal Opportunities Commission (EOC), which was created in 1975. It also shows how, at other moments in time, equal pay was defended for pragmatic rather than ideological reasons by male rank-and-file unionists, often at the risk of their own union careers. It explores the role of lawyers and legal services within unions in the more recent wave of litigation for equal pay. More generally, this chapter explores 'the effectiveness of the law', understood as an analysis of the 'concrete or symbolic, legal or extra-legal outcomes whether intended or not intentional, immediate or deferred' (Leroy, 2011) of the use of the law to defend women's interests. This analysis contributes to the existing literature on how trade unions have mobilized the law to produce positive change (McCann, 1994; McCann and Lowell, 2020). It shows how importing legal categories and strategies into trade unions' repertoires of actions can challenge discriminatory labour management methods and bargaining practices (Deakin et al, 2012; Guillaume, 2015b).

To shed light on these legal mobilizations, 41 interviews were conducted in 2012 and 2015 with activists from different unions (UNISON, GMB, UNITE, PCS, APEX), as well as lawyers and experts who have been involved in equal pay litigation since the 1970s (Table 4.1).

These interviews were supplemented by various archival investigations and secondary sources, including the abundant literature published on the subject in sociology, history, and law; the EOC reports; internal union documents; and archives brought together on the TUC website 'Winning Equal Pay: the Value of Women's Work',[1] available through their library. The existing jurisprudence on 'emblematic cases' was also compiled and analysed, along with the statistics published on employment tribunals, in order to have an idea of how litigation has evolved since the introduction of the first legislation in 1975.

Putting equal pay on the agenda: repeated mobilizations by women

Historians have demonstrated how, in the 19th century, unions were ambivalent or even opposed to the repeated demands for equal pay made by women workers from the 1830s onward. Craft unions, weakened by the Industrial Revolution, were particularly staunch opponents and ardent defenders of the ideology of the 'family wage' brought home by male heads of households. From the 1850s, they even opposed women's work by excluding women from their professions (and their unions) and stigmatizing married women workers (Rose, 1988). The TUC passed a motion for equal pay in 1888, but it was more to protect male workers against competition from lower female wages than to incorporate feminist demands into the labour movement. But lower wages for women were not only due to defensive strategies by craft unions; employers also had an interest in keeping women at the bottom of the wage hierarchy (Downs, 2002). In the automotive industry in the 1920s, they used separate and incommensurable wage scales for different categories of workers. Young people and women were paid less than men, and only men had a right to qualification and promotion. The so-called general unions organizing in low-skilled medial industries in the early 20th century were more ambivalent. They allowed women to join but also accepted separate pay scales and bargaining units for different occupational groups (Savage, 1988). In the rare cases where equal pay was granted by the union, for example by the ACT in the 1930s, only a minority of women were in fact covered by equal pay agreements, because sex segregation confined women to grades in which few men were employed (Galt, 2021).

Table 4.1: Interviewee profiles

Role	Union	Sex	Age
Unionists			
Former Senior Policy Officer	TUC (ex NALGO)	Woman	65–69
Senior Policy Officer	TUC	Woman	40–44
Women's Equality Officer	TUC	Woman	30–34
National Women's Officer	UNISON (ex NALGO)	Woman	55–59
Former National Equality Officer	UNISON (ex COHSE)	Woman	50–54
National Officer	UNISON (ex COHSE)	Man	45–49
National Officer	UNISON (ex NALGO)	Man	35–39
Senior Regional Officer	UNISON (ex NALGO)	Woman	50–54
Regional Organizer	UNISON (ex NUPE)	Man	45–49
Regional Women's Officer	UNISON (ex NALGO)	Woman	35–39
Regional Organizer	UNISON	Woman	45–49
Researcher	UNISON (ex GMB)	Woman	60–64
Employment Lawyer	UNISON	Man	45–49
Employment Lawyer	UNISON	Woman	30–35
Assistant General Secretary	UNITE (ex TNG)	Woman	60–64
Assistant General Secretary	UNITE (ex MSF)	Woman	60–64
Former National Officer	UNITE (ex TNG)	Woman	65–69
National Officer	UNITE (ex MSF)	Woman	40–44
Regional Organizer	UNITE (ex GMB)	Man	50–54
National Officer for Equalities	UNITE (ex AEU–TNG)	Woman	40–44
Former Equality Officer	UNITE (ex GPMU)	Woman	50–54
Head of Legal Department	UNITE	Man	45–50
Equality Officer	GMB	Woman	35–40
Head of Legal Department	GMB	Woman	45–50
National Officer	PCS	Man	50–54
Regional Organizer	UNISON (ex NUPE)	Man	50–54
Legal professionals			
Employment Judge	Employment Tribunal	Woman	45–49
Employment Judge	Employment Tribunal	Woman	55–60
Head of Equality Department	Thompsons Solicitors	Woman	60–64
Solicitor	Thompsons Solicitors	Woman	50–54
Solicitor	Stefan Cross Solicitors	Man	50–54

Table 4.1: Interviewee profiles (continued)

Role	Union	Sex	Age
Solicitor	Leigh Day & Co Solicitors	Man	30–34
Former Equal pay campaigner	Action 4 Equality (ex GMB)	Woman	60–64
Former Equal pay campaigner	Action 4 Equality (ex GMB)	Man	60–64
Former Equal pay campaigner	Action 4 Equality (ex NUPE)	Man	50–54
Barrister	Old Square Chambers	Man	40–45
Barrister	Cloisters	Man	55–60
Former Barrister	Old Square Chambers	Woman	65–69
Experts			
Former Head of Equal Pay Unit	EOC	Woman	65–69
Independent expert in job evaluation		Woman	60–64
Head of Equality Department	ACAS	Man	55–59

The TUC took almost no action on the subject in the 1960s. But the pressure was building in the rank and file, particularly in the public sector unions. Women's strikes for equal pay were initially visible during the widespread integration of women into formerly male professions, like in the war industries between 1914 and 1918 (women demanded 'war bonuses', for example) and then again between 1939 and 1945, with a movement coordinated by the Equal Pay Campaign Committee, created in 1943.[2] Following the 1943 equal pay strike at the Rolls Royce factory in Glasgow, the equal pay for equal work campaign became a priority for the labour movement for the remainder of the war, leading to numerous resolutions on equal pay at the TUC Women's Conferences (Summerfield, 1984). The government was obliged to open public debate on this issue, in 1917 with the investigation by the War Cabinet Committee on Equal Pay, and in 1946 with the Royal Commission on Equal Pay. But only a handful of qualified public sector professions (schoolteachers and certain ranks of public servants) were granted the principle of equal pay from 1946. A movement was organized to apply this principle, through demonstrations and petitions, with the support of professional organizations and some unions who included equal pay in their platforms. Although the principle was enacted in 1955, it became effective in only 1961 and 1962, excluding manual grades (Boston, 2015). Furthermore, women workers remained predominantly confined to sex-segregated employment in secretarial and factory work. The TUC officially demanded a law on equality in 1963 and the Labour Party incorporated that into its electoral platform in 1964, but certain unions with large numbers of women members were frustrated by the lack of concrete strategies associated with these on-paper promises (Meehan, 1985). Once in power, however, the Labour government pushed back the adoption of such a law, claiming a risk of inflation in a context of economic recession and hostility among employers (Carter, 1988), in spite of the repeated demands from women's groups within the party.

The growth of rank-and-file mobilizations

A more militant phase began in 1968, the year of the 50th anniversary of women's suffrage in England, with a series of women's strikes in the automotive sector supported by the nascent second-wave feminist movement. The early win by women workers at Ford's Dagenham plant, demanding a regrading of their jobs, launched a wave of other strikes in the sector in autumn 1968. These local strikes were supported by feminists, often highly educated and middle class, whether they were socialist or liberal. In 1967, for example, the Fawcett Society[3] advised women to join unions and go on strike if necessary, to obtain equal pay (Carter, 1988). They were also supported by young radical feminists[4] who drew media attention to their struggles in the newspapers that were being set up at the time, such as *Spare Rib* or *Women's Voice*. These feminists also supported mobilizations by women workers, as was the case for the organizing campaign for cleaning ladies at the TGWU which led to a lawsuit for equal pay (Rowbotham, 2006).

During the TUC Congress in June 1968 the organization called for its various affiliated unions to take action to adopt a motion demanding the Labour government ratify International Labour Organization (ILO) conventions 100 and 111 and propose a Bill on the subject before 1970. During the conference on equal pay organized by the TUC in November 1968, representatives from different feminist groups[5] accused TUC leaders of having been duped by the Labour government. A coordinating committee bringing together striking women workers, unionists, and feminists was organized around the action at Ford and they held a march to London on 18 May 1969, which attracted 30,000 people.[6] The first National Women's Liberation conference, organized the following year at Ruskin College in Oxford, put equal pay first on the list of their four priorities, before equal opportunity and education, free contraception and abortion rights, and, finally, free childcare.

In the context of strikes and public debates, the Employment Minister, Barbara Castle (who was seen as quite remote from the feminist movement), managed to pass the Equal Pay Act in May 1970 (see Box 4.1), just before Labour's defeat at the elections. This legislation was voted in by a new generation of Labour MPs who believed that it would protect the weak (women and migrants) and was compatible with the paradigm of class-based inequality. Above all, it was a way to avoid the risk that a more restrictive text would be imposed by the European Union, which the UK was then seeking to join. This legislation was followed in 1975 by the Sex Discrimination Act,[7] which introduced the notion of indirect discrimination, inspired by US law, and by the creation of a government agency specialized in gender discrimination, the Equal Opportunities Commission. This body was to assist victims by investigating cases, studying existing jurisprudence, and conducting formal inquiries.

Box 4.1: Primary developments in the evolution of legislation and jurisprudence on the question of equal pay

The initial legislation dates back to May 1970 and the Equal Pay Act, which came into effect on 1 January 1976. It covers remuneration in the broadest sense, including wages, bonuses, paid leave, and company pensions. It outlines equal treatment between a man and a woman within the same employment, defined as 'like work' or work that is 'rated as equivalent'. It covers only employees who are currently in the position in question or have left in the last six months. An amendment for 'work of equal value' was adopted in 1983 and came into effect on 1 January 1984, following a complaint by the EOC to the European Court of Justice.[8] Work of 'equal value' must be paid at the same rate, unless the gap in wages is justified by a 'material factor' that is not linked to gender. This modification of the law was associated with the implementation of complex procedures and the possibility for employers to justify their discriminatory practices by material factors, such as differences in qualification or experience, geographical disparities, or constraints linked to working conditions (shift work, night work, and so forth).

In 2006 the government obliged public sector employers to introduce gender equality duty, which requires them to adopt proactive strategies to reduce gender inequalities, in consultation with unions.

In 2010 the Equality Act replaced the previous legislation, including the Equal Pay Act 1970, the Sex Discrimination Act 1975, and the measures included in the Pensions Act 1995. The objective of this new legislation was to integrate and simplify the existing provisions. One single Equality Audit was established, covering gender, race, and disability. This resulted in weakened powers to constrain employers; no union consultation is required, and no sanctions exist if the audit is not performed. However, as of 2017, any organization that has 250 or more employees must publish and report specific figures on their gender pay gap. Employers that fail to report on time or report inaccurate data are in breach of the regulations and risk facing legal action from the Equality and Human Rights Commission (EHRC), leading to court orders and fines.

Although the legislation remains relatively limited, several European Court of Justice (CJEU) decisions have established jurisprudence in this area:

- In 1993 the CJEU found in favour of speech therapists in a Bristol hospital[9] who demanded an equivalent salary to their colleagues in male-dominated medical professions (clinical psychologists and hospital pharmacists), thus invalidating the possibility for the employer to argue the existence of separate collective agreements to justify the pay gap, and also limiting the argument of a scarcity of labour.
- In 1993 an individual case of sex discrimination was brought by the EOC before the CJEU against the NHS, resulting in an increase in the threshold of possible compensation.[10] This case led to a modification in the law for all employers, the Sex Discrimination and Equal Pay (Remedies) Regulations 1993, abolishing the threshold of compensation (previously set at £6,250).
- In 1998 two other decisions by the CJEU[11] extended the number of years for which compensation could be paid (back pay extended to six years). In 2000, the maximum time limit to file for compensation was conditionally extended to six months after the end of the contract.[12] Since 2012, if the six-month time limit has expired, some employees may bring their claim in the courts within the normal breach of contract time limit, which is much longer, namely six years.[13] Equal pay claims can now be raised in the civil courts by former employees up to six years after their employment ends (five years in Scotland). However, bringing claims in the civil courts instead of the tribunal involves greater financial risk, as the losing party usually has to meet the winning party's costs.

The 1970 law was undeniably a catalyst (McCann, 1994), initiating a cycle of women's strikes during the 1970s demanding equal pay and wage increases, and also promoting union rights and challenging restructuring. The TUC itself called on its affiliate unions to support these strikes during the moratorium period, to put pressure on employers who were reticent to revise their pay grades. An unprecedented peak in women's strikes was reached in 1973–74, often explicitly on the issue of equal pay. These strikes were the opportunity for joint mobilizations with feminists, resulting in the formulation of the Working Women's Charter in 1974. This charter was drawn up by the London Trades Council, where there were many radical feminists, and then spread through local groups around the country. For the first time, it brought together typical union demands (with equal pay at the top of the list, along with a minimum wage) with demands on 'women's issues' (contraception, abortion, childcare, maternity leave). Certain unions, like NALGO, adopted it entirely, particularly in the public sector, but the TUC did not include it as a motion in its 1975 Congress because of internal opposition to abortion.[14] However, the TUC drew up a Charter for Equality of Women in Unions in 1979, which led its affiliate unions to adopt procedures to promote women's rights at all levels of the union.

This first phase of contestation, which unfolded over a long period, emphasizes the role of women's mobilizations outside of institutions (Katzenstein, 2012) including unions. In fact, unions joined the struggle for equal pay only out of fear that the working conditions of their male members would be undermined. Equal pay was also hotly debated within the Labour Party, and the 1970 legislation was passed only because the government wanted to avoid both more restrictive legislation being imposed on them by the European Union, on the one hand, and on the other hand, the intensification of mobilization by women workers in factories. Interestingly, many of the women's strikes did not specifically demand equal pay with men, but simply the regrading of women's wages (see Box 2.2). However, once the law was passed, these women workers (sometimes with the support of feminist groups) increased their contestation in the workplace to put pressure on their employers, who had been given a five-year moratorium to come into line with the law and revise the pay grades, with the support of the unions. "Following the Equal Pay Act, there was a phase of intense negotiations in the workplace to get rid of separate pay systems for men and women. This was the priority of employers and unions" (Woman, age 45, Senior Policy Officer, TUC).

Limited use of the law in the 1970s

After 1975, individual sex discrimination cases flooded the courts; there were 2,500 in 1975 and 1,794 in 1976. Although the law did not allow for class actions, some of these claims were multiple cases brought against the same employer by female union members in the private sector. Almost no lawsuits were bought in the public sector, because the unions considered that women already had equal pay by way of the agreements negotiated in the 1950s for professional women.

'When the legislation came into effect in 1975, there were "like work" cases in the private sector where women were comparing themselves with men doing the same job. In the public sector, there was a shared belief in the unions that they had already won equal pay for their members through the negotiation of agreements in the 1950s for qualified women, teachers, public servants, professionals working in local government. They forgot to think about the question of equal pay for "work rated as equivalent" or of "equal value". It was not until the 1990s that there was a significant number of claims.' (Woman, age 65, job evaluation expert)

But then the influx of claims rapidly declined, to the point where there were only 39 cases in 1982. What was behind this drop in numbers? Firstly, there was the length of the procedures and the low success rate, which progressively instilled doubt as to the usefulness of bringing a case before the courts, which were considered pro-employers. Moreover, unions did not always actively support the claimants. They were not always well informed about how to put a legal case together, and often gave poor advice, constructed the victim's argument badly, or instructed the claimant to accept unfavourable out-of-court settlements (Leonard, 1987).

Secondly, the legislation also had a number of shortcomings and limitations that were criticized from the beginning by feminist groups and experts, such as the lack of legal aid for victims and the impossibility of feminists to act as experts in the legal sphere (following the principle of 'amicus curiae' which exists in the US). At the time, the law was based on a limited understanding of equal pay – formal equality of treatment with a man as the 'comparator' in a 'similar position' or a 'job rated as equivalent' according to methods of job evaluation (according to criteria such as effort, skills, or responsibility). Legal provisions displayed an individualistic framing of equality and were centred on a demand for individual compensation, preventing any kind of collective action or class action, unlike in the US. Above all, they did not force companies to modify their practices and thus the source of discrimination, even though they allowed for an examination of existing 'collective dispositions' such as collective bargaining agreements or salary regulations (sections 3, 4, and 5), with a possible appeal to the Central Arbitration Committee (CAC) to amend these collective dispositions.

These possibilities for legal challenges via the CAC were hardly ever mobilized by the unions.[15] The situation was uncomfortable for local union reps because they found themselves at odds with the agreements or regulations negotiated previously. These negotiators were also almost always men, better at defending the interests of male occupations even within unions with female members. In NUPE, for example, the union covering low-paid public sector workers, only two of the 25 union delegates sent to the 1971 National TUC Congress were women, and there was only one woman among the 90 full-time union officials (Meehan, 1985), even though about 60% of NUPE members were women at the time. Moreover, NUPE's opposition to the pay freeze in the public sector during the winter of 1978–79, known as the 'winter of discontent', led to the negotiation of agreements that discriminated against women. These allowed the introduction of a system of 'productivity bonuses' for certain male jobs, which would be the source of many equal pay claims in the 2000s. Yet, at the national level, NUPE had adopted policies to promote women; five seats had been allocated to women on the NEC since 1975, and there were women's officers and women's training programmes that were intended to encourage women's participation (Cunnison and Stageman, 1995).

The inconsistency between discourse and practice could also be criticized at the EOC, which could force employers to apply the law through formal investigation, even when there was no particular case against them, and yet almost never used this power of enforcement before the 1980s. Prior to 1979, only nine investigations were conducted, and only two of those were on equal pay. The discretion of the EOC, which prioritized responses to individual claims and avoided controversial actions, can be explained by a fear of weakening the institution in the event of the election of a Conservative government, along with the cost and length of the formal investigation, with their limited budget (Sacks, 1986). The lack of feminists among the first figures appointed to the board also reinforced the EOC's non-aggressive position (all the female applicants were rejected[16]).

Equal value: a struggle by 'insider feminists'

The struggle for equal pay took a different turn in the early 1980s, due to strategic action by feminists inside the unions, the EOC, and local government, who drew on European legislation to promote equal pay with the help of feminist lawyers. Faced with the difficulty of enforcement and the limitations of the law itself, these women demanded several key amendments, such as the reversal of the burden of proof, the possibility of class actions, or the creation of specific courts and tribunals. Above all, these women sought to ensure the ratification of the ILO's Convention 100 (on work of equal value) so that women's jobs without a male equivalent could be covered by the law, which was also what the European Commission demanded.

The EOC's litigation strategy

From the late 1970s, the EOC initiated a legal strategy at the national level, with numerous claims brought before the highest courts in England (Barnard, 1995), but these attempts failed, due to a very restrictive reading of the law by the Employment Appeals Tribunal (EAT), which was then presided by a judge who was unsupportive of equality legislation (Gregory, 1987). The EOC then changed strategies and used European law to contest the validity of English legislation in the light of EU norms. It argued a number of lawsuits that went to the European level, in the hope of creating jurisprudence that could be used by English judges. Surprisingly, this legal strategy came from an institution otherwise described as being very cautious, which made only moderate use of its formal powers. The EOC was subject to tensions between its paid experts, who were deeply committed to the cause of equality, and some of its commissioners, who were from unions and employers' associations and therefore reluctant to challenge the established discriminatory practices in workforce management. But the activism of certain employees and the single mandate (Kilpatrick, 1997) in the defence of equality for women seem to have tipped the balance in favour of court action which contributed to the passing of an 'equal value' amendment in 1983, which came into force on 1 January 1984.

As soon as it was adopted, the EOC used this amendment to take on the first 60 cases through a 'strategic litigation' approach, in other words preselecting strong cases (Lejeune and Orianne, 2014) that were likely to win and thus construct a strong body of case law. This was due to the fact that the Commission had limited means and was attempting to involve unions in the fight for equal pay.

'Before 1983, the unions did not draw much on the legislation for equal pay. They were very ambivalent about the EOC. On one hand the EOC was created to deal with equality issues, so they had the feeling that they could not deal with them. On the other hand, they could not bear the fact that the EOC was interfering in their prerogatives on wage negotiations. After obtaining the equal value amendment, we decided, within the EOC legal team, that we would make sure that this amendment brought results. We had to convince the unions. The EOC approached them the year prior to its promulgation. And we supported the first 60 equal value lawsuits.' (Woman, age 65, EOC)

In this it once again relied on the European Court of Justice and on certain tribunal judges known for supporting women's rights (Alter and Vargas, 2000). As the former manager of the equal pay team within the EOC at the time explains, "the golden age for defending equal pay in England was between 1983 and 1992". This was an era when there were not too many cases (120 equal value cases between 1984 and 1988), involving no more than 50 people (and therefore modest amounts of money), which came before judges who were more competent than in the past and often met favourable outcomes. For the EOC, this strategy of supporting individual plaintiffs was seen as more effective than the formal investigation approach.

'In the case of the speech therapists,[17] I prepared all the evidence. The EOC had two possible paths for action. We could support women's lawsuits or request a formal investigation. The second possibility would have involved a very long procedure. At the time I had just finished one investigation that lasted eight years. I was therefore unconvinced that this was the right approach, particularly given that the women would not have obtained any compensation. So, we submitted our recommendations to support individual claimants, stipulating that the

EOC had nothing to gain by being involved in such long, drawn-out procedures.' (Woman, age 65, EOC)

The EOC supported claimants in sectors where unions were weak, and also the action of a small number of women unionists who used the law to assist, or even induce, low-paid women workers to file lawsuits. The collective framing of the equal value law, the influence of a few women activists, and the desire to organize women[18] all contributed to certain unions mobilizing the law.

'Most of the lawsuits that we supported at the time, we supported with the claimant's union. Unlike the equal pay for equal work law, equal value allowed a collective approach to the issues. The unions were also trying to find a way to fight against declining unionization. They saw equal pay as a way to attract new members, particularly women. It was a time when women's voices were beginning to be heard in certain unions and there were some female regional officers and one or two national officers who strongly supported equality. The lawsuits came before the courts within two or three years. The EOC provided legal expertise, activist training, and covered half the costs. And that was a benefit for members and for unions, who, in return, gained a positive image with female workers.' (Woman, age 65, EOC)

The progressive influence of women in unions

These lawsuits in private sector companies were supported by unions that were generalist, but also decentralized and accustomed to company negotiations, like GMB or TGWU, as well as by more feminized unions like APEX (which represented employees, and whose General Secretary was a woman). The influence of the first women elected to the national bodies, or as women's officers, was also being felt. Some encouraged local (male) unionists to follow a minimum number of cases. This was the case for Martin, at APEX, who became involved in a collective lawsuit in his region.

'In 1978 I was hired by APEX as area organizer for the region of Northampton. There was very little union activity linked to equal pay. The union was particularly active in collective bargaining. In 1982 I was transferred to Coventry, which was a town that was historically very unionized. Two things jumped out at me: occupational segregation between men and women, and the fact that White employees earned more than Black employees. At the time, APEX was already conducting campaigns for women, for example, so that employers gave women time off to have screenings for cervical cancer. We had begun to promote women's interests within the branches and with employers. Pushed by Rita Steven, one of the first women national officers, we also began to talk about equal pay. Her idea was that each regional officer should support three equal pay lawsuits. She laid out quantified targets. We went around the factories and encouraged the women to file their claims. APEX had already supported cases before the 1975–78 period, there was a sort of legacy in that respect.' (Man, age 60, former regional organizer, APEX)

Other women union leaders became involved in assisting these lawsuits. Within the TGWU, well known for its involvement in the women's strike at Ford in 1968, the first female woman's officer saw the defence of equal pay cases in the automotive sector as an opportunity to organize women and identify future women leaders while also organizing training sessions for employees and union leaders.

'There were very good women who were beginning to get involved at the workplace level. I began to organize training sessions for women in the automotive sector around London and the South East. At the beginning it was a session for 20 people, but it was so popular that we held it three times in a row, on the weekends. Women from Ford, Vauxhall, Aston Martin, and Jaguar began to come together for the first time. We had women who were talking about their experience as women in this very male industry, in front of male union leaders who were really hearing them for the first time. We covered the question of wage inequality but also sexual harassment, work–life balance, and retirement. And we also supported an equal pay case against Vauxhall.' (Woman, age 65, former National Women's Officer, TGWU)

Most cases were settled out of court, but some show the length and complexity of the legal process. The first 'equal value' claim, filed by Julie Hayward in 1984,[19] took four years of proceedings before it was finally ruled on by the House of Lords. At age 16 Hayward was hired in the Cammell Laird naval shipyards in Birkenhead, along with many young men. They were craft workers (a painter, a joiner, and a thermal insulation engineer), she was the cook. Four years later, at the end of her apprenticeship, she discovered that she was paid less than her male colleagues. She said:

'friends told me that their pay went up when they turned 20, and I said that mine had not. They said that wasn't fair and that I should sort it out with the union. I went, and the union rep said he thought it wasn't fair either. He went to see the manager who said that my job was ranked as "labourer", so at the bottom of the pay grade.'[20]

Julie was well liked by her male colleagues and was friends with them outside of work, in the football club where she was a very active supporter. She decided to file a claim to obtain the same pay as her colleagues, comparing herself to three of them, all craftsmen but in different professions. The employer conceded that the applicant received less favourable basic pay and overtime rates than the men, but argued that, looking at their contracts as a whole, including provisions for sickness benefit and meal breaks, she was as favourably treated as the men. The Court of Appeal ruled that, in determining whether a woman's contract is less favourable than a man's, matters such as paid meal breaks, holidays, and sickness benefits form part of their pay. The appeal was dismissed. Miss Hayward then appealed to the House of Lords, which reversed the judgment and accepted this argument, ruling that, under the Act, the appellant was entitled to parity in terms of pay without consideration of whether under the contract as a whole she was treated as favourably as male employees performing work of equal value. The victory of this shipyard cook in Liverpool, supported by her union, GMB, and her male colleagues, would become a symbol of the potential of this new law.

Despite these legal gains, the role of the first women responsible for equality within male-dominated unions was not an easy one. As most of the research conducted in the 1980s and 1990s shows (Cunnison and Stageman, 1995), the progressive feminization of unions 'from above' conceals the difficulty that women had in participating in negotiations within their workplace or branch. This was the case for Patricia.

Patricia, a women's officer in a male world

After leaving school in 1979, Patricia was hired as a researcher by the National Graphical Association (NGA), one of the unions in the printing sector, which was essentially made up of skilled male workers. Her sister also worked for the union and she came from a strong union background. There were very few women officers in this very male-dominated union. A Women's Committee and an annual conference were progressively established in the 1980s but did not play a major political role. In 1992, when the NGA merged with SOGAT to form GPMU, Patricia found herself one of only a handful of women in the new union structure. The former General Secretary of SOGAT had left because she did not want to become a deputy. One female senior official retired and another woman, who was responsible for equality, clashed with the new management because she was ostensibly a member of the Communist Party, which was not acceptable within this union. Patricia therefore became the GPMU women's officer by default, without formally being an elected official, which did not make her job any easier. Women made up only of 17% of members, very few of them were branch secretaries, and the Women's Committee had very little influence in the running of the new union. "We never had the critical mass necessary to really change things." Unlike some of her very head-on female colleagues, Patricia defines herself as "socialist-feminist" and tried "to be pragmatic and move forward slowly". On the issue of equal pay things were more difficult still. There were very few lawsuits. Women were often unaware of inequalities because they worked in bookbinding workshops, did not have much contact with the men working in typography, and were also not aware of legislation on equal value. It was the local reps in the branches who transferred claims to the national level for legal assistance. "But at the time, the first reflex was to obtain an out-of-court settlement with the employer. The courts were a last resort." Patricia tried to organize training for women, "but it was very difficult to have the women come, because either they had childcare problems, or because their husbands did not want them to". The idea of women having access to Grade 1 jobs was progressively discussed and accepted among male workers, but the sticking point remained the regrading of 'women's jobs' at Grade 3. "Unionists always kept their distance from the least qualified jobs, and always wanted to maintain a wage hierarchy. The idea that women's work could have the same value was unacceptable." In fact, an agreement on regrading these jobs, negotiated by SOGAT, would never be implemented, because of the massive restructuring of the sector that took place between 1990 and 2000. In 2005, the GPMU, which was in major financial difficulties because of loss of membership, merged with AMICUS. Patricia could not see herself in this new environment and decided to return to study.

The glory days of 'municipal feminism'

In the public sector, where the rate of women union members was higher and expanding, lawsuits emerged more slowly. Because equal pay was obtained for qualified women in the 1950s, the issue seemed less urgent. In a sector marked by a tradition of separate (national) negotiations, women unionists struggled to implement the modalities of the law that involved finding a male comparator. Public sector unions were also more centralized and less militant, less driven by their rank and file, with the exception of NALGO, which represented qualified women. A feminist awareness eventually emerged within the public sector unions following the development of a 'municipal feminism' (Bruegel and Kean, 1995) that was very active in the 1980s. In local government, particularly in the region around London, feminists (often highly qualified) worked with left-wing councils to defend public services and oppose the Thatcher government's economic restructuring policies (Conley and Page, 2015). In 1978 the Women's Rights Working Party, created by groups of women in Lewisham borough, asked the council to take action to promote women's rights. By 1986 more than 30 councils had women's groups.

In certain councils within Greater London, highly qualified women who were unionists and radical feminists or socialists organized within the London Equal Value Steering Group (LEVEL). In 1987 they produced a study on pay inequalities for white collar workers. These women helped to train branch officers through textbooks and guides. Most of them participated in the Pay Equality Campaign, an activist group made up of unionists, academics, lawyers, and political activists. As one of the lawyers interviewed said, "we were like a small club. Everyone knew everyone else, unionists like Diana Holland, and Margaret Prosser before her at TGWU, activists from UNISON, external experts like Lorraine Patterson, and lawyers like Tess Gill and me." Elizabeth, now a labour court judge, recounts her experience.

Elizabeth, a pioneer of equal pay law

Elizabeth became a barrister in 1974. During her studies she quickly became aware of gender inequalities, because in the pub where she worked as a student she was paid 6p less than her male co-workers. "That was in 1972, the law had been passed, it was illegal. I hardly needed convincing that labour law was important in women's rights." She spent a year in the US and came back even more convinced of the importance of antidiscrimination legislation. She taught for a few years and began her placement to practise as a barrister in 1981.

> 'I began working at the right time. There was lots of work. At the beginning I was above all working on litigation on workplace discrimination. Most of the cases my firm worked on came from unions. The law was becoming more complex in the 1980s and unions progressively stopped handling their cases alone. And, at the time, a junior barrister was not very expensive.'

Alongside this, Elizabeth was involved with others on the issue of sexual harassment, as part of an organization called WASH (Women Against Sexual Harassment). Before the 1984 amendment, she handled a few cases on equal pay for like work, and she defended her first equal value case in 1987. She went on to handle a great many more, all through unions, and particularly in the banking sector. At the time, she realized that she was a little naive as to the unions' motives and that some of these lawsuits were in fact intended to ensure that women would not cost less than men. "What I thought was an altruistic struggle for the defence of women's rights was in fact a form of male protectionism." The attitudes of the judges were also not exempt of sexism, in relation both to equal pay and to the presence of women in the legal profession. The law is a complex thing, and union resources are limited, by comparison with those of employers, who often make intensive use of the legal defences available to them. The claimants are also often alarmed by the possible consequences of a trial for their working conditions, or the number of hours they will be given, particularly when they work part time. "You had to work a lot, be very sharp, but we won quite a lot of the claims." Along with Sue Hasting, a specialist in job evaluation techniques, who is today retired, Elizabeth created the Equal Value Advisory Network and trained many people. In 1998 she decided to become a labour court judge, and she is regularly called on to judge equal pay disputes. Hearings last between 15 days and three weeks. These cases are grouped together and lodged by unions on behalf of low-skilled women, or they may be individual cases brought by high-skilled young women in the banking sector, who are suing for gender and pay discrimination. For Elizabeth, "in both cases, it is the same feminist struggle".

★★★

Some of these lawyers worked in the union's legal services before practising the law. This is the case of Tess Gill, a very well-known women's rights lawyer, who is now retired. Inversely, some feminists working in local government later joined the union movement through research positions, or directly as women's officers in the 1980s. Vicky, for example, considers herself representative of this generation who joined the unions as part of this feminist wave, after working for a civil rights lobbying group and then working in human resources in a local council. When she was recruited in 1988 at the TUC as Senior Women's Officer, she was able to bring her experience to the union, and also her network of lawyers and academics committed to feminist issues.

'I am this awkward combination of a feminist and unionist. ... But they don't always go well together. Firstly, I worked for the Lewisham Council near London in 1984. Back then it was not yet the Greater London Council,[21] and it was basically lots of lefties like me. That was our generation, the 1970s, and half of my friends had a job there. And we developed very progressive policies. ... It was an exciting time. I was advisor on women's employment, or something like that. And they set up a whole department on equality, but I was not part of that. I was in personnel, which was quite interesting, because I was inside. My whole job was gender equality in employment, which meant developing equal pay policies, but also developing training for women in traditionally male professions. Basically, it was an affirmative action programme. Later, I was hired by the TUC. I managed to persuade them to organize a series of training sessions over two years, on the "equal value amendment" voted in 1984. We went around regional areas. We invited experts, but also quite a lot of lawyers. I knew all the high-flying progressive lawyers who worked in the area. And they were very generous with their time and expertise.' (Woman, aged 65, former senior officer, TUC)

In 1988 the TUC created an 'equal rights unit' and got involved in training and negotiation assistance. In the same year they published a manual on the content of the 1984 amendment and the stages in bringing an equal value case before the courts. This was followed in 1991 by another manual to help unionists negotiate equal pay, emphasizing the role of the law as leverage in negotiations.[22] The role of certain women job evaluation experts, like Sue Hasting, was also central in implementing equal value in union practices. Used as experts in the courts, in the implementation of new agreements on pay grades, and also in union training, these women were often mentioned in the interviews and played a critical role in the understanding and implementation of equal value legislation. But they did not all define themselves as 'feminists'.

'I would not describe myself as a feminist. I come from a left-wing background, but I'm not very comfortable with that term. I always said that I would work for anyone who was discriminated against. When it comes to pay, it is women. But I have also worked on claims filed by men. I have never campaigned for equal pay. I consider myself more a technician, I am not an activist, unlike women unionists.' (Woman, age 65, job evaluation expert)

It is rare that radical feminists, close to the extreme Left, chose to join the unions or were hired by the EOC. However, whether they were in the courts, in the EOC, or in the unions, they all contributed to interpreting and implementing the legislation. As Michael McCann (1994) emphasized, the role of these leaders from different spheres is particularly important in raising awareness about ongoing inequalities and the potential power of the law. At the time, the legal approach and the technical approach were combined without being in opposition, but very rapidly equal pay experts realized the difficulties in litigation and sought to train rank-and-file unionists to encourage employers to adopt organizational responses (Edelman, 1992) to conform to the law. They emphasized the importance of revising collective bargaining agreements or implementing equal opportunity policies that would develop over the course of the 1980s.

Resistance from employers: justified by 'the market'?

Legal mobilization in the 1980s enabled the development of jurisprudence on the concepts of equal value and indirect discrimination, inspired by

European law, along with innovations in job evaluation methods. But it also demonstrated the difficulty in incorporating these notions into the individualistic framework of the Equal Pay Act (Fredman, 2008), particularly in the context of repeated appeals by employers. Within the courts, employers made full use of the 'market forces' clause in the law, and continue to do so. This operated as a counterweight to the equal value amendment, arguing that higher wages for men were necessary to attract them and keep them loyal to the company.[23] In spite of a few significant wins, most of the equal value cases took a long time to reach a verdict. As a result of these delays, a certain number of smaller unions, but also the EOC, who accompanied some of these cases withdrew their support en route or refused to support other similar cases, partly due to the cost of these long drawn-out procedures.

'Initially, the legal process was much less formal, and the cases were taken on by the unionists themselves. And then employers began to appeal and get help from lawyers. It became much more legalistic. Many of these cases were simple and settled out of court. But then with increased resistance from employers, everything became more technical, and more expensive.' (Woman, age 63, former legal officer, APEX/GMB)

Certain unions nevertheless managed to use the threat of court proceedings to encourage employers to negotiate. The banking sector union, BIFU, and the LBSA (Lloyds Bank Staff Association) thus assisted with cases against Lloyds Bank in 1988, and obtained the introduction of job evaluation schemes in most major banks (Arthurs, 1992). The retail sector union, USDAW, supported cases against Sainsburys in 1989 and ensured that major shops where the union was active (Sainsburys, Tesco) negotiated agreements with job evaluation schemes. As Chris Howell (1996) argues, 'the USDAW's success recruiting women supermarket workers was due to its aggressive use of the equal pay legislation'. In the energy sector, a certain number of privatized public companies also renegotiated their job evaluation system to try to curtail the number of claims (Gilbert and Secker, 1995). Since then, these agreements have not been modified, which, according to certain experts, left the door open for other possible claims (that were indeed filed against major retailers in the 2010s).

'In the 1980s and 1990s there was a series of grouped claims in the private sector. The response of major companies was to introduce job evaluation schemes, the whole banking sector, the supermarket sector, and major industrial companies. Since then, their systems have deteriorated. They have simplified them in the extreme and classified jobs in categories that are very broad and vague in terms of the descriptions of the work involved. So workers know what grade they are, but their specific job is not evaluated. These new systems cannot lead to equal pay. I suggested that UNITE look into this, but they are very reluctant to do so. They have the feeling that there are other issues for workers, and the banks have also introduced performance-based pay, which causes more problems for workers than the question of which grade they are on.' (Woman, age 65, job evaluation expert)

In the public sector, a fear of ending up before the courts, along with the mobilization by four unions (TGWU, NUPE, NALGO, and COHSE) against low-paid part-time work, forced local government bodies to reclassify manual jobs. This undertaking involved 200 people preparing and evaluating 540 job types between 1986 and 1987 (Dickens et al, 1988). The new classification system had six grades and improved the situation for certain categories of employees, particularly home help, in exchange for more flexibility. But it did not impact on the bonuses systematically attributed to male-dominated professions (garbage and sanitation, for example), and preserved the principle of separate negotiation for different professional groups. This frequently recurring issue of bonuses would be at the heart of the litigation in the 2000, and is a good illustration of the difficulty unions had in reforming their discriminatory negotiation practices, as Harry describes.

Harry, a progressive awareness of gender inequalities

Harry left school very young and was employed in the cleaning service of Middleborough Council, in the North East of England, in 1969. At age 19 he became a union rep and joined the Communist Party. Shortly after he was hired there was a major strike, called the 'Dirty Job Strike'. "It was a time when pay was frozen and the only way to get a raise was to introduce bonuses." In the years that followed there was intense negotiation on these bonus systems for male jobs. A few questions were raised at the time about the fact that women did not get bonuses. "But the answer was always that women were already very efficient, while men were not. At the beginning, the bonuses were around 30% of the salary and then they increased up to 60%, which created big wage gaps between men and women." Harry progressed in his career and became team manager in a warehouse and branch secretary for NUPE. It was a major branch, with over 3,000 members. He was himself involved in negotiating these bonuses.

'What is surprising, when you see my political background, is that I also thought that it was normal that men got bonuses and women didn't. I didn't even question it. I was working in a team that was 100% male, I wasn't responsible for negotiating for women. At one point, I did find it unfair, and I went to see the Deputy General Secretary who was responsible for negotiations as a whole, and he told me that it was the "winter of discontent" that had brought us to this point, but that none of the unions had the intention of going to court.'

The situation got worse because NUPE continued to negotiate out of fear of annoying male members, and because the employers were very clear about the fact that equal pay would be awarded only if they gave up their bonuses. Similarly, NALGO, who represented qualified women, did not want employers to embark on a job evaluation scheme, out of fear that some of their members would lose pay and status. "It very quickly became clear that it would be low-skilled women who would benefit most from equal pay." When Labour came to power in 1997, the unions did not want to rock the boat and preferred to avoid defending equal pay (which would have been expensive) in exchange for a government agreement to create jobs in the public sector. Shortly afterwards, Harry heard about an equal pay case brought by GMB with the support of Thompsons Solicitors, in a nearby council. "UNISON joined GMB on this case simply because they were afraid that GMB would steal their female members." Following the merger between NUPE, NALGO, and COHSE, many manual workers did in fact leave to join GMB, out of fear that their interests would not be correctly represented by the more qualified leaders of the new union. Harry decided to file a lawsuit against his employer. He was then subject to disciplinary action by the council, in league with his union, and was fired. He was not supported by his branch, which had merged with the NALGO members, and he had lost his power base. His unfair dismissal case spent five years in the courts, during which time he managed to remain an elected official in his union, up until 2000, when he was irrevocably excluded from UNISON. Harry became depressed and was unable to find any work other than part-time, badly paid jobs. In 2003 he was hired by Stefan Cross (an independent lawyer, discussed further later) and launched an information campaign on equal pay in his former council (and then in the region) among women who knew him and trusted him. He fought against the unions that pushed women to accept the unfavourable deals proposed by their employers. He set up a network of women throughout the region. "They weren't feminists, but women aware of the fact that they had been done over by the unions and that they could have more compensation through the courts." He worked with Stefan Cross for years, "but it was hard work, stressful, immensely so, given how many claims there were". He fully understood Cross's decision to close his practice in England and he himself retired in 2013.

★★★

This momentum was hindered by the economic restructuring of the public sector, waged by the Thatcher government against a backdrop of economic crisis and full frontal assaults on union rights. From 1988 the battle for equal pay unfolded in a context of attacks on public services that particularly degraded the working conditions for low-paid women in the public health sector and local government, and made it difficult for them to resort to the law. In a context of decreasing public budgets, the 1988 compulsive competitive tendering legislation forced local governments to outsource and privatize their maintenance services (cleaning, restoration, repairs). In most cases, low-paid women working part time in these services were fired and then rehired under less favourable conditions, on temporary contracts with fewer hours, paid less, and without social protection. The unions failed to ensure that these service contracts respected the principle of non-discrimination based on gender, even though, paradoxically, they respected the principle of non-discrimination on ethnicity (Race Relations Act 1976). Along with the EOC, some unions condemned the gendered effects of this privatization of public services (Escott and Whitfield, 1995). While the male-dominated professions that were outsourced sometimes saw salaries and bonuses increase in exchange for increased production, female-dominated professions paid the cost of a social 'race to the bottom'.

In the late 1990s very few claims were filed in the private sector, because of the development of decentralized and individualized pay mechanisms that made it difficult to resort to the law (Gregory, 1996; Colling and Dickens, 1998). Moreover, an employer-driven counteroffensive was organized around the *Opportunity 2000* campaign, launched in 1991, widely criticized by the unions. This was driven by the Business in the Community association, which proposed to reconsider inequality issues in terms of management. Equality policies were no longer about defending the interests of minority groups, but about resolving problems to do with recruitment, mobility, productivity, and quality (Forbes, 1997). The policies that were put in place by major companies essentially benefited a handful of highly qualified women (Cockburn, 1991) and the question of equal pay dropped off the agenda, to be replaced by questions to do with the glass ceiling and work–life balance. This was facilitated by the fact that union presence in the private sector had been declining dramatically.

When male unionists and lawyers join the fray

Towards the end of the 1990s multiple claims re-emerged[24] in the public sector, primarily filed by male unionists to fight against the government's privatization policies and the degradation of employment conditions. In a context where unions were hesitant as to the most effective strategy to fight the outsourcing policies that were developing in local councils, these rank-and-file unionists saw the legal battle for equal pay as a way to avoid the widespread strikes reminiscent of the 'winter of discontent' in 1978–79, or as a way to negotiate with employers, which certain unions like NUPE refused (Foster and Scott, 1997).

Male unionists ahead of their time?

In 1990 a UNISON unionist brought a claim against the North Yorkshire council[25] on behalf of 1,300 canteen workers whose pay had decreased in comparison with that of non-outsourced male workers in the same category. The trial lasted five years but ended with a decision by the House of Lords ruling that 'no material factor' other than gender could justify this difference in salary. The canteen workers were awarded £2 million in compensation as well as the regrading of their jobs. In 1997 another claim,[26] representing 1,600 women (nurses, orderlies, cleaners), was filed by another UNISON unionist as a way to push back the privatization of a North Cumbria hospital and frighten possible private investors. Although the privatization did take place, this action before the courts led to a settlement between the parties of £300 million in 2005.

These two cases are exemplary of the large number of claims brought before the courts in the 2000s, and are often cited as proof of the unions' commitment to the struggle for equal pay. In reality, they often reflect individual initiatives by local unionists who made the decision to support, or induce, the claims. Women, and particularly those with low-level qualifications, are not always very conscious of the law. This was stressed by one of the lawyers at Thompsons Solicitors interviewed here, who had worked with the unions for 20 years. It is unionists who identify inequalities and tell the women they can press charges. The TUC Equal Pay Archives thus reveal how a single TGWU unionist, Pete Allen, was responsible for initiating 18 claims – of which 17 were won – by women in the food sector between 1983 and 2002.[27] Allen was recruited as a full-time officer in 1977 and developed an interest in equal pay after his wife, also a union activist, opened his eyes to the discrimination inherent in the measures negotiated by the union in 1975, which stipulated that part-time women workers should be fired before full-time male workers. He supported eight equal value claims between 1983 and 1987, using a strategy to raise awareness among women workers, informing them of their rights, and helping them to deconstruct certain assumptions about the value of their work (Cunnison, 1988).

Other interviews with men who were involved in the struggle for equal pay in the 1970s and 1980s reveal their early and intense efforts at the local level, fighting against their own union hierarchy to support the claims. Although this commitment by men can be seen as the expression of a 'humanist register that considers feminism as an element within a broader political struggle' (Jacquemart, 2012) and therefore equal pay as a 'bread and butter classic issue', it also demonstrates a precise knowledge of the mechanism of occupational segregation for low-paid women. This can be seen in Paul's comments.

Paul, a struggle for equal pay at the cost of a union career

Paul was born in Cumbria, in the North West of England. After leaving school at 18 he took a job doing home help for elderly people. Most of his colleagues were women. He became a steward with NUPE while continuing his career. "When I was elected shop steward, I represented the interests of these women. I knew their jobs and their working conditions. I was always very proud that they trusted me." After a few years he became a full-time official at NUPE and then, two years later, at age 39, got a job as a regional organizer with GMB. As part of his union role he participated in many negotiations on the implementation of the single status agreement[28] in the local government bodies in his region, and observed significant inflexibility among his unionist colleagues and employers. There was no progress, in spite of GMB's threats to take court action. So he made the decision to act and support claims, particularly given that the situation of low-paid women had deteriorated in the councils because of the pay cuts that had been imposed on them. "I was lucky because, at that time, my boss, the Regional Secretary, had decided to campaign to become General Secretary. He supported me because he thought it would win him votes." Paul decided to join forces with UNISON and call on Thompsons Solicitors, the law firm with whom the unions worked the most often, to look at the potential benefit of a multiple claim for the 2,960 workers at Cumbria County Council.[29] Stefan Cross, who was then working for Thompsons, helped him to prepare this case, which ended with an out-of-court settlement in 2006 in favour of 1,700 of the claimants, after Paul had left GMB. His action was frowned upon by his union colleagues who "had not understood that fair pay meant giving up unfair bonuses for male jobs". Paul was a member of the younger generation of unionists recruited to transform union practices, but once his boss became General Secretary he was side-lined by the new regional executive and negotiated his departure. Stefan Cross also left Thompsons and set up his own firm in Newcastle, offering Paul a job with him. He was responsible for the Manchester region and his work consisted in conducting research on the different city councils to evaluate possibilities for litigation. How many people worked there? How much were the men and women paid? Who got bonuses? "I describe myself as an agitator. I organized big public meetings with women employees to explain their rights to them. I spoke in the local papers, on the radio." The local unions, GMB and UNISON, tried to stop his action and tried to negotiate settlements with the employers, but they were also forced to support claims. In certain councils, women were able to file claims with the help of either Stefan Cross or the lawyers working for the unions. This was the case in the litigation against the Birmingham City Council, which took years to reach a verdict and gave rise to many strikes by male workers. In 2012 Paul was still occasionally working with Stefan Cross but he had returned to university to study history and political science. He was very proud of what he had contributed on behalf of the women, and remained a staunch unionist. However, he is still waiting for unionists of both sexes to adopt a genuinely more radical and feminist position on the question of equal pay.

★★★

Some of these unionists also 'stumbled' across the question of equal pay in their search to defend workers against pay cuts. It was the lawyers whom they turned to for advice who pointed out that they also had the option of making a claim for wage discrimination.

> 'I was the one who started the first litigations in 1995 when I was working for Thompsons. At Cleveland Council, the employer had set up a series of measures to reduce jobs and salaries. Ironically, one of the UNISON unionists had suggested cutting the budgets and pay for canteen workers rather than for male jobs. Out of inter-union competition, GMB – that was the minority union – decided to oppose the proposition, and came to me. They wanted to fight against the pay cuts, not for equal pay. I was the one who told them that there was a problem with undervaluing women's jobs, since the agreement that they had signed in 1988. These jobs were at the same grade level as their male counterparts, but they did not have a right to bonuses that had in fact become systematic. So there was a potential lawsuit for gender discrimination due to lowering women's wages, as well as an equal pay lawsuit. And we won. The wages were not cut, and we won £1,000,000 compensation. The unionists who defended these cases had problems with their union afterwards though. One was fired, the other was transferred to another region.' (Man, age 50, no win no fee lawyer)

These unionists often became full-time officials younger than their colleagues and were less accustomed to the existing collective bargaining practices. They were also more likely to trust the potential of the law. As one lawyer interviewed emphasized, "I think that the most pragmatic among them understood that lawyers could help them get results." Their court action relied on the essential support of specialized lawyers who became their main allies against a union hierarchy that was often either suspicious or indifferent, as David explained.

David: a solitary struggle for equal pay

David began working in 1977 in a job in the penitentiary system, and he joined the PCS union right away. From 1984 to 1985 he became more active in the union and was appointed the leading rep for administrative workers. The prison was a very segregated working environment. There were 30,000 guards, who were mostly men, and 4,000 administrative workers, who were mostly women. There were various dichotomies that reflected this division of labour: operational vs non-operational; front-line staff vs back-office staff; uniformed staff vs non-uniformed staff. There were two separate systems of collective bargaining and two unions, POA for the prison guards (with a unionization rate of 90%) and PCS for the other categories of workers (60% unionized). In 1987 the administration decided to negotiate a new pay agreement, called Fresh Start, which further enshrined the wage disparities between male and female jobs. For ten years the women complained to their union and their employer about this, and the latter finally agreed to a job evaluation for all prison jobs in 1996. As David remarks, "this approach was very useful because it allowed us to position these jobs on equal footing with those of the prison guards". But the employer was slow to implement the new pay grade. In 1999 PCS decided to take legal action. This was the beginning of a legal saga that lasted for 8 years, with 75 days of hearings before the court. David was involved from beginning to end, first as the leading rep and then as PCS full-time officer responsible for the prison sector from 2003. Early on he worked with Thompsons Solicitors, who mandated Tess Gill as barrister. Just as management was not taking this case very seriously, not even hiring a lawyer for the first hearing, the union hierarchy was equally unconcerned about the case and let David manage things. "Formally, it went before the executive office, but they didn't pay any attention to it. Years later, they realized that it had cost a fortune." Over 3,500 equal value claims were filed, mostly by women, but also by men in the same professions.[30] The employer then began a strategy of repeated appeals, which delayed the verdict. Eventually PCS had to pay for a job evaluation expert and lawyers. Given the extent of the costs, David tried to send the invoices off to different services of the union, out of fear of being reprimanded. He dedicated an enormous amount of time to this case, on top of his other union duties. "Sometimes, it was nearly impossible. I worked lots of weekends, evenings, because we had deadlines. It was interesting, but I would not say I enjoyed it. I was always afraid that we would lose, and my superiors would say to me 'do you realize how much money we have lost!'" He was very relieved when a settlement was reached in 2005 (in response to political pressure from the Labour government), with a revaluation of women's wages and financial compensation for past discrimination. But, like in many places, things have not changed much since, the classification agreements have not evolved, and equal pay has been taken off the bargaining table. Interestingly, when interviewed a few years later, the head of the PCS legal department, already in place at the time, never mentioned this legal action.

★★★

Whether they left the union movement or stayed, these unionists stress the risks that they took to defend women's interests, whether because they were suspected of trying to gain power in the organization by obtaining women's support, because they took significant financial risks, or more often because they contributed to revealing discriminatory collective bargaining practices. But these mobilizations were criticized by feminists and some lawyers. They were considered characteristic of the fact that unions tended to instrumentalize litigation for equal pay in order to defend the interests of male workers, like in the case of the Ford sewing machinists, where the equal pay claim was supported by the unions because they hoped to avoid a revision to the classification of male jobs (Cohen, 2013). In the 1970s litigation for equal pay was also used to increase wages in the context of the pay freeze imposed by the government, as a former regional officer for COHSE explains: "when there was a pay freeze policy, you could use an equal pay claim for a group of workers as leverage for overall wage negotiations. Employers tended to agree to an increase for that group and the others as well."

More recently, the threat of equal pay lawsuits was used quite creatively to fight against the privatization of the public sector. Investigation into the union responses to the outsourcing policies in local councils shows that certain unions, including NUPE, did not hesitate to use litigation as a way to oppose the privatization projects in their areas, sometimes without the support or agreement of the national level (Foster and Scott, 1997). In certain cases, equal pay litigation was used as a threat to discourage private companies from standing as candidates for outsourcing, given that the workers they would have to rehire were among the potential claimants. In other contexts, equal pay cases meant pay rises for the few men in traditionally female-dominated jobs, as was the case in the prison administration described by David, where the re-evaluation benefited 3,000 women, and also 1,000 men. As one lawyer explains,

'equal pay litigation is a formidable mechanism to obtain pay increases that have nothing to do with gender. The lawsuits can benefit men too. Once the women have obtained a pay rise by comparing themselves to men's jobs, the minority men in the same professional group can compare themselves to the women and also get a pay rise.'

Above all, these initial multiple claims contributed to unleashing a vast process of judicialization in the public sector which has been highly controversial.

The intervention of 'no win no fee lawyers'

Because they identified a major legal risk linked to the structural under-evaluation of women's jobs and the maintenance of unjustified bonuses for male jobs, lawsuits in hospitals and local councils led John Major's government to embark on an overhaul of the job classification system. A certain number of other evolutions in jurisprudence, such as the European Court of Justice's decision on speech therapists, which invalidated the possibility for an employer to argue separate collective agreements to justify equal pay, also played a role in the government's decision to take preventative action (see Box 4.1). In 1997 single status agreements (SSA) were signed for local government, with the objective of harmonizing working conditions and salaries among managers and non-managers in a single classification, applying the principle of 'equal pay for work of equal value'. A similar agreement, Agenda for Change, was also signed in the hospital sector in 2004, after five years' negotiation. In both cases, the National Job Evaluation methodology was proposed, with the help of Sue Hasting in the latter case.

As innovative as they may be, these two agreements revealed substantial discrepancies in pay between workers at the same grade (stretcher bearers or orderlies, for example), in terms of both basic salary and bonuses. This paved the way for a widespread litigation process. Objectivating these pay gaps indeed gave rise to an awareness of past discriminations that low-paid women had been subject to in the previous system, reinforced by the media attention on successful court cases[31] and the comparability of claims from staff in the same category (canteen workers, carers, and so forth). Several lawsuits were filed after 2004, first and foremost under the initiative of Stefan Cross, former lawyer with Thompsons Solicitors. Having set up his own firm and being by now a specialist in the structure of job classification systems and the content of ongoing negotiations, he called on former unionists, like Paul described earlier, to launch an information campaign in local governments and hospitals to encourage low-paid women to file their claims.

In the space of one year, between 2004 and 2005, he alone was responsible for initiating 10,000 claims (Table 4.2). His litigation work continued to increase, drawing UNISON and GMB with it in its wake.[32] In 2007–08 more than 60,000 equal pay claims were lodged, some of which were defended by UNISON (40,000 between 2004 and 2008) and GMB (30,000), and some by private lawyers like Stefan Cross (30,000).

Although criticized by the unions, Stefan Cross's action drew on the fact that negotiations with local government were difficult and drawn out, the SSA having been designed as a process for decentralized negotiation, unlike Agenda for Change. Two unexpected difficulties emerged over the course of negotiations (Oliver et al, 2014). Firstly, there was the cost of 'pay protection' measures designed to spread loss of salary out over time for workers who had been downgraded in the new classification or who would lose their bonuses, and secondly, there was the cost of back pay compensation for workers who had been discriminated against in the old system. Although the first agreements that were negotiated successfully minimized these costs by only partially compensating women who had been discriminated against (Deakin

Table 4.2: Evolution of the number of equal pay claims since 1995

	1999–2000	2000–1	2001–2	2002–3	2003–4	2004–5	2005–6	2007–8	2008–9	2009–10	2010–11
Claims received	4712	17153	8762	5053	4412	8229	17268	62700	45700	37400	34600
Claims disposed of	590	1288	2252	1158	1563	3943	11323	9471	20148	20100	25600
Claims withdrawn	233	936	665	484	668	1493	4373	4899	16335	14300	15300
Claims conciliated with ACAS	229	208	381	173	578	1559	1441	1512	2000	2300	3000
Claims struck out without a hearing	18	89	1021	409	240	778	1614	2189	1629	3100	5300
Claims dismissed at preliminary hearing	26	9	8	3	3	17	23	83	62	110	36
Successful claims	9	11	149	47	51	20	3722	678	36	200	280
Claims unsuccessful at hearing	75	35	28	43	23	76	124	105	82	77	1700
No ruling made	NA	NA	NA	NA	NA	NA	26	5	4	10	7

Source: Employment Tribunal and EAT Statistics reports, Ministry of Justice, 1999–2011.

Box 4.2: Extract from an article published in the *Guardian*, 28 April 2010

Female Birmingham council workers win £200m equal pay case
More than 4,000 female council workers have won the right to be paid the same as their male colleagues in a case which could lead to payouts worth about £200m. An employment tribunal found in favour of female workers employed by Birmingham City Council in 49 different jobs, including lollipop ladies and cleaners, who complained of being excluded from bonuses – worth up to 160% of their basic pay – paid to men. In one year, a refuse collector took home £51,000, while women on the same pay grade received less than £12,000. The bill for the council based on the 4,000 test cases was about £200m. However, if a further 20,000 women came forward and lodged claims, the figure could rise to £1bn.

---

et al, 2015), the cost of implementing them was particularly dissuasive for major public bodies with a diversified workforce, to the point where the state did not plan for any additional means. In 2009, less than half of local governments had implemented the SSA (Oliver et al, 2014); only 30% of councils had implemented it, and 40% of the councils who had not yet done so said they had equal pay claims underway. Following on from Stefan Cross, UNISON and GMB were also involved in legal action, pushed by the intense media coverage of the trials (Box 4.2) and the comparability of the claims.

Although the number of claims has dropped since 2011, largely because Stefan Cross closed his firm in England (but not in Scotland) and most of the litigation in local government has dried up, the judicialization essentially froze all negotiation on equal pay and left unionists suspicious of job evaluation practices (Gilbert, 2012), out of fear of leaving themselves open to possible court action. Having been attacked in the courts by Stefan Cross for not having sufficiently defended the interests of their female members,[33] and overwhelmed by the influx of claims, unions attempted to disconnect claim management from the everyday activities of unionists by centralizing all claims and systematically hiring lawyers to deal with them. UNISON and GMB also organized their own legal practices, recruited skilled lawyers to manage their internal legal department (Guillaume, 2018b), and set up equal pay units in the regions.

Sally, manager of an equal pay unit

Sally graduated from a polytechnical school and was hired as a benefits advisor in a council in the Midlands. She came from a very unionized background and considered that working in the public sector provided more security than working in the private sector, even in the 1980s. She joined NALGO and became branch secretary just when UNISON was created, in 1991, thanks to the equality policy put in place by the union. "Due to rules about proportional representation, the oldest activists in the branch were looking for someone who could get more involved. I was a woman, young, and able to control what I said." A few years later, a position as full-time officer was advertised in the paper. She applied, and was recruited in 1997 as regional women's officer. In theory she was also responsible for equal pay, but initially there were very few claims. "UNISON did not have a strategy to encourage claims. At the beginning, our position was training, negotiating, and legal action as a last resort. And in fact, in my heart of hearts, I think that we are really a 'bargaining organization' and not a 'legal organization'." Litigation began only in 2005. Since then, Sally has spent nearly all her time on the subject. She has helped lawyers, found comparators, talked to claimants, tried to find settlements with employers. Where she struggles the most with litigation is "that we lose all negotiating power overnight. When lawyers come on the scene, the stakes change completely. In certain councils, negotiations had been underway for two years, with male workers striking and all sorts of employer strategies to 'protect men's pay'." For her, the biggest difficulty was both fighting for equal pay and continuing to represent male members, while also maintaining good relationships with the employer. "Lawyers don't have this problem. They come and then they go." Of course, UNISON's commitment to equal pay also allowed them to attract many new female members. "They aren't female members who are particularly active. Individual claims don't lead to organizing practices. It is more like an extreme form of servicing. Join up and we will support your claim." For her, it is now difficult to "put the genie back in the bottle", and she considers that "it is one of the last major feminist struggles that we must continue to fight".

★★★

Many women's officers, particularly in the private sector or male-dominated unions like UNITE, consider that court action is not a good way to defend women's interests. But the experience of the cases brought against GMB is still present in people's minds and all the unions are very careful about the settlements they negotiate with employers.[34]

> 'Most equal pay claims are filed by low-paid women, apart from a few claims by female senior managers in the city. If they go to court, they won't get much. When we see the amount of stress and time that is required for these lawsuits. Of course, we support claims if they are well founded, but we prefer to negotiate a settlement with the employer because they don't have much chance of winning. Unions have been criticized for that, like in the case of Allen vs GMB, so we are very cautious. We always tell our members the amount of compensation

they might obtain if they go to court.' (Woman, age 40, women's officer, UNITE)

In most unions, the management of claims is now centralized, and legal process is managed by external firms. Recently, GMB even preferred to refer claimants working for the major supermarket chain Asda to a law firm without getting involved, so that they did not have to be directly responsible for the claim and thus disrupt their relationship with the employer in a context of economic austerity.

'The case of Asda is interesting because it was initiated in 2008 by GMB in the name of its 400 members in Manchester. They had male members in the distribution centres and women in the shops. The men were better paid. So, they filed a claim, and nothing happened. The union continued to negotiate with the employer and the legal process didn't progress because both parties agreed to negotiate. In December 2013 the case was supposed to be heard by the court and just beforehand the two parties agreed to set up a working group for four years to find a solution. At the end of those four years the employer did not want to change its position, and the union said nothing. Asda is owned by Walmart, which is not known for being pro-union, so maybe GMB was happy just being recognized and invited to the negotiating table.' (Man, age 35, no win no fee lawyer).

More generally, after 2013, the costs of bringing a case before the Employment Tribunal increased significantly,[35] following the introduction of fees (a decision now overturned following legal action by UNISON). All the unions set up filters to try to find non-legal responses to problems and to sort claims according to the likelihood of success before the courts. If they considered there was a 50% chance of winning, the union supported the claim and paid representation costs. In addition, since 6 May 2014 all claimants (with very few exceptions) have been required to comply with the Early Conciliation Procedure before they can lodge a claim in the Employment Tribunal.[36] ACAS, Advisory, Conciliation, and Arbitration Service, will then offer a free conciliation service for the parties in the dispute. All things considered, in reality, very few discrimination claims reach the stage of hearing, and the success rate before the courts is very low (see Table 4.2).

Moreover, unlike in the 1980s and 1990s, the EOC (which became the Equality and Human Rights Commission, the EHRC, in 2007) legal action on equal pay completely dried up, due to a lack of resources and of lobbying by feminist associations. In the 2000s it even called a moratorium on equal pay claims in the local government sector to create space for negotiations. According to certain interviewees, the EHRC's role was weakened in the 2000s by the Labour governments, who had a strong commitment toward equality that used other administrative and ministerial avenues to implement their policies.[37] The arrival of New Labour also marked the reframing of equality in terms both of diversity management and of women's contribution to the economic performance of companies, without questioning the effects of the neoliberal privatization and restructuring policies put in place by the Conservatives (Conley and Page, 2015). Determined to move away from a strictly legal and adversarial approach to the problem of discrimination, the government modified the legislation to call on employers to act responsibly.

Several 'positive equality duties' were imposed for public sector employers from 2001 (see Box 4.1), so that they could promote equality and thus avoid litigation. This approach was intended to bring parties together, particularly the unions and management, to ensure that corrective measures were taken. Each time that a local government or hospital wanted to modify how it operated or was organized, an equality impact assessment had to be conducted to gauge the potential impact the proposed modifications would have on the different groups protected under legislation. These assessments could also serve as the basis for court action in the context of a judicial review,[38] a procedure which comes under administrative law and which examines the legality of a decision made by a public body. These 'equality duties' were criticized for being inconsistent and were fused into a single 'duty' in 2011 after the new Equality Act was passed in 2010. However, there were no specific measures included to cover the question of equal pay. The only binding measure taken since is the obligation (after 2017) for any organization that has 250 or more employees to publish and report specific figures about their gender pay gap. Employers that fail to report on time or report inaccurate data will be in breach of the regulations and risk facing legal action from the EHRC, leading to court orders and fines.

The legacy of the Labour Party in favour of equal pay is considered controversial, even though it was Tony Blair's government that introduced a minimum wage in Great Britain, in 1999, which benefited low-paid women. As an employer, the state fought tooth and nail against the claim brought by Stefan Cross against the hospital sector (NHS), which was forced to drop the case for lack of means. The state also refused to fund the implementation of the SSA in local governments, which left councils facing a drastic choice. They could either grant equal pay to women but reduce the total number of jobs, or sell some of their heritage assets to pay for compensation for women who were victims of discrimination. On the legal front, the state also did everything possible to hinder the action of no win no fee lawyers and prioritized conciliation measures, particularly via ACAS.

'The Labour Party only did things that didn't cost them anything, or which brought them something else. They paid for the Agenda for Change because having a single classification system for all staff can make things easier when some parts are privatized. They also decided to put an end to the speech therapists' case by settling out of court, even though the previous government had been ready to fight all the claims individually. However, they offered very little assistance to local governments. They ended up setting up a fund to help them get out of the impasse, but it was too little too late. They introduced the Equality Act, which in principle was a good thing. They merged the different equality commissions, which should also have been a good thing. Their principles were good, but they never wanted to pay for anything, unless they had another reason to do so.' (Woman, age 65, job evaluation expert)

It is true that the involvement of no win no fee lawyers and the extensive judicialization that followed were widely criticized, within both the legal profession and the union movement. Inspired by certain recent efforts to simplify legal proceedings, and particularly to extend the 'material' arguments to the defence before pursuing the trial, the appeal strategy by employers contributed to an engorgement of the system. Procedures that were very useful for obtaining information from employers were also removed, such as equal pay questionnaires prior to hearings (which also allowed claimants to obtain essential information on the nature of jobs and wages).

'The efficiency of the law is a disaster. At different points we tried to make the judges understand these difficulties, to have them appoint a single judge for example. In cases of multiple claims, certain claims were judged by an employment tribunal judge, and at the same time there might be an appeal being judged on other claims in the same "lot" which would then go back down to another level of the employment tribunal. Nothing was coordinated.' (Woman, age 65, former barrister)

The involvement of lawyers who were paid on their successes was considered suspicious by lawyers working with the unions and by the unionists themselves, who did not see this as a militant or feminist engagement, but as a sort of cash cow, profiting from the difficulties of low-paid women. It was rare that unionists acknowledged the validity of Stefan Cross's actions, for example, but some admitted that they did secure significant compensation for low-paid employees whose interests were side-lined in negotiation practices. Stefan Cross was in fact appointed an honorary Queen's Counsel (QC) in recognition of his contribution to pay equality, one of only a small number of solicitors to be awarded this venerable distinction. In 2018, Southampton

Law School (where Cross had graduated in 1982) launched the Stefan Cross Centre for Women, Equality & Law (SCC), thanks to a donation from Stefan Cross QC (Hons). The university website states that

> The SCC will be the first centre of its kind in the country dedicated to tackling this issue. It will be staffed by academics and doctoral researchers who will work with experts across a wide range of disciplines and backgrounds and hold regular public events to spark conversations about where gender inequality occurs and understand the roots of the problem. They will also undertake research projects on the broad range of social, cultural and legal issues associated with gender discrimination to identify what needs to change to reduce the problem.

Other unionists emphasize the fact that these trials would not have been able to come to light if the unions had not attempted to provide an organizational response to equal pay legislation by negotiating innovative classification agreements using job evaluation methods. Unlike the diversity policy in the US (Edelman, 2016), these agreements were not used for defence in the court room but were used against the unions and employers that had negotiated them. As Jérôme Pélisse (2014) notes, 'implementing the law is a complex operation in which specialized and lay intermediaries come together to interpret the rules and produce legal and organizational responses'. The example of the struggle for equal pay in Great Britain underlines to what extent organizations are both constitutive of and reactive to their legal environments, and how the forms of internalization of the law (Edelman, 1992) can interact with judicialization processes (Pélisse, 2009). These interactions may be complimentary or substitutive (Deakin et al, 2015; Guillaume, 2015b), and they may evolve, depending on the context and period.

Much of the research on equal pay has emphasized the conflictual nature of the negotiation process (Acker, 1989; Hart, 2002), but this seems particularly exacerbated in the British case because of interactions between the production of norms through collective bargaining and the judicialization that is associated with it. The use of the courts demonstrates the difficulty unions and employers have in addressing the systemic aspect of gender inequality through negotiation. The adversarial approach of certain unions has come up against a number of limits that have been well identified in the literature, including a difficulty to collectivize workers' interests in a context of activist movement fragmentation (McCann, 1994) and employers' tougher negotiating positions. The fact that unions have managed to collectivize some claims may, however, be considered a 'counterhegemonic' use of the law (Hunt, 1990), able to legitimate the social interests of certain underrepresented (or even oppressed) categories of employees, and to challenge certain implicit social norms such as representations associated with women's work and its value (Guillaume, 2015a).

Conclusion

The history of the struggle for equal pay provides a complex, evolving, and detailed reading of the possible links between the descriptive and substantive representation of women. Like other research on 'feminist insiders' (Banaszak, 2010), it has shown the involvement of 'critical actors', both male and female, within institutions which have sometimes been very hostile to the defence of equal pay, first and foremost among them the unions. Women have mobilized for equal rights and their implementation, from within the unions or outside, in structures like the EOC or associations like the Fawcett Society (Conley, 2012). Without their action and commitment, the struggle for equal pay would have probably remained a secondary issue. These women, often highly educated, and sometimes from working-class backgrounds, are characteristic of the second-wave feminists who joined these institutions through the first equality policies that were implemented. They are very similar to their American counterparts, studied by Michael McCann (McCann, 1994), in the context of the 'equity campaigns' conducted in the 1980s. What is less known is the role of certain low-level male unionists, often low paid and from male-dominated unions, who stood up to their union hierarchy and employers to use the legislation to obtain equal pay for their female colleagues. They often risked their own careers in the union, even though this engagement was made in the name of the union movement, with a view to attracting new female members and fighting management policies that deteriorated employment conditions, but also in the name of social justice.

These men and women sometimes worked together, sharing a socialist and feminist understanding of the fight for equal pay. This fight was very quickly understood and presented as a struggle for revaluing low-paid, female-dominated jobs. Initially it benefited White women in the 1970s–1990s, and then increasingly benefited BAME women in the 2000s, who are overrepresented in low-paid public sector jobs. Although there were some legal campaigns that benefited professional women (such as in the case of the speech therapists), they above all had an impact on low-paid women in the public sector, as well as the private sector in certain periods. From this perspective, the extent of the equal pay movement and then the equal value movement was broader than in the US, even though the context was hostile to workers' rights, particularly between 1979 and 1997. This difference can most likely be explained by the much greater influence of unions in Great Britain, but also by the possibilities offered by European law.

The second aspect of the struggle that is unusual, but similar to other American experiences (McCann, 1994), is the fact that the different actors were able to combine 'conventional' forms of contestation, such as the use of collective bargaining, training, or good practice guidelines, with large-scale litigation. Marginal within their institutions, they were able to call on allies in the legal and political fields, both at the national and European level, to build networks and tackle the interpretation, diffusion, and implementation of legal norms in organizational practices. Although the political and economic context was hostile to workers' rights, these actors were able (depending on the periods) to benefit from windows of opportunity, such as that provided by the UK's desire to join the European Union. Although their action partially benefited from the support of an increasing number of women within unions – and thus the effect of the equality policies implemented earlier by unions – the connections between this 'critical mass' of women and the work of these 'critical actors' were not automatic (Chaney, 2012). In the most feminized and, especially feminist unions, such as NALGO or APEX, the work of unionists to defend equal pay was supported and encouraged by the first women union leaders, but other people, particularly men, got involved in this cause even though their unions did not have many female members.

One of the most striking moments in this history is undoubtedly the introduction of the concept of equal value into British legislation and its application through the first claims lodged in the 1980s. Although the individual nature of equal pay legislation, and antidiscrimination law more generally, has often been criticized (Colling, 2006; Dickens and Hall, 2006; Dickens, 2007; Pollert, 2007; Fredman, 2008), the notion of equal value, associated with that of indirect discrimination, had a potential for overall transformation that the feminists of the time understood perfectly. Like in the US, the changes to the law in 1984 allowed the creation of a 'new language that shifted the focus of fighting discrimination from discrete acts of individual "ill will" to systemic biases in institutional practices and policies' (McCann, 1994: 50). The implementation of job evaluation strategies, generally associated with equal value implementation (or rulings in the event of claims), often stumbled when it came to the numerous difficulties well identified in the American literature on pay equity campaigns (Fudge and Mcdermott, 1991). These include management's control of implementation mechanisms, the creation of competition between skilled and low-skilled women's interests (Acker, 1989), the consolidation of wage hierarchies (Blum, 1991), and the difficulty of bringing about these approaches in a context of economic restructuring and redundancy (Khan and Figart, 1997; Hallock, 2000). But this approach to equal pay remains the only one that enables: (1) a collective approach to wage inequalities; (2) an understanding of the systemic and organizational nature of wage inequalities and the reform of job classification practices.

Moreover, and this is undoubtedly one of the most remarkable aspects of the different experiences of the way unions use the law in the UK and the US, the struggle for equal pay gave rise to increased awareness of rights among women unionists and employees. By adopting evaluation procedures covering all jobs and abandoning separate negotiation practices for different professional groups, equal value or comparable worth practices managed to avoid the effects of professional segregation that had made gender pay gaps invisible. The use of litigation also played a central role in raising awareness among women victims of discrimination, some of whom actively participated in putting together cases and recruiting claimants. Like the unionists responsible for these claims, these women acted as intermediaries between lawyers and claimants, spreading information, explaining the foundations and constraints of the law, reassuring claimants about the risks of going to court. Like in the US (McCann, 1994), the struggle for equal pay was a way to attract many women members, even though their actual participation was very variable between workplaces. In the case of class actions in centralized public administrations, such as prisons, the management of the lawsuits made it impossible to actively bring together the 4,000 claimants. However, in some smaller public bodies, like local councils, litigation relied on the participation of members and helped to identify new women activists.

All this shows how a particular cause might seem decisively lost at any given time, for example in a political context hostile to women's and workers' rights, and then rise up again, driven by other actors outside institutions, depending on legal opportunities and individual strategies. Stefan Cross was a particularly high-profile example of this for many years and is a good illustration of seemingly unexpected shifts in events; but he also demonstrates the ability of individuals to act as 'dormant structures' (Taylor, 2005) in a cause everyone seems to have tired of. His actions, along with his no win no fee lawyer colleagues, were widely criticized as parasitic and counterproductive with regard to the unions' attempts to find compromises in the defence of the contradictory interests of their members. But they also helped to depoliticize the question of equal pay (Beirne and Wilson, 2016) and enable new forms of empowerment for women who could, if they wished, call on lawyers to promote their rights without having to turn to the unions, and could indeed challenge the compromises negotiated by their union. As Michael McCann emphasizes, 'counterhegemonic movements most often evolve incrementally through a series of more limited local struggles over quite concrete, often trivial ends' (1994: 307). Within unions, this lawyer-driven action also allowed certain women unionists to more actively invest in the cause of equal pay through means other than collective bargaining. From this perspective, the battle for equal pay led to an objective – but controversial – legitimation of unions in terms of the representation of employees' and members' interests. Since the 2008 financial crisis, the TUC and public sector unions in particular have revived the question of women's jobs and pay from another perspective, through campaigns emphasizing the effects of austerity policies on women as both public service users and employees.

5

Conclusion: Lessons for Future (Comparative) Research

Comparative research is always a challenge. However, it is also necessary if we are to develop robust interpretations and encompassing theories (Hyman, 2001), with a view of displaying both similarities and differences, as well as identifying 'best practice' (Ledwith and Hansen, 2013). The two studies presented in this book approach international comparison in different ways. The first, on women's underrepresentation in trade unions, uses a 'career' methodology to analyse the variation in 'inequality regimes' (Ackers, 2006) across two countries. The second proposes a socio-historical analysis of legal mobilizations (Lehoucq and Taylor, 2020) in favour of equal pay in the UK as an example to draw useful lessons for other national contexts (notably France) on the effectiveness of mobilizing the courts as a union repertoire of action. In doing so, both studies offer different contributions to (comparative) research in industrial relations.

Designing a longitudinal case study

The first contribution of this research is methodological. Our aim in this comparative endeavour was to overcome some of the difficulties encountered in comparative research on industrial relations (Hyman, 2001), and to avoid a deterministic and overarching perspective investigating institutions and structures (for example, industrial relations systems, gender equality regimes) at the expense of social processes (for example, social construction of gender inequalities). At the same time, while previous research has shown that there is a universalism in the way women are treated in the workplace and a strong resilience of the gendered order over time (Kirton and Healy, 2013a), scholars have argued for contextually and/or historically grounded analysis as a means of understanding the structure and dynamics of 'inequality regimes' (Acker, 2006). Studies have established that several institutional characteristics contribute to the variations in the extent to which equality is achieved in different union contexts; they include size (Kirton, 2015), the internal union labour market (Guillaume and Pochic, 2011) and internal democracy (Healy and Kirton, 2000; McBride, 2001), the framing of gender equality strategies (more or less feminist and/or intersectional), and the articulation of class and gender (Dean 2015; Guillaume, 2018a). Moreover, socio-historical studies have highlighted the fact that the union representation of women is inscribed in and should be understood in the context of specific social, economic, and institutional configurations. These studies have shown that the issue of gender inequality in the trade union movement cannot be addressed without understanding the specific institutional dimensions of each trade union, and in particular the links with feminist movements and the evolution of internal political orientations.

In her recent book, Ruth Milkman (2016) has put forward the hypothesis that there are major variations in the way women have been represented by American unions, depending on the periods when the unions were founded. She thus distinguishes different cohorts of unions founded between the mid-19th century and the 1960s, which are characterized by distinct configurations in their social gender relations within society, their activity sectors, and their more or less inclusive union practices. According to the author, the combination of these different elements has given these unions a particular vision of women employees, which has also influenced their equality policies. Thus the 'old' male-dominated trade unions created in the 19th century inherited a tradition of hostility toward women workers and continued to exclude women sometimes up until the 1940s. Although most have now disappeared, it is rare that they were known for progressive equality policies. By contrast, the major industrial unions created in the 1930s were more feminized from the outset. Driven by rising demands for equality in society, many of them were active in obtaining antidiscrimination legislation and tried to facilitate the representation of women internally.

Frances Galt's rich analysis of the relationship between women and the entertainment union ACT(T)/BECTU, representing workers in the British film and television industries, through periods of both militancy and inertia, also offers a superb analysis of the ACT(T)/BECTU 'inequality regime' and its permanence over time, despite the introduction of progressive equality policies and periods of intense activism by women. The combination of rich archival records and oral history interviews provides a detailed examination of the constraints and levers for the participation of women in this male-dominated craft union, and of the ways by which the union has shaped women's experiences of work. It reveals how the union has strived to exclude women through a gendered definition of jobs and skills. When forced to represent feminized jobs, it has consistently made women's interests subordinate to the defence of male occupations, particularly in contexts of economic recession and job insecurity.

Fanny Gallot's research (2015) on French textile and electrical appliance workers since the 1960s provides another example of the value of an in-depth longitudinal case study. Her work shows how the representation of women's rights in the union has evolved in response to mobilization by women workers, the progressive positioning of women in representative roles, and the evolutions of labour law in favour of equality. She also looks at the impact of the contrasting ways this issue has been framed and the attitudes of the two representative unions – the CFDT and the CGT – in different periods. Although women workers had to conduct an unrelenting fight to obtain legitimacy within these two unions, along with recognition of the deeply unfair and sexist nature of the discrimination they were subject to, the variation in union responses demands a contextualization that reveals the internal and external constraints in these two contexts.

These and other research cited in this book have called for a methodology attentive to the articulation of structural, organizational, and individual dimensions in the making and/or weakening of gender inequalities in trade unions. They have also documented the conditions that enable progress in some unions, including individuals' agency and equality/diversity policies. Research has pointed to the centrality of women's agency in the union context (Briskin, 2006; Kirton, 2006b; Kirton and Healy, 2013a); how women negotiate barriers and constraints, how they seek to challenge the existing masculine culture and practices, and what kind of individual resources and strategies might help them, including job qualifications (Guillaume and Pochic, 2013) and feminist orientations (Kirton and Healy, 2012, 2013b; Pochic, 2014).

To bring together the analysis of the different union 'inequality regimes' (Ackers, 2006), their embeddedness in specific social, economic, institutional, and micro-level agency processes, we therefore adopted a 'case study' methodology (Yin, 2014). In contrast to comparative investigations (Mazur, 2003) that start from a multiplicity of national institutional assumptions such as the characteristics of gender regimes or industrial relations regimes (Rubery and Fagan, 1995) to explain variations in the success of feminist policies across national contexts, this approach aimed at understanding how and why institutional contexts at different levels (European, national, local) interfere (Demazière et al, 2013), constrain, or facilitate the development of unions' internal and external equality policies. In choosing 'contrasting contexts' (Crompton, 2001) within the same country and in different countries, the comparison aimed to bring out the typical difficulties the trade union movement has in representing women (and their interests), but also what was specific to each institutional context, depending on the period.

We chose individuals as the unit of analysis in order to conduct this comparison. Using what Rosemary Crompton (2001) calls a 'biographical matching and comparative analysis', we compared the careers of trade unionists – men and women – in two countries and four unions. This methodology, developed through previous research (Guillaume and Pochic, 2011, 2013), has provided a comprehensive, multi-spaced and dynamic understanding of career development, therefore addressing some of the gaps and limitations of comparative research in industrial relations (Rubery and Fagan, 1995; Hyman, 2001). While this methodological approach could have been enriched by further historical investigation into trade unions' archives, the analysis of individual careers in different time periods has enabled us to gauge the impact of changing equality policies (and legislation) on women's representation in different unions. We strongly believe that future research should further embrace the in-depth longitudinal case study approach developed by labour historians (Galt, 2021).

Adopting an intersectional perspective

The second contribution of this book, which echoes the call of other colleagues before us (for example, Kirton and Ledwith, 2013; Ledwith and Hansen, 2013, to name but a few), is to stress the importance of adopting an intersectional approach in analysing 'inequality regimes', which we have partially succeeded in doing. According to Joan Acker's conceptualization (2006), this concept should enable an identification of the way in which gender, class, and ethnicity interact to produce multiple barriers to certain minority groups and contribute to the underrepresentation of their interests (Bradley and Healy, 2008; Healy et al, 2011). However, while this intersectional perspective (Walby et al, 2012; McBride et al, 2015) is today mobilized by most research on gender and trade unions, it does not escape the conceptual and methodological difficulties identified in other academic fields (Bilge and Roy, 2010). Although it aims to identify the heterogeneity of women's lived experiences, a lack of data means that it is often difficult to objectivate what Acker calls the 'foundation' of inequality regimes in union organizations. Unions now tend to record the gender of activists and members in most of the statistics they produce, but other characteristics such as education level, race, disability, or sexuality are generally not recorded, particularly in France. The data collected by British unions are richer and allow for analysis incorporating other social characteristics. A number of studies have looked at the role of BAME workers (Virdee and Grint, 1994; Kirton, 2019) in unions, sometimes in connection with the participation of women (Kirton and Greene, 2002). Others have instead studied the representation of LGBTI members (Colgan, 1999; Bairstow, 2007) or members with disabilities (Humphrey, 1998). However, this group-centred approach can lead to a certain reification of categories of domination and can struggle to capture the power relations between minority groups (Briskin, 2008).

Some rare studies have looked at the intersections of race, class, and gender within trade unions. Anne Munro's investigation into the British hospital sector documented the discriminatory practices observed among unionists against low-skilled Asian women (hospital orderlies), whose demands were played down or even contested by their White colleagues. Their interests and requests were very rarely transmitted by union representatives even though clear progress had been made for more qualified workers, particularly White nurses (Munro, 1999). The participant observation conducted by Joan Acker in the late 1980s (Acker, 1989) as an expert in implementing comparable worth for Oregon state employees (US), also revealed how gender and class relations not only were embedded in organizational and ideological functioning but were also reproduced over the course of the actions that were implemented to correct them. Beyond the intrinsic bias of the evaluation method used, which did not provide a grasp of the complexity of women's work, nor challenge the technical appreciation of these jobs, Acker showed how consultants worked with management to avoid increasing value/worth associated to 'relational skills' and to the notion of stress in low-skilled (and feminized) jobs. She also revealed unions' ambivalent attitude in refusing to participate in joint collective bargaining out of fear of losing control over certain employee categories. Unions were clearly reticent about possible wage freezes for men, which the employer considered a necessary condition to redress women's salaries. In this very feminized sector, this investigation emphasized the complexity of the situation for low-paid women whose interests were both supported and threatened by male-dominated unions. These unions allocated both time and means to the reclassification process but also attempted to preserve the interests of men (and of highly qualified women) in a context of budgetary constraints and employer strategies that sought to decrease their power in collective bargaining.

Another comparative study on women's experiences of union leadership in Great Britain and in the US (Kirton and Healy, 2013a) investigated the processes that hinder and/or facilitate women's participation in unions, articulating gender, class, and race. Out of the 134 women leaders who were interviewed or participated in focus groups in the two countries (half in each), 36% clearly identified as 'women of colour' or 'black and minority ethnic' (BAME). This internal diversity among women provided greater depth to the analysis of organizational barriers and leverages in women accessing positions of leadership within unions. The authors particularly emphasized the role of gender, class, and racial stereotypes conveyed by both men and women. Thus, according to the interviewees, women did not always identify other women as potential union leaders, particularly when they were in low-paid jobs. 'Minority' women, and particularly BAME women, were often judged more harshly on their skills than qualified White women, who benefited more from mentoring by established leaders (men or women) and who relied on their educational qualifications to compensate for the lack of training provided by the union. Similarly, British BAME activists were quite critical of the (rare) women-only spaces within their unions which demonstrated a neglect of their interests as Black women (who were often also in low-paid jobs).

Although the study presented in this book has not allowed to explore the issue of racial inequalities because of the very small number of BAME activists interviewed (the same is true of inequalities based on disability or sexuality), it has demonstrated very clearly the difficulties that low-paid women in precarious jobs face in joining and participating in unions – and even more in pursuing a union career. This is true for all unions but appears to be a particularly important obstacle in Great Britain, where there is an erosion of both employment conditions and union rights in the public sector, as well as a smaller union presence in the private sector, both of which have a strong impact on the representation of low-paid women. Yet job security, full-time work, and access to union rights all encourage women to join the union and facilitate the typical career that leads to paid union officer positions. Although organizing casual and temporary workers is an important issue for French unions, the existence of union rights and the strength of sectoral collective bargaining continue to enable women in these insecure positions to access a form of union representation. By contrast, UNISON and the GMB seem to be more proactive in terms of organizing women workers (who are often also migrants) on insecure contracts than the CFDT, and even more than Solidaires, which is limited by its low resources. Nearly 30% of new UNISON members come from the private sector (or the privatized public sector), but the organizing campaigns conducted by UNISON in these areas reveal the difficulty in identifying activists, and above all keeping them in the union through successive privatizations (especially if they fear they may lose their job or immigration rights). However, it is the issues at stake in unionizing and organizing that helped to put feminization on the agenda.

The 'intersectionality perspective' is making progress in the field of employment relations (McBride et al, 2015), even if it is only rarely theorized by unions themselves, or is so through a model of superposition of independent social characteristics (Jaunait and Chauvin, 2012). The difficulty in grasping the complexity of social relations and the specificity of configurations within which these relations are mutually constructed often leads to a union approach based on the defence of categories of workers who are seen as suffering discrimination because of cumulative social and economic disadvantages – migrant women on precarious contracts, for example. This is an approach that does not look at either the systemic mechanisms that reproduce inequalities or the mechanisms for compensation or reversal of discrimination, depending on the context. However, in terms of research, it seems more important than ever to consider the making of gender inequalities as being at the intersection of mutually constitutive relations of class, race and other forms of discrimination. This is something that this book illustrates, albeit imperfectly, for want of data but certainly also for lack of prior theoretical framing.

Thinking outside the box of industrial relations theory

Finally, the third contribution of this book is to encourage scholars to free themselves from the classical analytic categories in industrial relations to explore other potentially effective repertoires of action (Kelly, 1998) in the fight against workplace discrimination. Industrial relations scholars have a predilection for analysing the traditional repertoires of trade union action, whether it be collective bargaining or industrial disputes. The use of litigation by trade unions remains under-researched. Notwithstanding remarkable seminal work (McCann, 1994; Willemez, 2003; Pélisse, 2007) and recent developments (Guillaume, 2015a, 2015b, 2018b, 2020; Chappe et al, 2016, 2019; Guillaume et al, 2016; Lejeune and Yazdanpanah, 2017; Willemez, 2017; Chappe, 2019; Louis, 2019; Kirk, 2020), scholars have rarely studied trade unions acting as 'legal intermediaries' (Pélisse, 2019), echoing the trade union movement's suspicion of judicial institutions (Colling, 2004, 2006, 2012). And yet, trade unions have frequently participated in individual and collective litigation to obtain or enforce statutory rights at the national and European levels. The juridification of employment relations and workers' rights has been noted in both decentralized and corporatist industrial relations systems (Bondy and Preminger, 2021). While the mobilization of the courts has been positioned counter to collective labour relations (Colling, 2004, 2006; O'Sullivan et al, 2015; Giraud, 2017), many studies have also demonstrated the limits of collective bargaining on gender equality in France (Milner and Gregory, 2014; Milner et al, 2019; Pochic et al, 2019) and of positive equality duties in the British public service (Conley and Page 2015; Wright and Conley, 2018).

By contrast, the example of unions' legal mobilizations for equal pay in Great Britain, discussed at length in this book, demonstrates to what extent the use of antidiscrimination legislation, particularly European law, is an undeniably precious resource for those who promote equality and the fight against discrimination in unions (Chappe et al, 2019). Although action by internal structures and leaders responsible for equality has probably had a certain impact on the representation of women and their interests, the recent advances in the defence of women's rights, whether in terms of equal pay or part-time employees' rights, in Great Britain have been the product of a collective mobilization of the law. This adversarial use of the legal system has led to the evolution of union practices in terms of negotiations on job classification and pay, forcing unions and employers to address the recurring issue of women's work being undervalued. From this perspective, and despite all the debates on the limits of the law and individual rights (Dickens, 2012), litigation seems to have had greater effects than the production of rules and regulations through collective bargaining. This observation should encourage us to reflect more intensively on how collective bargaining, litigation, and forms of responsive regulations (Ayres and Braithwaite, 1992; Wright and Conley, 2018) can operate together, complement, or replace each other, depending on periods and contexts. An overly naive belief in the value of social dialogue in a context of austerity (Conley and Page, 2015), economic recession (Milner et al, 2019), and now the COVID-19 pandemic, overlooks the great inertia of collective bargaining practices and the difficulty both unions and employers seem to have in making equality a priority.

Notes

Chapter 2

[1] This case led to the women correctors' union being excluded from the Labour Exchange following the use of women workers to replace striking male workers in Nancy.

[2] Louis Couriau was a typesetter who was expelled from the union for having signed up his wife, Emma.

[3] National and Local Government Officers Association.

[4] The Manufacturing, Science and Finance Union (MSF) is today part of UNITE, the second-largest British union, resulting from the merger of several private sector unions.

[5] The Communication Workers Union (CWU) represents the employees of the telecommunications sector and the postal service. Today it has around 200,000 members.

[6] Society of Graphical and Allied Trades.

[7] The term 'closed shop' refers to a system in which the employer can hire only union members. The union has a monopoly over recruitment.

[8] Sources: *Trade Union Membership 2014, Statistical Bulletin, Office for National Statistics*; Thomas Amossé, 'Mythes et réalités de la syndicalization en France', *Premières Synthèses*, DARES, n°44, 2004.

[9] Two main sources were used here: the CFDT archives on equality policy, and the TUC Collection at London Metropolitan University.

Chapter 3

[1] Sources: *Women in the Labour Market* – Full report – September 2013, Office of National Statistics; *The Impact on Women of Recession and Austerity*, TUC report, 2013; *Les inégalités entre les hommes et les femmes* – Données Focus DARES – June 2018.

[2] This situation does not exist for Solidaires, which has very few paid activists.

[3] Law n° 2015-994 of 17 August 2015 relating to industrial negotiations and employment. Article L. 2314-24 -1 stipulates that for any electoral constituency, the ballots mentioned in article L 2314-24 with several candidates must be made up of a number of men and women reflecting the proportion of men and women enrolled to vote. These electoral ballots are made up of candidates of alternating genders until there are no further candidates of a particular gender. Where para.1 of the present article does not lead to an even number of candidates being designated for each gender, they will be arithmetically rounded as follows: (1) rounded up to the next whole number in case of a decimal equal to or above 5; (2) rounded down to the next whole number in case of a decimal below 5. In cases where an uneven number of seats are to be filled, and of strict equality between men and women on the electoral ballot, the ballot will include either an additional man or a woman. This article applies to the election of delegates and deputies.

[4] These reforms had a profound impact on the structure of employee representation in France, establishing the Social and Economic Council (*Comité social et économique* – CSE),

which has now replaced elected workplace representatives. This council combines all the staff representative bodies, staff reps (DP), work council (CE), and the health and safety committee (CHSCT).

[5] In 2016 there were around 600,000 staff representatives (unionized or not) in the sales sector in France, of whom 330,000 were union members and 100,000 union delegates, see Thomas Breda, *Les représentants du personnel en France*, Paris, Presses de Sciences Po, 2016. By comparison, the figures from UNISON, the second-largest British union, list 6,000 shop stewards. British unions also have a large number of union reps, but do not have (many) work council-type structures. As a result, there are far fewer union roles with facility time available in Great Britain than in France.

[6] The Social and Economic Committee (*Comité social et économique* – CSE) is now the only representative body for workers and is compulsory for all businesses with at least 11 employees. It was introduced by ruling n°2017-1386 of 22 December 2017, and the decree implementing it, known as *'Ordonnances Macron'*, is n° 2017-1819 of 29 December 2017. In businesses with between 11 and 49 employees the CSE replaces staff reps. In companies with more than 50 employees, it combines and replaces the works council, staff reps, and the health and safety committee (CHSCT).

[7] Agenda for Change is the name of the new national classification and pay system, negotiated by the unions and the central management of the NHS in 2004, applicable to all NHS workers except doctors.

[8] The Single Status Agreement was negotiated in 1997 to standardize pay and conditions for manual workers and white-collar officers. This national agreement gave rise to negotiations in each local authority.

[9] In 2016 at UNISON, women made up more than 60% of organizers, at level 1 in the union employment grade, in the regions.

[10] A number of roles within companies have been added to roles within the union. Roles within private companies: *délégué syndical* (shop steward), *délégué syndical central* (central shop steward), *délégué du personnel* (union rep), *élu du Comité Economique et Social* (work council member), *élu du Comité Economique et Social central* (Central work council member), *élu du Comité Economique et Social Européen* (European work council member), *élu du Comité Economique et Social de Groupe* (Group Work Coucil member), *élu du CHSCT* (Health and Safety Council rep). Equivalent positions exist in the public sector. Finally, there are union roles in external public institutions that deal with social security, retirement, housing, and unemployment issues. Many trade unionists also sit as labour court lay judges (*Prud'hommes*).

[11] Although the employment sector does have an impact on the feminization of members, including among union leaders, it is not in itself a sufficient explanation for the presence of women. Although it is likely that there are more women in leadership positions in employment sectors with more women workers (social work, health, teaching, services), these are also industries where atypical contracts are widespread, and therefore less conducive to union activism.

[12] Source: Central Executive Council Special Report. GMB Women's Project. Progress Report to Annual Congress, 2015.

[13] Source: CFDT Diversity Plan 2013 (our translation).

[14] 'Gender and unity in the labour movement', *The Guardian,* 16 September 2015.

[15] In 1998, UNISON introduced the *Women's Development Project* targeting the training and career development of women managers.

[16] *Diversity: the CFDT Action Plan* 'Mixité: le plan d'action de la CFDT. Mode d'emploi', *Syndicalisme Hebdo*, supplement to n°3395, 28 February 2013.

Chapter 4

[1] www.unionhistory.info/equalpay/ These online archives are the result of a partnership between the London Metropolitan University and the TUC, with the financial support of the EQUAL programme of the European Social Fund.

[2] This group was coordinated by Labour MPs, but included a public service union, NALGO, professional organizations (British Medical Association, London County Council Staff Association), and the Communist Party.

[3] Association promoting women's rights, created in 1866 to defend women's suffrage.

[4] International Marxist Group, the Revolutionary Socialist Student Federation, the Internationalist and the Communist Party.

[5] These groups were the following: The Status of Women Group, Fawcett Society, TUC Women's Congress, National Council of Labour Women, Child Poverty Action Group; cf Pugh (2000).

[6] National Joint Action Campaign Committee for Women's Equal Rights (NJACCWER), of which the secretary was Fred Blake, the Dagenham local union rep of the National Union of Vehicle Builders.

[7] It followed on from the laws on racial discrimination passed in the 1960s, with the Race Relations Act in 1965, amended in 1968 and 1976. This law was extended to include transsexual people in 1999 following a decision from the European Court of Justice, and then transformed into the Gender Recognition Act in 2004.

[8] This consisted in introducing the 1975 European directive on Equal pay (75/117/EEC) into European law.

[9] *Enderby v Frenchay Health Authority and Secretary of State for Health* (1993).

[10] *Marshall v. Southampton and South West Hampshire District Health Authority* (1993).

[11] *Magorrian and Cunningham v Eastern Health and Social Services Board and Department of Health and Social Services C-246/96; B.S. Levez.*

[12] *Preston and Others v Wolverhampton NHS Trust (2000).*

[13] *Birmingham City Council v Abdulla and others (2012, SC).*

[14] The TUC nevertheless revised its internal charter 'Twelve Aims of Women at Work' (TUC 1975), deleting the reference to abortion.

[15] Out of 68 full lawsuits on equal pay over the period 1980–82, only 17 concerned (exclusively female) 'pay schemes', and their success rate was half that of individual cases (36% compared to 18%); cf Leonard (1987). This strategy was recommended by a feminist expert, a militant at ASTMS, involved in a project on the implementation of equal pay, who said 'the issues of equal pay and opportunity need to be taken up and fought for in the workplace rather than before tribunals', cf Snell (1979).

[16] In the appointments of 'knowledgeable and expert' figures in the area, to the administrative council, the Labour government sought to balance the representation of unions, employers, and administrative bodies from different parties and regions, but they excluded feminist expert groups on this issue (Fawcett Society or NCCL, National Council for Civil Liberties).

[17] *Enderby vs Frenchay Health Authority and Secretary of State for Health* (1993).

[18] Some of the cases brought by declining unions, such as the NUM (National Union of Mineworkers), which sought to organize women by regrading their wages, would take years to accept even the principle of comparison with male jobs in separate establishments and would eventually be abandoned, due to privatization of the company and the statute of limitations, see *British Coal Corporation v Smith and others* (1996).

[19] *Hayward v Cammell Laird Ship Building* (1988).

[20] Extracts from this interview are available on the website: www.unionhistory.info/equalpay/index.php.

[21] The Greater London Council was directed by Ken Livingston, known as Red Ken. It was dismantled in 1986.

[22] *TUC Equal Value Manual.*

[23] In 1987 the House of Lords accepted that a shortage of manpower could be used as an argument justifying higher wages for doctors in hospitals; cf *Rainey v Greater Glasgow Health Board* (1987).

[24] Like in France, in Great Britain class actions are not authorized under labour law, but in order to respond to a growing number of similar claims, judges can decide to admit multiple claims and select a limited number of 'test cases'.

[25] *Ratcliffe v North Yorkshire County Council (1995).*

[26] *Wilson v North Cumbria NHS Trust (2005).*

[27] Cf Hull Fish Packers equal pay claim, *Equal Pay Archive.*

[28] The Single Status Agreement is a national classification agreement that was negotiated in 1995 in the local government sector, with a moratorium period awarded to local governments to implement it.

[29] *Joss v Cumbria County Council (2002).*

[30] *Home Office v Bailey and others (2005).*

[31] Articles were regularly published in the *Guardian* or the *Daily Mail* whenever a claim involving large amounts of compensation was won.

[32] Stefan Cross even attacked the GMB for not having sufficiently defended the interests of their members, cf *GMB v Mrs Allen and others* (2007).

[33] *GMB v Mrs Allen and others* (2007).

[34] However, in a subsequent case, *Nichols v Coventry City Council*, the EAT found that employers, and not trade unions, are liable for equal pay (Conley et al, 2019).

[35] This led to an 80% drop in the number of claims over just four months. Between October and December 2013, 9,801 claims were filed, compared to 45,710 for the same period in 2012. Antidiscrimination claims were particularly affected, with 1,222 sex discrimination claims between January and March 2014, compared to 6,017 for the same period in 2013.

[36] The Employment Tribunals (Early Conciliation Rules of Procedure, Schedule to the Employment Tribunals (Early Conciliation: Exemptions and Rules of Procedure) Regulations 2014, SI 2014/254.

[37] Since the Conservative victory in 2010, the situation at the EHRC seems even more uncertain, with redundancies in 2012 and dramatic budget cuts.

[38] This legal proceeding allows a judge to decide whether the decision or action by a public body is lawful. Decisions can be challenged on three main grounds: (1) illegality, the lawfulness of the decision in view of the law specifically regulating the field of activity of that body; (2) irrationality, and whether the decision was 'reasonable'; (3) irregularity, whether the decision was made in accordance with procedural rules (including proper consultation, for example) or natural justice. This procedure does not determine whether the decision was just in itself, but whether the decision-making process was lawful. The organization can therefore make the same decision, if the process that leads to it conforms to the legal norms in place, seems reasonable, or respects the forms of consultation required. In reality, the number of judicial reviews accepted by the Administrative Court is very low. In 2007, out of 6,692 claims received, only 955 were upheld by the judges. Only 425 were heard in court. The rate of withdrawals for claims is also low, however (13 out of 426 in 2007). For those that reach hearing, the success rate is also high (187 out of 425). See the report by the Ministry of Justice, 'Judicial Review Statistics, 2007–2011', available online.

References

Abbott, J. (1997) 'On the Concept of Turning Point', *Comparative Social Research*, 16: 85–105.

Abdelnour, S., Collovald, A., Mathieu, L., Péroumal, F. and Perrin, E. (2009) 'Précarité et luttes collectives: renouvellement, refus de la délégation ou décalages d'expériences militantes?', *Sociétés contemporaines*, 2(74): 73–95.

Acker, J. (1989) *Doing Comparable Worth. Gender, Class and Pay Equity*, Philadelphia: Temple University Press.

Acker, J. (2006) 'Inequality Regimes: Gender, Class and Race in Organizations', *Gender & Society*, 20(4): 441–464.

Acker, J. and Van Houten, D. (1974) 'Differential Recruitment and Control: The Sex Structuring of Organizations', *Administrative Science Quarterly*, 19(2): 152–163.

Agrikoliansky, E. (2002) *La Ligue française des droits de l'homme et du citoyen depuis 1945. Sociologie d'un engagement critique*, Paris: L'Harmattan.

Alter, K.J. and Vargas, J. (2000) 'Explaining Variation in the Use of European Litigation Strategies: European Community Law and the British Gender Equality Policy', *Comparative Political Studies*, 33(4): 452–482.

Ardura, A. and Silvera, R. (2001) 'L'égalité hommes/femmes: quelles stratégies syndicales?', *La revue de l'IRES*, 37(3): 1–25.

Arthurs, A. (1992) 'Equal Value in British Banking: The Midland Bank Case', in P. Kahn and E. Meehan (eds) *Equal value / Comparable Worth in the UK and the USA*, Basingstoke: Macmillan, pp 119–136.

Avril, C. (2014) *Les Aides à domicile: un autre monde Populaire*, Paris: La Dispute.

Auzias, C. and Houel, A. (1982) *La grève des avalistes. Lyon, juin-juillet 1869*, Paris: Payot.

Bacon, N. and Hoque, K. (2012) 'The Role and Impact of Trade Union Equality Representatives in Britain', *British Journal of Industrial Relations*, 50(2): 239–262.

Bairstow, S. (2007) '"There isn't Supposed to Be a Speaker Against!" Instigating Tensions of Safe Space and Intra-group Diversity for Trade Union Lesbian and Gay Organization', *Gender, Work and Organization*, 14(5): 393–408.

Banaszak, L.A. (2010) *The Women's Movement: Inside and Outside the State*, New York and Cambridge: Cambridge University Press.

Bard, C. (1993) 'L'apôtre sociale et l'ange du foyer: les femmes et la C.F.T.C. à travers "Le Nord-Social" (1920–1936)', *Le Mouvement social*, 165: 23–41.

Bargel, L. (2014) 'Apprendre un métier qui ne s'apprend pas. Carrières dans les organisations de jeunesse des partis', *Sociologie*, 5(2): 171–187.

Barley, S. (1989) 'Careers, Identities, and Institutions: The Legacy of the Chicago School of Sociology', in M. Arthur, D. Hall and B. Lawrence (eds) *Handbook of Career Theory*, Cambridge: Cambridge University Press, pp 41–65.

Barnard, C. (1995) 'A European Litigation Strategy: The Case of the Equal Opportunities Commission', in J. Shaw and G. More (eds) *New Legal Dynamics of European Union*, Oxford: Clarendon, pp 254–272.

Barthélémy, M., Dargent, C., Groux, G. and Rey, H. (2012) *Le réformisme assumé de la CFDT*, Paris: Presses de Sciences Po.

Beaujolin-Bellet, R. and Grima, F. (2011) 'Le talent des leaders syndicaux. Comment mener la résistance contre un plan social? Le cas du travail d'influence des leaders syndicaux', *Revue internationale de Pyschosociologie*, 17(41): 247–258.

Becker, H. (1966) *Outsiders*, New York: Glencoe Free Press.

Beirne, M. and Wilson F. (2016) 'Running with "wolves" or waiting for a happy release? Evaluating routes to gender equality', *Work, employment and society*, 30(2): 220–236.

Benquet, M. (2011) *Les damnées de la caisse. Enquête sur une grève dans un hypermarché*, Paris: Editions du Croquant.

Bereni, L. (2007) 'Du MLF au Mouvement pour la parité. La genèse d'une nouvelle cause dans l'espace de la cause des femmes', *Politix*, 78: 107–132.

Bereni, L. and Prud'homme, D. (2019) 'Servir l'entreprise ou la changer: Les responsables diversité entre gestion, critique et performance de la vertu', *Revue française de sociologie*, 60(2): 175–200.

Béroud, S. (2013) 'Une campagne de syndicalisation au féminin. Une expérience militante dans le secteur de l'aide à domicile', *Travail, genre et sociétés*, 30: 111–128.

Béroud, S., Denis, J-M., Desage, G. and Thibault, M. (2011) *L'Union Syndicale Solidaires: une organisation au miroir de ses militants*, Lyon: Laboratoire Triangle.

Berrey, E. (2015) *The Enigma of Diversity: The Language of Race and the Limits of Racial Justice*, Chicago: University of Chicago Press.

Bilge, S. and Roy, O. (2010) 'La discrimination intersectionnelle: la naissance et le développement d'un concept et les paradoxes de sa mise en application en droit antidiscriminatoire', *Canadian Journal of Law and Society*, 25(1): 51–74.

Blaschke, S. (2011) 'Determinants of Female Representation in the Decision-making Structures of Trade Unions', *Economic and Industrial Democracy*, 32(3): 421–438.

Blum, L. (1991) *Between Feminism and Labor. The Significance of the Comparable Worth Movement*, Berkeley: University of California Press.

Bondy, A. and Preminger, J. (2021) 'Collective Labor Relations and Juridification: A Marriage Proposal', *Economic and Industrial Democracy*, 1–21.

Borzeix, A. and Maruani, M. (1982) *Le temps des chemises. La grève qu'elles gardent au cœur*, Paris: Syros.

Boston, S. (2015) *Women Workers and the Trade Unions*, London: Lawrence and Wishart.

Boussard, V. (2016) 'Celles qui survivent: dispositions improbables des dirigeantes dans la finance', *Travail, genre et sociétés*, 35: 47–65.

Bradley, H. and Healy, G. (2008) *Ethnicity and Gender at Work: Inequalities, Careers and Employment Relations*, London and New York: Palgrave Macmillan.

Breda, T. (2016) *Les représentants du personnel en France*, Paris: Presses de Sciences Po.

Breitenbach, E., Brown, A., Mackay, F. and Webb, J. (eds) (2002) *The Changing Politics of Gender Equality in Britain*, Basingstoke: Palgrave.

Briskin, L. (1993) 'Union Women and Separate Organizing', in L. Briskin and P. MacDermott (eds) *Women Challenging Unions, Feminism, Democracy and Militancy*, Toronto: University of Toronto Press, pp 89–108.

Briskin, L. (2002) 'The Equity Project in Canadian Unions', in F. Colgan and S. Ledwith (eds) *Gender, Diversity and Trade Unions. International Perspectives*, London: Routledge, pp 28–47.

Briskin, L. (2006) 'Victimisation and Agency: The Social Construction of Union Women's Leadership', *Industrial Relations Journal*, 37(4): 359–379.

Briskin, L. (2008) 'Cross Constituency Organizing in Canadian Unions', *British Journal of Industrial Relations*, 46(2): 221–247.

Briskin, L. (2011) 'The Militancy of Nurses and Union Renewal', *Transfer: European Review of Labour and Research*, 17(4): 485–499.

Briskin, L. (2014) 'Strategies to Support Equality Bargaining inside Unions: Representational Democracy and Representational Justice', *Journal of Industrial Relations*, 56(2): 208–227.

Briskin L. and MacDermott P. (eds) (1993) *Women Challenging Unions, Feminism, Democracy and Militancy*, Toronto: University of Toronto Press.

Bruegel, I. and Kean, H. (1995) 'The Moment of Municipal Feminism: Gender and Class in 1980s Local Government', *Critical Social Policy*, 44/45: 147–169.

Buscatto, M. (2009) 'Syndicaliste en entreprise: une activité si masculine', in P. Roux and O. Fillieule (eds) *Le sexe du militantisme*, Paris: Presses de Sciences Po, pp 75–91.

Campbell, R., Childs, S. and Lovenduski, J. (2010) 'Do Women Need Women Representatives?', *British Journal of Political Science*, 40(1): 171–194.

Carter, A. (1988) *The Politics of Women's Rights*, London and New York: Longman.

Celis, K. (2008) 'Studying Women's Substantive Representation in Legislatures: When Representative Acts, Contexts and Women's Interests Become Important', *Representation*, 44(2): 111–123.

Celis, K., Childs, S., Kantola, J. and Krook, M-L. (2008) 'Rethinking Women's Substantive Representation', *Representation*, 44(2): 99–110.

Chabot, J. (2003) *Les débuts du syndicalisme féminin chrétien en France (1899–1944)*, Limoges: Presses universitaires de Limoges.

Chaignaud, F. (2009) *L'affaire Berger-Levrault: le féminisme à l'épreuve (1897–1905)*, Rennes: Presses universitaires de Rennes.

Chaney, P. (2012) 'Critical Actors vs Critical Mass: The Substantive Representation of Women in the Sottish Parliament', *The British Journal of Politics and International Relations*, 14: 441–457.

Chappe, V-A. (2019) *L'égalité au travail: Justice et mobilisations contre les discriminations*, Paris: Presses de Mines.

Chappe, V-A., Guillaume, C. and Pochic, S. (2016) 'Négocier sur les carrières syndicale pour lutter contre les discriminations: une appropriation sélective et minimaliste du droit', *Travail et Emploi*, 145: 121–146.

Chappe, V-A., Denis, J-M., Guillaume, C. and Pochic, S. (2019) *La fin des discriminations syndicales? Luttes judiciaires et pratiques négociées*, Paris: Editions du Croquant.

Charpenel, M., Demilly, H. and Pochic, S. (2017) 'Égalité négociée, égalité standardisée?', *Travail, genre et sociétés*, 37(1): 143–147.

Childs, S. (2004) *New Labour's Women MPs: Women Representing Women*, London: Routledge.

Childs, S. and Krook, M.L. (2009) 'Analyzing Women's Substantive Representation: From Critical Mass to Critical Actors', *Government and Opposition*, 44(2): 125–145.

Cobble, D.S. (1990) 'Rethinking Troubled Relations between Women and Unions: Craft Unionism and Female Activism', *Feminist Studies*, 16(3): 519–549.

Cockburn, C. (1983) *Brothers. Male Dominance and Technological Change*, London: Pluto Press.

Cockburn, C. (1989) 'Equal Opportunities: The Short and Long Agenda', *Industrial Relations Journal*, 20(4): 213–225.

Cockburn, C. (1991) *In the Way of Women: Men's Resistance to Sex Equality in Organizations*, London: ILR Press.

Cockburn, C. (1995) *Strategies for Gender Democracy*, Luxembourg: European Commission, working paper.

Cockburn, C. (1999) 'Les relations internationales ont un genre. Le dialogue social en Europe', *Travail, genre et sociétés*, 2: 111–137.

Cohen, S. (2013) *Notoriously Militant. The Story of a Union Branch*, London: Merlin Press.

Cohen, L.E., Broschak, J.P. and Haveman, H.A. (1998) 'And Then There Were More? The Effect of Organizational Sex Composition on the Hiring and Promotion of Managers', *American Sociological Review*, 63(5): 711–727.

Colgan, F. (1999) 'Recognizing the Lesbian and Gay Constituency in UK Trade Unions: Moving forward in UNISON?', *Industrial Relations Journal*, 30(5): 444–463.

Colgan, F. and Ledwith, S. (1996) 'Sisters Organizing – Women and Their Trade Unions', in S. Ledwith and F. Colgan (eds) *Women in Organizations*, Basingstoke: Macmillan, pp 152–185.

Colgan, F. and Ledwith, S. (2000) 'Diversity, Identities and Strategies of Women Trade Union Activists', *Gender Work and Organization*, 7(4): 242–257.

Colgan, F. and Ledwith, S. (2002) *Gender, Diversity and Trade Unions, International Perspectives*, London: Routledge.

Colling, T. (2004) 'No Claim, No Pain? The Privatization of Dispute Resolution in Britain', *Economic and Industrial Democracy*, 25(4): 555–579.

Colling, T. (2006) 'What Space for Unions on the Floor of Rights? Trade Unions and the Enforcement of Statutory Individual Employment Rights', *Industrial Law Journal*, 35(2): 140–160.

Colling, T. (2012) 'Trade Union Roles in Making Employment Rights Effective', in L. Dickens (ed) *Making Employment Rights Effective: Issues of Enforcement and Compliance*, London: Hart Publishing, pp 183–204.

Colling, T. and Dickens, L. (1998) 'Selling the Case for Gender Equality: Deregulation and Equality Bargaining', *British Journal of Industrial Relations*, 36(3): 389–411.

Collovald, A. and Mathieu, L. (2009) 'Mobilisations improbables et apprentissage d'un répertoire synodical', *Politix*, 86: 119–143.

Conley, H. (2012) 'Using Equality to Challenge Austerity: New Actors, Old Problems', *Work, Employment and Society*, 26(2): 349–359.

Conley, H. (2014) 'Trade Unions, Equal Pay and the Law in the UK', *Economic and Industrial Democracy*, 35(2): 309–323.

Conley, H. and Page, M. (2015) *Gender Equality in Public Services. Chasing the dream*, New York: Routledge.

Conley, H., Gottardi, D., Healy, G. and Mickolajczyk, B. (2019) *The Gender Pay Gap and Social Partnership in Europe: Findings from 'Close the Deal, Fill the Gap'*, Abingdon: Routledge.

Contrepois, S. (2006) 'France: un accès encore inégal et partiel aux différentes sphères de la représentation syndicale', *Recherches Féministes*, 19(1): 25–45.

Cooper, R. (2012) 'The Gender Gap in Union Leadership in Australia: A Qualitative Study', *Journal of Industrial Relations*, 54(2): 131–146.

Cristofalo, P. (2014) 'Négocier l'égalité professionnelle: de quelques obstacles à la prise en charge syndicale de la thématique', *Nouvelle revue de psychologie*, 18: 133–146.

Crompton, R. (2001) 'Gender, Comparative Research and Biographical Matching', *European Societies*, 3(2): 167–190.

Cunningham, I. and James, P. (2010) 'Strategies for Union Renewal in the Context of Public Sector Outsourcing', *Economic and Industrial Democracy*, 31(1): 34–61.

Cunnison, S. (1988) 'Equal Pay: A UK First for Hull Women', Occasion paper 1, Hull Centre for Gender Studies.

Cunnison, S. and Stageman, J. (1995) *Feminising the Unions. Challenging the Culture of Masculinity*, Aldershot: Avebury.

Darmon, M. (2008) 'The Concept of Career: An Interactionist Instrument of Objectivation', *Politix*, 82(2): 149–167.

Dawson, P. (2014) 'Collective Bargaining and the Gender Pay Gap in the Printing Industry', *Gender, Work and Organization*, 21(5): 381–394.

Deakin, S., McLaughlin, C. and Chai, D. (2012) 'Gender Inequality and Reflexive Law: The Potential of Different Regulatory Mechanisms', in L. Dickens (ed) *Making Employment Rights Effective. Issues of Enforcement and Compliance*, Oxford: Hart Publishing, pp 115–138.

Deakin, S., Fraser Butlin, S., McLaughlin, C. and Polanska, A. (2015) 'Are Litigation and Collective Bargaining Complements or Substitutes for Achieving Gender Equality? A Study of the British Equal Pay Act', *Cambridge Journal of Economics*, 39(2): 381–404.

Dean, D. (2015) 'Deviant Typicality: Gender Equality Issues in a Trade Union that Should Be Different', *Industrial Relations Journal*, 46(1): 37–53.

Dean, D. and Greene, A. (2017) 'How Do We Understand Worker Silence Despite Poor Conditions – as the Actress Said to the Woman Bishop', *Human Relations*, 70(10): 1237–1257.

Dean, M. and Perrett, R. (2020) 'Overcoming Barriers to Women's Workplace Leadership: Insights from the Interaction of Formal and Informal Support Mechanisms in Trade Unions', *Industrial Relations Journal*, 51(3): 169–184.

Defaud, N. (2009) *La CFDT (1968–1995). De l'autogestion au syndicalisme de proposition*, Paris: Presses de Sciences Po.

Demazière, D. and Dubar, C. (1997) *Analyser les entretiens biographiques. L'exemple des récits d'insertion*, Laval: Presses Universitaires de Laval.

Demazière, D., Giraud, O. and Lallement, M. (2013) 'Comparer. Options et inflexions d'une pratique de recherche', *Sociologie du travail*, 55(2): 136–151.

Denis, J-M. (2001) *Le groupe des Dix: un modèle syndical alternatif?*, Paris: La Documentation Française.

Denis, J-M. and Thibault, M. (2015) 'Des organisations syndicales en quête de renouvellement. Trajectoires militantes et expériences syndicales de jeunes militants de l'Union Syndicale Solidaires', *Nouvelle revue de psychosociologie*, 2(18): 117–131.

Dickens, L. (1989) 'Women – a Rediscovered Resource?', *Industrial Relations Journal*, 20(3): 167–175.

Dickens, L. (1997) 'Gender, Race and Employment Equality in Britain: Inadequate Strategies and the Role of Industrial Relations Actors', *Industrial Relations Journal*, 28(4): 282–291.

Dickens, L. (2000a) 'Collective Bargaining and the Promotion of Gender Equality at Work: Opportunities and Challenges for Trade Unions', *Transfer: European Review of Labour and Research*, 6(2): 193–208.

Dickens, L. (2000b) 'Promoting Gender Equality at Work – A Potential Role for Trade Union Action', *Journal of Interdisciplinary Gender Studies*, 5(2): 27–45.

Dickens, L. (2007) 'The Road is Long: Thirty Years of Equality Legislation in Britain', *British Journal of Industrial Relations*, 45(3): 463–494.

Dickens, L. (2012) *Making Employment Rights Effective: Issues of Enforcement and Compliance*, Oxford: Hart Publishing.

Dickens, L. and Hall, M. (2006) 'Fairness – up to a Point: Assessing the Impact of New Labour's Employment Legislation', *Human Resource Management Journal*, 16: 338–356.

Dickens, L., Townley, B. and Winchester, D. (1988) *Tackling Sex Discrimination through Collective Bargaining. The Impact of Section 6 of the Sex Discrimination Act 1986*, Manchester: EOC Research Series.

Doeringer, P. and Piore, M. (1971) *Internal Labor Markets and Manpower Analysis*, D.C. Heath: Lexington.

Dorgan, T. and Grieco, M. (1993) 'Battling against the Odds: The Emergence of Senior Women Trade Unionists', *Industrial Relations Journal*, 24(2): 151–164.

Dovi, S. (2007) 'Theorizing Women's Representation in the United States', *Politics and Gender*, 3(3): 297–319.

Downs, L.L. (2002) *L'inégalité à la chaîne. La division sexuée du travail dans l'industrie métallurgique en France et en Angleterre*, Paris: Albin Michel.

Dulong, D. and Lévêque, S. (2002) 'Une ressource contingente. Les conditions de reconversion du genre en ressource politique', *Politix*, 60: 81–111.

Dunezat, X. (2005) 'Syndicalisme et domination masculine en France: parcours bibliographique féministe. *Recherches Féministes*, 19(1): 69–96.

Dutoya, V. and Hayat, S. (2016) 'Prétendre représenter. La construction sociale de la représentation politique', *Revue française de science politique*, 66(1): 7–25.

Edelman, L. (1992) 'Legal Ambiguity and Symbolic Structures: Organizational Mediation of Civil Rights Law', *American Journal of Sociology*, 97(6): 1531–1576.

Edelman, L. (2016) *Working Law. Courts, Corporations, and Symbolic Civil Rights*, Chicago: University of Chicago Press.

Escott, K. and Whitfield, D. (1995) *The Gender Impact of Compulsive Competitive Tendering in Local Government*, Manchester: EOC Research Series.

Fairbrother, P. and Yates, C. (2003) *Trade Unions in Renewal: A Comparative Study*, London: Continuum.

Fillieule, O. (2010) 'Some Elements of an Interactionist Approach to Political Disengagement', *Social Movement Studies*, 9(1): 1–15.

Fillieule, O. and Mayer, N. (2001) 'Devenirs Militants', *Revue française de science politique*, 51(1): 19–25.

Fillieule, O., Monney, V. and Rayner, H. (2019) *Le métier et la vocation de syndicaliste*, Lausanne: Editions Antipodes.

Forbes, I. (1997) 'The Privatization of Equality Policy in the British Employment Market for Women', in F. Gardiner (ed), *Sex Equality Policy in Western Europe*, London: Routledge, pp 161–179.

Foster, D. and Scott, P. (1997) 'Conceptualising Union Responses to Contracting out Municipal Services, 1979–97', *Industrial Relations Journal*, 29(2): 137–150.

Frader, L. (1996) 'Femmes, genre et mouvement ouvrier en France au XIXe et XXe siècle: bilan et perspectives de recherche', *Clio. Femmes, Genre, Histoire*, 3, available from https://doi.org/10.4000/clio.472

Franzway, S. (2000) 'Women Working in a Greedy Institution: Commitment and Emotional Labour in the Union Movement', *Gender, Work and Organization*, 7(4): 258–268.

Fredman, S. (2008) 'Reforming Equal Pay Laws', *Industrial Law Journal*, 37(3): 193–218.

Frege, C. and Kelly, J. (2003) 'Union Revitalization Strategies in Comparative Perspective', *European Journal of Industrial Relations*, 9(1): 7–24.

Fudge, J. and Mcdermott, P. (1991) *Just wages. A Feminist Assessment of Pay Equity*, Toronto: University of Toronto Press.

Gallot, F. (2015) *En découdre. Comment les ouvrières ont révolutionné le travail et la société*, Paris: La Découverte.

Gallot, F. and Meuret-Campfort, E. (2015) 'Des ouvrières en lutte dans l'après 1968. Rapports au féminisme et subversions de genre', *Politix*, 109: 21–43.

Galt, F. (2021) *Women's Activism behind the Screens. Trade Unions and Gender Inequality in the British Film and Television Industries*, Bristol: Bristol University Press.

Gavin, M., McGrath-Champ, S., Stacey, M. and Wilson, R. (2020) 'Women's Participation in Teacher Unions: Implications of a "Triple Burden" for Union Gender Equality Strategies', *Economic and Industrial Democracy*, 1–23.

George, J. (2011) *Les féministes de la CGT. Histoire du magazine Antoinette (1955–1989)*, Paris: Éditions Delga.

Gilbert, K. (2012) 'Promises and Practices: Job Evaluation and Equal Pay Forty Years On!', *Industrial Relations Journal*, 43(2): 137–151.

Gilbert, K. and Secker, J. (1995) 'Generating Equality? Equal Pay, Decentralization and the Electricity Supply Industry', *British Journal of Industrial Relations*, 33: 190–207.

Giraud, B. (2017) '"Quand on va au juridique, c'est qu'on a perdu". Le droit comme contrainte dans les mobilisations syndicales', *Politix*, 2(118): 131–155.

Glucksmann, M. (1982) *Women on the Line*, New York: Routledge.

Glucksmann, M. (1986) 'In a Class of Their Own? Women Workers in the New Industries in Inter-war Britain', *Feminist Review*, 24: 7–37.

Goffman, E. (1963) *Stigma: Notes on the Management of Spoiled Identity*, New York: Penguin.

Gregory, J. (1987) *Sex, Race and the Law. Legislating for Equality*, London: Sage.

Gregory, J. (1996) 'Dynamite or Damp Squib? An Assessment of Equal Value Law', *International Journal of Discrimination and the Law*, 1: 313–333.

Greene, A-M. and Robbins, M. (2015) 'The Cost of a Calling? Clergywomen and Work in the Church of England', *Gender, Work and Organization*, 22(4): 405–420.

Guilbert, M. (1966) *Les femmes et l'organisation syndicale avant 1914*, Paris: CNRS.

Guillaume, C. (2007) 'Le syndicalisme à l'épreuve de la féminisation: la permanence paradoxale du "plafond de verre" à la CFDT', *Politix*, 78: 39–63.

Guillaume, C. (2011) 'La formation des responsables à la CDFT: de la "promotion collective" à la sécurisation des parcours militants', *Le Mouvement Social*, April–June: 105–119.

Guillaume, C. (2013) 'La mobilisation des syndicats anglais pour l'égalité salariale', *Travail, genre et sociétés*, 30(2): 93–110.

Guillaume, C. (2014a) (ed) *La CFDT, sociologie d'une conversion réformiste*, Rennes: Presses Universitaires de Rennes.

Guillaume, C. (2014b) 'Devenir permanent-e syndical-e: une carrière déviante?', in C. Guillaume (ed) *La CFDT, sociologie d'une conversion réformiste*, Rennes: Presses Universitaires de Rennes, pp 133–150.

Guillaume, C. (2015a) 'Understanding the Variations of Unions' Litigation Strategies to Promote Equal Pay. Reflection on the British Case (1970–2000)', *Cambridge Journal of Economics*, 39(2): 363–379.

Guillaume, C. (2015b) 'Les syndicats britanniques et le recours au contentieux juridique', *Nouvelle Revue du Travail*, 7: 25–37.

Guillaume, C. (2018a) 'Women's Participation in a Radical Trade Union Movement that Claims to Be Feminist', *British Journal of Industrial Relations*, 56(3): 556–578.

Guillaume, C. (2018b) 'When Trade Unions Turn to Litigation: Getting All the Ducks in a Row', *Industrial Relation Journal*, 49(3): 227–241.

Guillaume, C. (2020) 'Legal Expertise: A Critical Resource for Trade Unionists? Insights into the Confédération Française Démocratique du Travail', *Industrial Law Journal*, published online, 31 October 2020.

Guillaume, C. and Gayral, C. (2011) *La fabrication des carrières syndicales. Enquête auprès des cadres 'intermédiaires' de la CFDT*, Paris: Rapport de recherche, IRES.

Guillaume, C. and Pochic, S. (2007) 'La fabrication organisationnelle des managers: un regard sur le plafond de verre', *Travail, genre et sociétés*, 17: 79–103.

Guillaume, C. and Pochic, S. (2009a) 'La professionnalisation de l'activité syndicale: talon d'Achille de la politique de syndicalisation à la CFDT?', *Politix*, 85: 31–56.

Guillaume, C. and Pochic, S. (2009b) 'Un engagement incongru? Les cadres et le syndicalisme, l'exemple de la CFDT', *Revue française de science politique*, 59(5): 535–568.

Guillaume, C. and Pochic, S. (2009c) 'Quand les politiques volontaristes de mixité ne suffisent pas: les leçons du syndicalisme anglaise', *Cahiers du genre*, 47: 145–168.

Guillaume, C. and Pochic, S. (2011) 'The Organizational Nature of Union Careers: The Touchstone of Equality Policies? Comparing France and the UK', *European Societies*, 13(4): 607–631.

Guillaume, C. and Pochic, S. (2013) 'Breaking through the Union Glass Ceiling in France: Between Organizational Opportunities and Individual Resources', in S. Ledwith and L.L. Hansen (eds) *Gendering and Diversifying Trade Union Leadership: International Perspectives*, London: Routledge, pp 245–264.

Guillaume, C. and Pochic, S. (2014) 'Les succès inégaux d'une politique confédérale de syndicalisation', in C. Guillaume (ed) *La CFDT, sociologie d'une conversion réformiste*, Rennes: Presses Universitaires de Rennes, pp 69–90.

Guillaume, C. and Pochic, S. (2021) 'Understanding the Underrepresentation of Women in Union Leadership Roles: The Contribution of a "Career" Methodology', in C. Elliott, S. Mavin and V. Stead, *Handbook on Research Methods in Gender and Management*, London: Edward Elgar, pp 249–265.

Guillaume, C., Pochic, S. and Chappe, V-A. (2016) 'The Promises and Pitfalls of Collective Bargaining for Ending Union Victimization. Lessons from France', *Economic and Industrial Democracy*, https://doi.org/10.1177/0143831X16639657

Guillaume, C., Pochic, S. and Silvera, R. (2015) 'Dans les syndicats: du volontarisme à la contrainte légale', *Travail, genre et sociétés*, 34: 193–198.

Halford, S. and Leonard, P. (2000) *Gender, Power and Organizations: An Introduction*, New York: Palgrave Macmillan.

Hall, P.A. and Soskice, D. (eds) (2001) *Varieties of Capitalism. The Institutional Foundations of Comparative Advantage*, Oxford: Oxford University Press.

Haller, Z. (2017) 'Genre et investissement syndical chez les enseignants', *La nouvelle revue du travail*, 10, https://doi.org/10.4000/nrt.3062.

Hallock, M. (2000) 'Pay Equity: What Is the Best Union Strategy?' *Labor Studies Journal*, 25: 27–44.

Hart, S.M. (2002) 'The Pay Equity Bargaining Process in Newfoundland: Understanding Cooperation and Conflict by Incorporating Gender and Class', *Gender, Work and Organization*, 9(4): 355–371.

Healy, G. and Kirton, G. (2000) 'Women, Power and Trade Union Government in the UK', *British Journal of Industrial Relations*, 38(3): 343–360.

Healy, G. and Kirton, G. (2013) 'The Early Mobilization of Women Union Leaders – A Comparative Perspective', *British Journal of Industrial Relations*, 51(4): 709–732.

Healy, G., Bradley, H. and Forson, C. (2011) 'Intersectional Sensibilities in Analyzing Inequality Regimes in Public Sector Organizations', *Gender, Work and Organization*, 18(5): 467–487.

Heery, E. (2006a) 'Equality Bargaining: Where, Who, Why?', *Gender, Work and Organization*, 13(6): 522–542.

Heery, E. (2006b) 'Union Workers, Union Work: A Profile of Paid Union Officers in the United Kingdom', *British Journal of Industrial Relations*, 44(3): 445–471.

Heery, E. and Kelly, J. (1989) 'A Cracking Job for a Woman – a Profile of Women Trade Union Officers', *Industrial Relations Journal*, 20(3): 192–202.

Heery, E., Simms, M., Delbridge, R. and Salmon, J. (2000) 'Organizing Unionism Comes to the UK', *Employee Relations*, 22(1): 58–75.

Hege, A., Dufour, C. and Nunes, C. (2001) 'Les femmes secrétaires de comités d'entreprise, une parité trompeuse?', DARES, *Premières Synthèses*, 15, available from: https://travail-emploi.gouv.fr/IMG/pdf/publication_pips_200104_n-15-2_femmes-secretaires-comite-dentreprise.pdf

Howell, C. (1996) 'Women as the Paradigmatic Trade Unionist? New Work, New Workers and New Trade Union Strategies in Conservative Britain', *Economic and Industrial Democracy*, 17: 511–543.

Huffman, M., Cohen, P. and Pearlman, J. (2010) 'Engendering Change Organizational Dynamics and Workplace Gender Desegregation, 1975–2005', *Administrative Science Quarterly*, 55(2): 255–278.

Humphrey, J. (1998) 'Self-organize and Survive: Disabled People in the British Trade Union Movement', *Disability and Society*, 13(4): 587–602.

Humphrey, J. (2000) 'Self-organization and Trade Union Democracy', *The Sociological Review*, 48(2): 262–282.

Hunt, A. (1990) 'Rights and Social Movements: Counter-Hegemonic Strategies', *Journal of Law and Society*, 17(3): 309–328.

Hunt, G. and Rayside, D. (eds) (2007) *Equity, Diversity and Canadian Labour*, Toronto: University of Toronto Press.

Hyman, R. (2001) 'Trade Union Research and Cross-National Comparison', *European Journal of Industrial Relations*, 7(2): 203–232.

Jacquemart, A. (2012) 'Du registre humaniste au registre identitaire. La recomposition du militantisme féministe masculin dans les années 1970', *Sociétés contemporaines*, 85: 65–83.

Jacquemart, A., Le Mancq, F. and Pochic, S. (2016) 'Femmes hautes fonctionnaires en France, l'avènement d'une égalité élitiste', *Travail, genre et sociétés*, 35: 27–45.

Jaunait, A. and Chauvin, S. (2012) 'Représenter l'intersection. Les théories de l'intersectionnalité à l'épreuve des sciences sociales', *Revue française de science politique*, 62(1): 5–20.

Jewson, N. and Mason, D. (1986) 'The Theory and Practice of Equal Opportunities Policies: Liberal and Radical Apporaches', *Sociological Review*, 34(2): 307–334.

Kaminski, M. and Yakura, E. (2008) 'Women's Union Leadership: Closing the Gender Gap', *The Journal of Labor and Society*, 11(4): 449–475.

Kanter, M.R. (1977) *Men and Women in the Corporation*, New York: Basic Books.

Katzenstein, M. (2012) 'Quand la contestation se déploie dans les institutions', *Sociétés contemporaines*, 85: 111–131.

Kelly, J. (1998) *Rethinking Industrial Relations: Mobilization, Collectivism and Long Waves*, London: Routledge.

Kelly, J. and Heery, E. (1994) *Working for the Union: British Trade Union Officers*, Cambridge: Cambridge University Press.

Kergoat, D. (1982) *Les ouvrières*, Paris: Le Sycomore.

Kergoat, D., Imbert, F., Le Doaré, H. and Senotier, D. (1992) *Les infirmières et leur coordination, 1988–1989*, Paris: Editions Lamarre.

Khan, P. and Figart, D.M. (1997) *Contesting the Market: Pay Equity and the Politics of Economics Restructuring*, Detroit: Wayne State University Press.

Kilpatrick, C. (1997) 'Effective Utilization of Equality Rights: Equal Pay for Work of Equal Value in France and the UK', in Frances Gardiner (ed), *Sex Equality Policy in Western Europe*, New York: Routledge, pp 25–45.

Kirk, E. (2020) 'Contesting "Bogus Self-Employment" via Legal Mobilisation: The Case of Foster Care Workers', *Capital and Class*, first published 17 February 2020.

Kirsch, A. and Blaschke, S. (2014) 'Women's Quotas and Their Effects: A Comparison of Austrian and German Trade Unions', *European Journal of Industrial Relations*, 20(3): 201–217.

Kirton, G. (1999) 'Sustaining and Developing Women's Trade Union Activism: A Gendered Project?', *Gender Work and Organisation*, 6: 213–223.

Kirton, G. (2006a) *The Making of Women Trade Unionists*, Aldershot: Ashgate.

Kirton, G. (2006b) 'Alternative or Parallel Careers for Women: The Case of Trade Union Participation', *Work, Employment and Society*, 20(1): 47–66.

Kirton, G. (2015) 'Progress towards Gender Democracy in UK Unions 1987–2012', *British Journal of Industrial Relations*, 53(3): 484–507.

Kirton, G. (2017) 'From "a Woman's Place is in Her Union" to "Strong Unions Need Women": Changing Gender Discourses, Policies and Realities in the Union Movement', *Labour and Industry: A Journal of the Social and Economic Relations of Work*, 27(4): 270–283.

Kirton, G. (2018) 'Anatomy of Women's Participation in Small Professional Unions', *Economic and Industrial Democracy*, 39(1): 151–172.

Kirton, G. (2019) 'Unions and Equality: 50 Years on from the Fight for Fair Pay at Dagenham', *Employee Relations*, 41(2): 344–356.

Kirton, G. and Greene, A.M (2002) 'The Dynamics of Positive Action in UK Trade Unions: The Case of Women and Black Members', *Industrial Relations Journal*, 33(2): 157–172.

Kirton, G. and Greene, A.M. (2019) 'Telling and Selling the Value of Diversity and Inclusion – External Consultants' Discursive Strategies and Practices', *Human Resource Management Journal*, 29(4): 676–691.

Kirton, G. and Healy, G. (2008) *Women and Trade Union Leadership. Key Theoretical Concepts form UK-Based Literature*, Centre for Research in Equality and Diversity, working paper.

Kirton, G. and Healy, G. (2012) '"Lift as You Rise": Union Women's Leadership Talk', *Human Relations*, 65(8): 979–999.

Kirton, G. and Healy, G. (2013a) *Gender and Leadership in Unions*, New York: Routledge.

Kirton, G. and Healy, G. (2013b) 'Commitment and Collective Identity of Long-term Union Participation: The Case of Women Union Leaders in the UK and the USA', *Work, Employment and Society*, 27(2): 195–212.

Klandersman, B. (2004) 'The Demand and Supply of Participation: Social-psychological Correlates of Participation in Social Movements', in D.A. Snow, S.A. Soule and H. Kriesi (eds) *The Blackwell Companion to Social Movements*, Oxford: Blackwell Publishing, pp 360–379.

Kopel, S. (2005) 'Les surdiplômés de la fonction publique', *Revue française de gestion*, 31(156): 17–34.

Krook, M.L. and Mackay, F. (eds) (2015) *Gender, Politics and Institutions. Toward a Feminist Institutionalism*, New York and London: Palgrave Macmillan.

Latté, S. (2002) 'Cuisine et dépendance. Les logiques pratiques du recrutement politique', *Politix*, 60: 55–80.

Laufer, J. (1982) *La féminité neutralisée? Les femmes cadres dans l'entreprise*, Paris: Flammarion.

Lawrence, E. (1994) *Gender and Trade Unions*, London: Taylor and Francis.

Le Brouster, P. (2006) 'La CFDT et les associations féministes de 1970 à nos jours', in D. Tartakowsky and F. Tétard (eds) *Syndicats et associations: concurrence ou complémentarité?*, Rennes: Presses Universitaires de Rennes, pp 409–418.

Le Brouster, P. (2009) 'Le débat sur la mixité des structures au sein de la CFDT (1976–1982)', *Sens Public*, 5: 3–12.

Le Brouster, P. (2011) 'Une syndicaliste-féministe: le parcours de Jeannette Laot à la CFDT, 1961–1981', in C. Bard (ed) *Les féministes d'une vague à l'autre*, Rennes: Presses Universitaires de Rennes, pp 109–120.

Le Brouster, P. (2014) 'Quelle stratégie syndicale pour les femmes? Regard sur l'histoire de la CFDT de 1960 à nos jours', in C. Guillaume (ed) *La CFDT, sociologie d'une conversion réformiste*, Rennes: Presses Universitaires de Rennes, pp 53–68.

Ledwith, S. (2009) 'Vive la différence? Women and Trade Unions in Britain', *Revue Française de Civilisation Britannique*, XV(2): 87–112.

Ledwith, S. (2012) 'Outside, Inside: Gender Work in Industrial Relations', *Equality, Diversity and Inclusion: An International Journal*, 31(4): 340–358.

Ledwith, S. and Hansen, L.L. (eds) (2013) *Gendering and Diversifying Trade Union Leadership. International Perspectives*, London: Routledge.

Ledwith, S. and Munakamwe, J. (2015) 'Gender, Union Leadership and Collective Bargaining: Brazil and South Africa, *The Economic and Labour Relations Review*, 26(3): 411–429.

Ledwith, S., Colgan, F., Joyce, P. and Hayes, M. (1990) 'The Making of Women Trade Union Leaders', *Industrial Relations Journal*, 21(2): 112–125.

Lehoucq, E. and Taylor, W.K. (2020) 'Conceptualizing Legal Mobilization: How Should We Understand the Deployment of Legal Strategies?' *Law and Social Inquiry*, 45(1): 166–193.

Lejeune, A. and Orianne, J-F. (2014) 'Choisir des cas exemplaires. La *Strategic litigation* face aux discriminations', *Déviance et Société*, 38(1): 55–76.

Lejeune, A. and Yazdanpanah, H. (2017) 'Face au handicap: action syndicale et cadrages juridiques', *Politix*, 30(118): 55–7.

Lenzi, C. (2009) 'L'injonction à l'autonomie comme mode de sélection sociale des militants des SEL', in S. Nicourd (ed) *Le travail militant*, Rennes: Presses universitaires de Rennes, pp 95–106.

Leonard, A. (1987) *Judging Inequality: The Effectiveness of the Industrial Tribunals System in Sex Discrimination and Equal Pay Cases*, London: Cobben Trust.

Le Quentrec, Y. (2013) 'Militer dans un syndicat féminisé: la sororité comme ressource', *Travail, genre et sociétés*, 30: 53–72.

Le Quentrec, Y. (2014) 'Luttes revendicatives, syndicalisme et rapports sociaux de sexe: réflexion sur les conditions de possibilité du travail d'émancipation des femmes salariées', *Cahiers du Genre*, 2(57): 159–181.

Le Quentrec, Y. and Rieu, A. (2003) '*Femmes: engagements publics et vie privée*', Paris: Editions Syllepse.

Leroy, Y. (2011) 'La notion d'effectivité du droit', *Droit et Société*, 3(79): 715–732.

Lescurieux, M. (2019) 'La représentation syndicale des femmes, de l'adhésion à la prise de responsabilités: une inclusion socialement sélective', *La Revue de l'Ires*, 98: 59–82.

Loach, L. (1987) 'Campaigning for change', in H. Baehr and G. Dyer (eds) *Boxed in: Women and Television*, Mondon: Pandora, pp 55–69.

Loiseau, D. (1996) *Femmes et militantismes*, Paris: L'Harmattan.

Louis, J. (2019) 'La Confédération européenne des syndicats à l'épreuve du droit et de la justice: genèse, usages et limites d'un mode d'action syndicale en faveur de l'Europe sociale', PhD dissertation, Université de Strasbourg.

Lovenduski, J. (1997) *Feminizing Politics*, Cambridge: Polity Press.

Lovenduski, J. and Norris, P. (1993) *Gender and Party Politics*, London: Sage.

Lovenduski, J. and Norris, P. (1996) *Women in Politics*, Oxford: Oxford University Press.

Lovenduski, J. and Norris, P. (2003) 'Westminster Women: The Politics of Presence', *Political Studies*, 51: 84–102.

Mackay, F. (2010) 'Gendering Constitutional Change and Policy Outcomes: Substantive Representation and Domestic Violence Policy in Scotland', *Policy and Politics*, 38(3): 369–388.

Maruani, M. (1979) *Les syndicats à l'épreuve du féminisme*, Paris: Syros.

Mazur, A. (2003) 'Drawing Comparative Lessons from France and Germany', *The Review of Policy Research*, 20(3): 495–523.

McAdam, D. (1986) 'Recruitment to High-risk Activism: The Case of Freedom Summer', *American Journal of Sociology*, 92(1): 64–90.

McBride, A. (2001) *Gender Democracy in Trade Unions*, London: Routledge.

McBride, A. and Waddington, J. (2009) 'The Representation of Women and the Trade Union Merger Process', in J.R. Foley and P.L. Baker (eds) *Unions, Equity and the Path to Renewal*, Vancouver: UBC Press, pp 192–218.

McBride, A., Hebson, G. and Holgate, J. (2015) 'Intersectionality: Are We Taking Enough Notice in the Field of Work and Employment Relations?', *Work, Employment and Society*, 29(2): 331–341.

McCann, M. (1994) *Rights at Work: Pay Equity Reform and the Politics of Legal Mobilization*, Chicago: University of Chicago Press.

McCann, M. with Lowell, G. (2020) *Union by Law. Filipino American Labor Activists, Rights Radicalism, and Racial Capitalism*, Chicago: University of Chicago Press.

Meehan, E.M. (1985) *Women's Rights at Work. Campaigns and Policy in Britain and the US*, New York: Saint Martin's Press.

Melville, D. (1959) *Men Who Manage. Fusions of Feeling and Theory in Administration*, New York: John Wiley & Sons.

Meuret-Campfort, E. (2010) 'Luttes de classes, conflits de genre: les ouvrières de Chantelle à Nantes', *Savoir/Agir*, 12: 43–58.

Milkman, R. (1990) 'Gender and Trade Unionism in Historical Perspective', in L.A. Tilly and P. Gurin (eds) *Women, Politics, and Change*, New York: The Russel Sage Foundation, pp 87–107.

Milkman, R. (2007) 'Two Worlds of Unionism: Women and the New Labor Movement', in D.S. Cobble (ed) *The Sex of Class. Women Transforming American Labor*, Cornell: Cornell University Press, pp 63–80.

Milkman, R. (2016) *On Gender, Labor, and Inequality*, Chicago: University of Illinois Press.

Milkman, R. and Voss, K. (eds) (2004) *Rebuilding Labor. Organizing and Organizers*, Cornell: Cornell University Press.

Milner, S. and Gregory, A. (2014) 'Gender Equality Bargaining in France and the UK: An Uphill Struggle?', *Journal of Industrial Relations*, 56(2): 246–263.

Milner, S., Demilly, H. and Pochic, S. (2019) 'Bargained Equality: The Strengths and Weaknesses of Workplace Gender Equality Agreements and Plans in France', *British Journal of Industrial Relations*, 57(2): 275–301.

Mischi, J. (2016) *Le bourg et l'atelier. Sociologie du combat synodical*, Marseille: Agone.

Monaghan, K. (2020) *Investigation into Sexual Harassment and the Management of Sexual Harassment Complaints within the GMB*, Independent report.

Monney, V. (2020) 'Lutter pour l'égalité. La féminisation des syndicats en Suisse: entre avancée de la cause des femmes et maintien des inégalités', PhD Dissertation: Université de Lausanne.

Monney, V., Fillieule, O. and Avanza, M. (2013) 'Les souffrances de la femme-quota. Le cas du syndicat suisse Unia', *Travail, genre et sociétés*, 30: 33–51.

Moore, S. (2011) *New trade Union Activists – Class Consciousness or Social Identity?*, Basingstoke: Palgrave Macmillan.

Moreau, M.P. (2014) 'Usages et conceptions des organisations syndicales chez les enseignants du second degré: Une comparaison France-Angleterre', *Sociologie du Travail*, 56(4): 493–512.

Munro, A. (1999) *Women, Work and Trade Unions*, Aldershot: Ashgate.

Norris, P. (1986) 'Conservative Attitudes in Recent British Elections: An Emerging Gap?', *Political Studies*, 34: 120–128.

Norris, P. and Lovenduski, J. (1995) *Political Recruitment*, Cambridge: Cambridge University Press.

Oliver, L., Stuart, M. and Tomlinson, J. (2014) 'Equal Pay Bargaining in the UK Local Government', *Journal of Industrial Relations*, 56(2): 228–245.

Olmi, J. (2007) *Oser la parité syndicale. La CGT à l'épreuve des collectifs féminins 1945–1985*, Paris: L'Harmattan.

O'Sullivan, M., Turner, T., Kennedy, M. and Wallace, J. (2015) 'Is Individual Employment Law Displacing the Role of Trade Unions?' *Industrial Law Journal*, 44(2): 222–245.

Parker, J. (2003) *Women's Groups and Equality in British Trade Unions*, New York: Edwin Mellen Press.

Pélisse, J. (2007) 'Les usages syndicaux du droit et de la justice', in Jacques Commaille and Martine Kaluzynski (eds) *La fonction politique de la justice*, Paris: La Découverte, pp 165–189.

Pélisse, J. (2009) 'Judiciarisation ou juridicisation? Usages et réappropriations du droit dans les conflits du travail', *Politix*, 86: 73–96.

Pélisse, J. (2014) *Le travail du droit. Trois études sur la légalité ordinaire*, Mémoire original pour l'Habilitation à diriger les recherches: Institut d'Etudes Politiques de Paris.

Pélisse, J. (2019) 'Varieties of Legal Intermediaries: When Non-legal Professionals Act as Legal Intermediaries', *Studies in Law, Politics, and Society*, 81: 101–128.

Perrot, M. (1974) *Les ouvriers en grève, France 1871–1890*, Paris: Mouton et Ecole Pratique des Hautes Etudes.

Peugny, C. (2009) *Le déclassement*, Paris: Grasset.

Phillips, A. (1995) *The Politics of Presence. The Political Representation of Gender, Ethnicity, and Race*, Oxford: Oxford University Press.

Pignoni, M-T. (2017) 'De l'adhérent au responsable syndical. Quelles évolutions dans l'engagement des salariés syndiqués?', *Dares Analyses*, 15 (March).

Pitkin, H. (1977) *The Concept of Representation*, Berkeley: University of California Press.

Pochic, S. (2014a) 'Femmes responsables syndicales en Angleterre et identification féministe: neutraliser leur genre pour mieux représenter leur classe?', *Sociologie*, 5(4): 369–386.

Pochic, S. (2014b) 'Façons de sortir. Politiques et pratiques de reconversion des anciens permanents de la CFDT', in C. Guillaume (ed), *La CFDT, sociologie d'une conversion réformiste*, Rennes: Presses Universitaires de Rennes, pp 151–176.

Pochic, S. and Chappe, V-A. (2019) 'Battles through and about Statistics in French Pay Equity Bargaining: The Politics of Quantification at Workplace Level', *Gender, Work & Organization*, 26(5): 650–667.

Pochic, S., Chappe, V-A., Charpenel, M., Demilly, H., Milner, S. and Rabier, M. (2019) 'L'égalité professionnelle est-elle négociable? Enquête sur la qualité et la mise en œuvre d'accords et de plans égalité femmes-hommes élaborés en 2014–2015', *Dares Analyses*, 131 and 132.

Pocock, B. and Brown, K. (2013) 'Gendered Leadership in Australian Unions in the Process of Strategic Renewal: Instrumental, Transformative or Post-Heroic?', in S. Ledwith and L.L. Hansen (eds), *Gendering and Diversifying Trade Union Leadership*, London: Routledge, pp 27–46.

Pollert, A. (1981) *Girls, Wives, Factory Lives*, London: Macmillan.

Pollert, A. (2007) 'Britain and Individual Employment Rights: "Paper Tigers", Fierce in Appearance but Missing in Tooth and Claw', *Economic and Industrial Democracy*, 28(1): 110–139.

Prowse, J., Prowse, P. and Perrett, R. (2020) ' "Women take care and men take charge": The Case of Leadership and Gender in the Public and Commercial Services Union', *Economic and Industrial Democracy*, 1–20.

Puech, I. (2005) 'Mayant Faty, ménages et remue-ménage d'une femme de chambre', *Travail, genre et sociétés*, 13: 5–25.

Pugh, M. (2000) *Women and the Women's Movement in Britain, 1914–1959*, London: Palgrave Macmillan.

Ratto, M. and Gautier, A. (1996) 'Les syndicats féminins libres de l'Isère 1906–1936', *Clio. Femmes, Genre, Histoire*, 3, https://doi.org/10.4000/clio.465.

Rogerat, C. (2005) 'Mouvements sociaux et syndicalisme', in M. Maruani (ed) *Femmes, genre et sociétés. L'état des saviors*, Paris: La Découverte, pp 323–331.

Rose, S. (1988) 'Gender Antagonism and Class Conflict: Exclusionary Strategies or Male Trade Unionists in Nineteenth-Century Britain', *Social History*, 13(2): 191–208.

Rowbotham, S. (2006) 'Cleaners' Organising in Britain from the 1970s: A Personal Account', *Antipode*, 38(3): 608–625.

Rubery, J. and Fagan, C. (1995) 'Comparative Industrial Relations Research: Towards Reversing the Gender Bias', *British Journal of Industrial Relations*, 33(2): 209–236.

Ryan, M. and Haslam, A. (2005) 'The Glass Cliff: Evidence that Women are Over-represented in Precarious Leadership Positions', *British Journal of Management*, 16: 81–90.

Sacks, V. (1986) 'The Equal Opportunities Commission – Ten Years on', *The Modern Law Review*, 49(5): 560–592.

Sampson, R.J. and Laub, J.H. (2005) 'A Life Course View of the Development of Crime', *The ANNALS of the American Academy of Political and Social Science*, 602: 12–45.

Savage, M. (1988) 'Trade Unionism, Sex Segregation, and the State: Women's Employment in "New Industries" in Inter-war Britain', *Social History*, 13(2): 209–230.

Savage, M. and Witz, A. (eds) (1992) *Gender and Bureaucracy*, Oxford: Blackwell.

Saward, M. (2010) *The Representation Claim*, Oxford: Oxford University Press.

Seccombe, W. (1986) 'Patriarchy Stabilized: The Construction of the Male Breadwinner Wage Norm in the Nineteenth Century Britain', *Social History*, 11(1): 53–76.

Silvera, R. (2006) 'Le défi de l'approche intégrée de l'égalité pour le syndicalisme en Europe', *La Revue de l'IRES*, 50: 137–172.

Silvera, R. (2010) 'Le nouveau défi de l'égalité pour le syndicalisme français: l'exemple de la charte CGT', *Cahiers du MAGE*, 14: 35–42.

Silvera, R. (2014) *Un quart en moins. Des femmes se battent pour en finir avec les inégalités de salaires*, Paris: La Découverte.

Silvera, R. and Rigaud, T. (2016) 'Les freins et les leviers à l'accès et au maintien des femmes aux responsabilités syndicales. Le cas de la commission exécutive confédérale de la CGT', Etude IRES.

Siméant, J. (2001) 'Entrer, rester en humanitaire: des fondateurs de MSF aux membres actuels des ONG médicales françaises', *Revue française de science politique*, 51(1): 47–72.

Simms, M., Holgate, J. and Heery, E. (2013) *Union Voices. Tactics and Tensions in UK Organizing*, Ithaca: Cornell University Press.

Simonpoli, N. (2020) 'La Griffe Cégétiste. Une sociologie historique de la reconversion professionnelle des cadres syndicaux de la CGT 1970–2010', HDR dissertation, Nanterre University.

Smolović Jones, O., Smolović Jones, S., Taylor, S. and Yarrow, E. (2020) '"I Wanted More Women in, but ...": Oblique Resistance to Gender Equality Initiatives', *Work, Employment and Society*, 1–17.

Snell, M. (1979) 'The Equal Pay and Sex Discrimination Acts: Their Impact in the Workplace', *Feminist Review*, 1: 37–57.

Squire, J. (2008) 'The Constitutive Representation of Gender: Extra-parliamentary Representations of Gender Relations', *Representation*, 44(2): 187–204.

Stevenson, G. (2016) 'The Forgotten Strike: Equality, Gender, and Class in the Trico Equal Pay Strike', *Labour History Review*, 81(2): 141–168.

Summerfield, P. (1984) *Women Workers in the Second World War: Production and Patriarchy in Conflict*, London: Croom Helm.

Sundari, A., Pearson, R. and McDowell, L. (2018) 'From Grunwick to Gate Gourmet: South Asian Women's Industrial Activism and the Role of Trade Unions', *Revue Française de Civilisation Britannique*, XXIII(1): 1–24.

Taylor, V. (2005) 'La continuité des mouvements sociaux. La mise en veille du mouvement des femmes', in O. Fillieule (ed) *Le désengagement militant*, Paris: Belin, pp 229–250.

Terry, M. (2000) *Redefining Public Sector Unionism. UNISON and the Future of Trade Unions*, London: Routledge.

Tomlinson, J. (2005) 'Women's Attitudes towards Trade Unions in the UK: A Consideration of the Distinction between Full and Part-time Workers', *Industrial Relations Journal*, 36(3): 402–418.

Trat, J. and Zylberberg-Hocquard, M-H. (2000) *La participation des femmes aux instances de décision des syndicats*, GEDISST CNRS, working paper.

Virdee, S. and Grint, K. (1994) 'Black Self-organization in Trade Unions', *The Sociological Review*, 42(2): 202–226.

Voss, K. and Sherman R. (2000) 'Breaking the Iron Law of Oligarchy. Union Revitalization in the American Labour Movement', *The American Journal of Sociology*, 106(2): 303–349.

Wajcman, J. (1998) *Managing like a Man. Women and Men in Corporate Management*, Cambridge: Polity Press.

Wajcman, J. (2000) 'Feminism Facing Industrial Relations in Britain', *British Journal of Industrial Relations*, 38(2): 183–201.

Walby, C. (1986) *Patriarchy at Work: Patriarchal and Capitalist Relations in Employment*, Minneapolis: University of Minnesota Press.

Walby, S., Armstrong, J. and Strid, S. (2012) 'Intersectionality: Multiple Inequalities in Social Theory', *Sociology*, 46(2): 224–240.

Walters, S. (2002) 'Female Part-time Workers' Attitudes to Trade Unions in Britain', *British Journal of Industrial Relations*, 40(1): 49–68.

Watson, D. (1988) *Managers of Discontent*, London: Routledge.

Willemez, L. (2003) 'Quand les syndicats se saisissent du droit. Invention et redéfinition d'un role', *Sociétés contemporaines*, 52: 17–38.

Willemez, L. (2017) *Le travail dans son droit. Sociologie historique du droit du travail en France (1892–2017)*, Paris: LGDJ.

Wolf, G. (2011) 'L'espace de la cause des femmes à la création des syndicats SUD (1988–1998)', Masters thesis in history, Angers University.

Woodward, A. (2003) 'European Gender Mainstreaming: Innovative Policy or Disappearing Act', *Review of Policy Research*, 20(1): 65–88.

Wright, T. and Conley, H. (2018) 'Advancing Gender Equality in the Construction Sector through Public Procurement: Making Effective Use of Responsive Regulation', *Economic and Industrial Democracy*, published online, 21 March 2018.

Yates, C. (1996) 'Neo-liberalism and the Working Girl: The Dilemmas of Women and the Australian Union Movement', *Economic and Industrial Democracy*, 17(4): 627–665.

Yates, C. (2006) 'Challenging Misconceptions about Organizing Women into Unions', *Gender, Work and Organization*, 13(6): 565–584.

Yates, C. (2010) 'Understanding Caring, Organizing Women: How Framing a Problem Shapes Union Strategy', *Transfer: European Review of Labour and Research*, 16(3): 399–410.

Young, I.M. (2000) *Inclusion and Democracy*, Oxford: Oxford University Press.

Yin, R. (2014) *Case Study Research Design and Methods* (5th edn), Thousand Oaks: Sage.

Yu, K-H. (2014) 'Re-conceptualising Member Participation: Informal Activist Careers in Unions', *Work, Employment and Society*, 58(1): 58–77.

Zylberberg-Hocquard, M-H. (1978) *Féminisme et syndicalisme en France*, Paris: Editions Anthropos.

Index

References to figures appear in *italic* type;
those in **bold** type refer to tables. References to endnotes show
both the page number and the note number (74n7).

Lightning Source UK Ltd.
Milton Keynes UK
UKHW021250190522
403200UK00003B/277